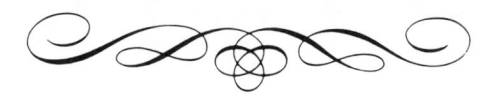

ENVIRONMENTAL ASSESSMENT AND DESIGN

ENVIRONMENTAL ASSESSMENT AND DESIGN

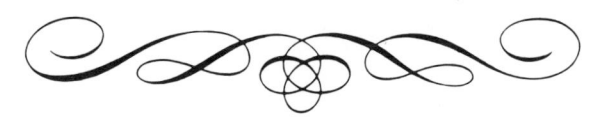

A New Tool for the Applied Behavioral Scientist

Robert K. Conyne
R. James Clack

PRAEGER

PRAEGER SPECIAL STUDIES • PRAEGER SCIENTIFIC

69125

Library of Congress Cataloging in Publication Data

Conyne, Robert K
   Environmental assessment and design.

   Bibliography: p.
   Includes index.
   1. Environmental psychology--Therapeutic use.
2. Psychology, Applied. I. Clack, R. James, joint author. II. Title.
BF353.C67   158'.3   80-24816
ISBN 0-03-057948-1

Published in 1981 by Praeger Publishers
CBS Educational and Professional Publishing
A Division of CBS, Inc.
521 Fifth Avenue, New York, New York 10175 U.S.A.

© 1981 by Praeger Publishers

All rights reserved

123456789 145 987654321

Printed in the United States of America

We dedicate this book to the memory of Robert K. Conyne, Sr., who was writing his own book; to the memory of Beatrice Parker Clack, who dedicated her "book" to her sons; and to our former major professor, our role model and friend, Dr. Shelley C. Stone.

FOREWORD

We are witnessing a change in our intellectual landscape. The last 20 years of social research reflect the beginning of a shift from person-centered explanations of social problems toward more environmentally oriented conceptions. Certainly this is not the first time in the history of social science that the pendulum has swung toward the environmental end of the explanatory continuum. Each time the pendulum does swing in this direction, however, the sophistication of our thinking about the impact of the environment on behavior increases.

In their book, *Environmental Assessment and Design*, Conyne and Clack carry on the tradition of Kurt Lewin by offering an environmentally based model of action research that involves a continuing cycle of assessment, change efforts, and evaluation of the impact of those efforts. While Lewin's conception of the environment was heavily psychological in nature, Conyne and Clack have broadened the meaning of the concept of environment. They offer us an environmental classification matrix that reflects diverse approaches to conceptualizing and measuring environmental dimensions. These dimensions include organizational structure, characteristics of the setting and habitants, the social climate of the setting, and the reinforcement contingencies that exist in those settings. Because of its breadth, the environmental classification matrix promises a degree of comprehensiveness in environmental assessment that has been missing from many previous efforts.

In addition, the authors describe a technology of environmental change. This technology involves a series of carefully designed feedback loops that serve the dual function of initiating change and then providing a new equilibrium in the living systems they consider.

Thus, the authors provide us with a new synthesis of environmental concepts and a new paradigm for thinking about human problems. Perhaps the most important function of new paradigms is that they provide us with a new view of the problem in question. Careful readers will find their views of human problems shifted from a conception that locates human problems within individuals to one that sees those problems located not either exclusively in individuals or in their environments, but in the interaction between the two.

Not only will readers find their understanding of human problems enlarged by this book, they will also find that the concept of "change agent" has taken on a new meaning as well. Change agents of all sorts including counselors, therapists, planners, organizational development experts, and others will find in this book a new and more sophisticated notion of the idea of the role of the change agent in a broad range of settings. Thus, Conyne and Clack have extended the spirit and the conception of Lewin's original work. Perhaps most important of all, they have understood his admonitions that "the theorist need not look toward applied problems with highbrow aversion," and at the same time, that "there is nothing so practical as a good theory."

Richard H. Price
Ann Arbor, Michigan
October 1980

PREFACE

Assessing and Changing Human Environments presents an ecologically based model for helping people that has its origins in the work of Kurt Lewin. Termed environmental design, this model takes a people-by-environment change perspective, where the interaction of behavior with environmental conditions becomes the change focus. Environmental design contains a technology that is used to assess and change human environments, rather than to assess and change people apart from their environments. As such, it is a revolutionary change approach for the helping fields and for the variety of change agents working with them.

We have written this book to offer to change agents (for example, counselors, consultants, trainers, action researchers, planners, therapists, group workers, administrators) a coherent model for conceptualizing environmental design and a concrete technology for carrying it out. In Chapter 1 we place environmental design in context by tracing many of the important historical forces that have preceded it and contributed to its evolution. Chapter 2 contains a comparative discussion of several frameworks for classifying human environments and it initiates an in-depth examination of five environmental design models (social ecological, ecosystem, open-systems, functions of physical settings, and cognitive/geographic mapping) that continues throughout subsequent chapters. Environmental assessment is the focus of Chapter 3. Methodologies are described in detail and examples of instrumentation are given. Chapter 4 defines environmental design conceptually and illustrates its relationship to the range of planned change models that are in use today. The shift from a conceptual to a practical emphasis occurs in Chapter 5, where the "Environmental Change Technology" is described. We present this step-by-step methodology as the action phase of environmental design. In Chapter 6 we share our views of some critical training, ethical, and value implications of environmental design and we offer practical guidelines that are meant to promote competent, ethical practice. Finally, a lengthy bibliography of related works is supplied in order to provide the reader with many other sources to use in exploring environmental design.

We hope that this book fulfills our intent of stimulating readers to learn more about and to use environmental design in their work. By doing so, not only will advancements be realized in the intervention itself but, far more importantly, in the human environments in which it is used.

ACKNOWLEDGEMENTS

Bob Conyne would like to gratefully acknowledge the assistance of Illinois State University and the Kellogg Foundation in granting him a sabbatical to devote more attention to this book than would be possible ordinarily; of Rick Price and Hal Korn of the University of Michigan's Community Psychology and Counseling Services, respectively, in providing a stimulating and reinforcing sabbatical work environment; of the several typists in Ann Arbor, Bloomington-Normal, and especially in Austin who labored on various pieces of the manuscript; and of Lynn Rapin, who helped this author get through the rough spots.

Jim Clark would like to gratefully acknowledge the contribution of The University of Texas at Austin and specifically the Counseling-Psychological Services Center, and its director, Dave Drum, for the resources and support made available; of Charles Lerman for his efforts in literature review, referencing, indexing, and his incisive editorial comments; of Dolores Hershey and Debi Rice for their long hours at the typewriters, typing and retyping while the authors figured out what they wanted to say; of Cindy Clack for her marvelous assistance in preparing the index; and of Linda, Angie, and Cindy for their love and support during the writing of the book.

CONTENTS

	Page
DEDICATION	v
FOREWORD	vii
PREFACE	ix
ACKNOWLEDGEMENTS	xi
LIST OF TABLES	xv
LIST OF FIGURES	xvi

Chapter

1   **THE ENVIRONMENT:**
    AN UNTAPPED FORCE FOR CHANGE   1

    Tracing Environment through Personality Theorists   3
    A Missing Link   12
    Summary   20

2   **ENVIRONMENTAL CLASSIFICATION:**
    UNDERSTANDING THE HUMAN ENVIRONMENT   21

    What is the Environment?   21
    Categories in Environmental Classification   27
    Environmental Classification Matrix: A Conceptual Tool   35
    Five Environmental Classification Models   35
    Summary   44

3   **ENVIRONMENTAL ASSESSMENT:**
    CHARTING THE PERSON-ENVIRONMENT INTERFACE   45

    What is Environmental Assessment   45

Environmental Assessment Approaches 48
Summary 77

**4 ENVIRONMENTAL DESIGN:
   ALTERING THE HUMAN ENVIRONMENT** 78

Applied Research in Environmental Design 78
Environmental Change:
  The Throughput of Environmental Design 82
Applied Research Revisited:
  Change Evaluation and Its Usages 112
Summary and Prospectus 114

**5 ENVIRONMENTAL CHANGE TECHNOLOGY:
   A METHOD FOR ENVIRONMENTAL DESIGN** 117

Development of Environmental Change Technology 117
A Guide to Environmental Change Technology 121
Illustrative Case 145
Summary 148

**6 ENVIRONMENTAL DESIGN IMPLICATIONS
   AND CONSIDERATIONS** 150

Brief Review of Key Points in Environmental Design 150
Implications for Practitioners 151
Implications for Training Programs 154
Implications for Clients 157
Value and Ethical Considerations 160
Summary 163

BIBLIOGRAPHY 165
INDEX 178
ABOUT THE AUTHORS 185

LIST OF TABLES

Table		Page
2.1	Two Environments of Reference (E_r)	26
3.1	Some Environmental Assessment Instruments for Campus Administrators	50
3.2	Group Environment Scale Subscale Descriptions	53
3.3	Examples of GES Items for Its Subscales	54
4.1	Predominant Assessment and Change Emphases for the Five Environmental Change Models	115
5.1	The Development of the Environmental Change Technology Model	119

LIST OF FIGURES

Figure		Page
1.1	Representation of Lewin's Conception of Life Space	9
2.1	An Environment of Reference (E_r)	23
2.2	Environmental Classification Matrix	36
2.3	A Framework Relating Environmental and Personal Variables with Outcomes	38
3.1	ER Example and Form	60
3.2	Six-Box Approach to Environmental Assessment in Organizations	62
3.3	The Six-Box Approach within the Open-System Model	63
3.4	"Model A:" Logic System Design	68
3.5	A Functions of Space Coding Sheet	72
3.6	Social Area Analysis—School Clusters Based on Student Demographic Data	75
3.7	Geocode Analysis of Math Scores by Student Address	77
4.1	Environmental Design Cycle	81
4.2	Environmental Design Cycle in Open System Format	82
4.3	A Force-Field Analysis Format	89
4.4	The Research, Development, and Diffusion Change Model	92
4.5	Comparing Lewin's Change Typology and Planned Change	93
4.6	A Diagrammatic Model for Action Research	97
4.7	An Overview of Model B.	105
4.8	Some OD Interventions Organized by Individual-Group and Task-Process	107
4.9	Some OD Interventions Organized by Target Groups	108
5.1	Environmental Change Technology Flow Chart	120
5.2	Categorization of Assessment Data	136

ENVIRONMENTAL ASSESSMENT AND DESIGN

1

THE ENVIRONMENT: AN UNTAPPED FORCE FOR CHANGE

An environment has potent effects upon its inhabitants. This observation has been widely accepted by applied behavioral scientists for a number of years. Environment is so pervasive in its effects upon human behavior that its very magnitude and complexity cause it to be ignored, taken for granted, or broken down into such miniscule subunits for study that application of results to human behavior becomes inappropriate, irrelevant, or of little consequence. In the past few years, however, a resurgence of interest in the effect of environment upon people has led to the development of budding new subspecialties in the social sciences. Social ecology, ecological psychology, population psychology, social engineering, systems analysis, and human ecology are examples of new movements that have joined the older disciplines of sociology and anthropology in addressing the environment-person interaction. It is probable that no credible psychologist, counselor, sociologist, architect, anthropologist, and so on would seriously question the notion that environment affects behavior and vice versa. In practice, however, those who work to improve the human condition have behaved too often as though they believed quite differently. Frequently people have been treated as though they were independent of their environment, and as though the environment were a static element, far removed from people. This misconception is compounded by an inaccurate view, arising from the save-the-environment ecology movement, that the environment is nature, to be thought of only in physical terms. The present analysis suggests that environment must be conceptualized more comprehensively than that view allows, if change agents are to have broader impact on clients. As long as change agents continue to use a narrow perspective of the environment and of its effects on people, both the number of individuals helped and the quality of that assistance will be limited.

The broader perspective presented in this book is exemplified by the definition of an environment. Briefly stated, an environment is viewed as including a physical component (both natural and built elements), a social component (people, their characteristics, behavior, and relationships), an institutional component (laws, policies, religions, and so on), and an ecological-climate dimension that evolves from an interaction of these three components with each other and with the perceptual framework of constituents. Further, it is posited that the environment shapes and is shaped by human behavior, suggesting that people are in transaction with their environment.

In order to be able adequately to assess environments that consist of such characteristics and then to change them for the benefit of their constituents, wide-screen vision is needed in order to view the phenomena and activities, and to recognize the ways in which they relate to each other.

The physical component of an environment includes both its natural and constructed features. It is exemplified by such elements as rivers, streams, parks, buildings, offices, family rooms, garages, sidewalks, thunderstorms, sunshine, temperature, and humidity. In short, people are affected to a greater or lesser extent by all those parts of the physical environment that impinge upon the senses of sight, smell, hearing, touch, and taste.

The effects of the social component of environment become apparent any time an individual comes into contact with another person, group, or mass of other people. From the most casual contact to an intimate relationship, from being alone with one's spouse, child, or lover, to being part of a cheering multitude at a football game, from a formal contact with a business associate to a night out at the local dance hall, all person-to-person(s) interactions have significant effects.

The institutional component of environment designates behavior in relation to the culture and society. Laws, codes, mores, policies, and procedures, of both formal and informal nature, chart the bounds of appropriate behavior. People are informed, either implicitly or explicitly when, where, and under what conditions they are to be quiet or noisy, run or walk, work or play, be creative or conform.

That individuals perceive, appreciate, and react to their environments in different ways is, by now, a fact. One may see Times Square as an over-populated, overlighted menagerie, whereas another will see it as a delightful source of stimulation and wonder; one will thrive on the ski slopes of Colorado, while another will find the same setting little but cold; one will find a cocktail party a place to make friends, while another finds it a bore; some find the 55-mile-per-hour speed limit necessary and appropriate for conservation of both natural resources and human lives, whereas others see it as an imposition upon the way in which they are making their living. Not everyone prefers the same environment. Its meaning is as variable as the number of individuals affected. The ecological climate, which is comprised of shared perceptions of and reactions to all aspects of an environment and to the product of the physical, social, and institutional components, is the direct link of individuals to their environment.

Therefore, it is through the ecological climate that individuals both experience and create their environment.

Environmental components are obviously not independent but synergistic. Change in one component brings about changes to a greater or lesser extent in others. A farmer whose land is flooded (physical component) may be aided and strongly moved by the help and care received from friends and neighbors (social component) and further affected by governmental efforts at flood control (institutional component). The farmer, although touched by all these separate environmental aspects, probably does not compartmentalize them in that way. It follows that although individuals may be more aware of certain parts of their environment than of others at any one point in time, the environment is usually experienced and reacted to as a whole. Breaking the environment into components is artificial in that it does not occur in "real life." It has been done here only to aid in identifying particular and differential environmental effects.

The everyday evidence of the effects of environment upon people and their behavior is clear. The scientific examination of human behavior is the domain of several academic disciplines, including psychology, sociology, anthropology, philosophy, and others. Psychology is most closely identified with the study of individuals and their behavior, and for this reason an overview of psychological theory, particularly that related to personality development, serves to introduce the relative importance ascribed to environmental effects on human behavior.

TRACING ENVIRONMENT THROUGH PERSONALITY THEORISTS

The relatively youthful profession of psychology has contributed much to the understanding of human behavior. Of particular note here is the work of personality theorists. One can observe that psychology has no parallel group of environmental theorists. This statement of fact underscores the previous observation that the environments of human beings, though frequently mentioned as important, are most often dealt with either implicity or not at all. While reviewing many of the classic books in the field that provide surveys of personality theory, some 13 in all, it was found that the word "environment" appeared in only one subject index. (This obvious exception is Krasner and Ullman's (1973) text *Behavioral Influence and Personality*.) Nevertheless, an analysis of selected personality theories reveals the theorists' recognition of environmental effects upon human behavior, although this environment-behavior relationship can be most often gleaned by implication.

In order to review, not inclusively one might add, the role given to environment in personality theory, selected theorists have been placed in three broad categories that cover the spectrum of personality theory and related psychotherapeutic practice: the psychoanalysts and neoanalysts, the behaviorists, and the phenomenologists. The summary of each theorist's position will focus primarily on the role of environmental influences in personality development.

The Analysts: Psycho- and Neo-

Two Psychoanalysts: Freud and Adler

Traditionally, Sigmund Freud has been recognized as the founder of personality theory and his works usually serve as a starting point in discussions of human behavior theory. This appears to be appropriate since his early 1900s expositions were the first in which a detailed conception of principles governing human personality functioning were presented.

Freud (1957) believed that all behavior emanated from innate instinctual drives, a conception that resulted in his notion of the psychic determinism or causality of behavior. Freud suggests that every human behavior pattern has a cause, and it is most likely that these causes are unrecognized or unconscious. Whether or not one will develop into a psychologically healthy person is deemed to be dependent upon an individual's psychosexual development, which in turn is a product of an infantile and early childhood developmental sequence. Freud considered adjustment or maladjustment to be determined by the experience of the young child from birth through roughly the sixth year, with much of this developmental process highly dependent upon child-parent interactions. Feeding procedures, toilet training, and the parents' sexual behavior as viewed by the child are thought to be some of the critical environmentally derived elements to be experienced and resolved. Freud was an environmentalist in the sense that he gave primacy to the environment created by parents during a child's early development.

In some of Freud's later and perhaps most popularly known work, he theorized the concepts of id, ego, and superego as explanations of an ongoing intrapsychic conflict experienced by all beyond the age of six. The id is representative of the innate and uncontrolled drives toward pleasure, the ego represents the forces of reality that mediate and control the drives of the id, and the superego roughly represents ideals and moral precepts. The development of two of these three basic concepts, the ego and the superego, are environmentally related. The ego develops as a result of frustration of the id by the external environment. When the environment thwarts the pleasure-seeking demands of the id for immediate gratification, the infant begins to differentiate between self and external reality, between what he or she can get away with and what he or she cannot. This brings about an adjustment to the external environment which comes to constitute the ego.

Like the ego, the superego develops through perceptions of the punishing effect of the environment, usually in the form of parents teaching and/or imposing their moral values upon the child. The child internalizes the parents' values via a process of identification, as a way of fighting the "wrong and immoral" impulses of the id. The ego and superego developed through the child's interactions with the environment created by the parents has substantial impact. Throughout an individual's life this environment, via the ego and superego, continues to mediate behavior.

Several of Freud's contemporaries as well as later theorists built on his original works to develop differing conceptions of human behavior. Alfred Adler (1935), the first of Freud's pupils to break from the fold, developed an individual psychology based on the contention that personality development is primarily a function of feelings arising from inferiority to others and a striving for power to overcome these feelings. He postulated that environmental effects are central in the development of individuals. In his view, individuals are born inferior, almost totally dependent upon others for their welfare, since they themselves are relatively weak and dependent throughout childhood. Adler stresses the important personality influences contained in the potentially deleterious environment, such as having older and more powerful siblings, neglectful parents, and other rejecting adults. In order to cope with the resulting sense of weakness and inferiority that naturally evolves, individuals strive to gain control or power over others. Therefore, the major developmental task, as viewed by Adler, is lodged in the interaction of individuals with others in their environment.

Adler (1939) identified additional major causes of maladjustment, including the adoption of unrealistic life goals and a lack of social interest in the concern for fellow humans. He saw the correction of maladjustment as being accomplished by assisting individuals to establish realistic goals and to develop social concern. Both of these objectives are environmentally oriented because goals tend to be realistic or unrealistic based upon environmental contingencies, and social concern is obviously directed toward others in the environment.

Three Neoanalysts: Horney, Sullivan, and Fromm

Neoanalysts are exemplary for the importance they place on the environment in personality development. Karen Horney, who was trained as a Freudian analyst, broke from the classical movement and developed her own theory in which the underlying determinant of behavior is the need for security. She thought that adjustment or maladjustment were closely related to child-parent interactions typified by overprotection, rejection, and punishment. Horney's (1937) basic concept revolves around the anxiety that results from child-parent situations such as lack of respect and warmth, under- or overprotection, too much or too little responsibility, an unjust or hostile family atmosphere, or isolation from other children. Situations that disrupt the security of a child produce basic anxiety, the seed of maladjustment. Conversely, appropriate parental behavior in regard to the above dimensions leads the child to experience a sense of security, and normal development can then be expected. The child learns to cope and compensate during early development, and the methods learned become more or less permanent strategies to be used throughout life. Horney, then, places a premium upon the social component of environment, created by parents, as a strong influencer of personality development.

Harry Stack Sullivan (1953, 1954), another of the neoanalysts, sees personality development primarily as a function of the quality of one's interpersonal relationships. He insists that personality cannot be studied or observed apart from interpersonal situations.

The self-system is one of many concepts that Sullivan created to conceptualize his interpersonal orientation to personality development. This self-system is composed of protective behavior controls developed by an individual to guard against interpersonal anxiety frequently resulting from restrictive societal norms. For example, the expression of disagreement with or anger toward one's parents or elders has traditionally been frowned upon within the society. Thus, a youth who feels considerable animosity toward a parent and yet is forbidden an outlet for this expression must develop behavioral control (a self-system) over the anger or face parental and societal censure as a result of its expression.

In Sullivan's theoretical position, therefore, the impact of environment is central, in that behavior is always viewed in an interpersonal context. All of Sullivan's innovative conceptual approach emanates from this interpersonal-environmental perspective.

Erich Fromm, who was trained in psychology and sociology as well as in psychoanalysis, developed a social psychological theory of human development in which behavior is viewed as a result of the sociocultural system in which a person resides. The major theme of Fromm's work (1941) is that individuals become lonely and isolated as a consequence of becoming separate from other people and nature. For example, children gain independence from their parents and then find themselves lonely and helpless in an alien world. Fromm states that the solution to this dilemma lies in people either joining together via reciprocal love and shared work or by conforming to the mandates of authority and society. Since the basic well-being of individuals is to be found only in relation to others and society, Fromm's social psychological approach places heavy emphasis upon environmental concerns.

Behaviorists

A second broad classification of psychologists who have had major influence upon the development of personality theory are the behaviorists. The origin of the modern behavioristic movement can be traced to the laboratory work and theory of Ivan Pavlov, John B. Watson, and Edward L. Thorndike. Pavlov (1906, 1927) was able to demonstrate the possibility of developing an objective psychology based only upon observed behavior. Watson (1916, 1925) led an assault on subjectivity in psychology by building an objective environmental point of view of human performance which he labeled "behaviorism." Coincidentally with Watson's work, Thorndike (1911, 1932) used animal research to develop his "law of effect," which states that any act in a given situation producing satisfaction becomes associated with that situation. When the situation recurs, the act is also likely to recur. Due to the work of Watson and Thorndike, as well as others such as Edward C. Tolman, Edwin R. Guthrie, and Clarke L. Hull, behaviorism became the predominant force in psychology in the United States in the 1930s and remains a major influence today.

From these early beginnings, two major streams of behaviorism as applied to behavior change have developed. In classical conditioning, a stimulus elicits a response with which it was not previously associated. For example, students in a classroom situation learn to respond to a bell signaling the end of class by gathering up their books and preparing to leave the room. The class instructor's lecture notes are repeatedly closed just prior to the end of the period (and the ringing of the bell). Thus the students become conditioned to gather their books and prepare to leave class when the instructor closes the lecture notes. In operant conditioning, on the other hand, an individual emits behavior and the events that closely follow it may serve temporarily as reinforcements, or consequences that either encourage or discourage the behavior. A student in a classroom volunteers to respond to an instructor's question and then presents an incorrect answer. The instructor replies, "The answer is incorrect but it was a good try and showed some real thinking," or replies "What a dumb answer! You ought to keep those to yourself." In the first case, the student would be liable to repeat the volunteering behavior, whereas in the latter case the student might be expected to maintain a low profile in the future. Most behavioral work with humans has been accomplished using the operant paradigm, and it is, therefore, with this approach that this study is most concerned. With this in mind, the works of such psychologists as B. F. Skinner, Leonard Ullman and Leonard Krasner, and Albert Bandura will now be considered.

B. F. Skinner

In the view of these theorists, the environment is crucial. Perhaps no behaviorist has applied this concept more succinctly than B. F. Skinner. Skinner took the animal and laboratory work of his predecessors and applied it to human problems. He offered the concept of operant behavior, which holds that a behavior that is followed by positive reinforcement is likely to be repeated. The focus of Skinner's work is upon the antecedents and consequences of behavior, rather than upon any hypothetical internal states. Skinner argues that most human behavior is a result of individuals acting within their environment, changing or being changed by the environment. As can be noted, the effect of the environment on behavior is paramount in Skinner's thinking. His most far-ranging work in terms of the implication of operant behavior for the scientist, and for society as well, is *Walden Two* (1948), in which he creates a utopian system based on learning and conditioning principles. His approach, since labeled "social engineering," calls for the creation of a planned environment that offers only those reinforcements that would assure desirable social behavior on the part of all inhabitants of the social system.

Leonard Krasner

Leonard Krasner, writing in Bergin and Garfield's *Handbook of Psychotherapy and Behavior Change* (1971), clearly indicates that the effects of environment in theoretical considerations of operant approaches to behavior therapy are dominant. He states (p. 644), "The aim of such programs (operant conditioning) is to arrange the environment in such a way that there is an increased likelihood of the individual learning new behavior more likely to elicit positive reinforcement from others in the environment." Krasner further notes that future research in operant conditioning will be aimed toward application of its principles to environmental design; if behavior is determined by environmental consequences, then the environment must be designed so as to maximize positive reinforcers. He suggests that behavior therapy will move away from a one-to-one treatment modality to a milieu or environmental manipulation focus, thus bringing about changes in individuals through changing their environments.

Albert Bandura

Albert Bandura is the main proponent of a behaviorist approach using social modeling as the therapeutic technology. Using this method, a therapist carries out efforts in the natural setting in which psychological problems arise. The therapist's task is often the training and supervision of persons who already have close and significant contact with a client. By altering conditions in an environment that foster a client's deviant behavior, the therapist promotes change, thereby performing an environmental manipulation function.

Phenomenologists

A third classification of theorists of human behavior is a diverse group labeled phenomenologists. Though their conceptions of human behavior indicate vast differences of opinion, all are tied together by their emphasis upon the experiences of individuals, particularly their world view. Phenomenologists forward the idea that each person perceives the world from a subjective point of view; that the meaning of the environment comes from an internal frame of reference, and the external is really what the person perceives it to be.

The earliest phenomenologists were German gestalt psychologists such as Max Wertheimer, Kurt Koffka, and Wolfgang Kohler. Their major contributions included the idea of "insight" as a method of learning, coupled with the notion that the perception of any object in a person's environment is dependent upon the relationship of the object to the perceptual field in which it appears.

Kurt Lewin

If there is any one theory of personality that sets the stage for environmental design as a method for modifying and improving the human condition, it is Lewin's field theory. Therefore, a more extended summary of Lewin's work than that allocated to other theorists is appropriate.

Kurt Lewin, a German philosopher and psychologist, was heavily influenced by the previously noted works of the gestaltists Wertheimer, Kohler, and Koffka, with whom he worked in the years immediately following World War I. A major principle of gestalt psychology is that the way an object or event is perceived is determined by the context in which the object or event is located. Further, that perception is determined by the relationship among the different parts of a perceptual field, rather than by any characteristic of an individual part. From this gestalt background, Lewin developed his field theory which was briefly summarized by Hall and Lindzey (1957) as follows: (1) behavior is a function of the total perceptual field which exists at the time a behavior occurs; (2) analysis of behavior begins with the situation as a whole, from which are differentiated the component parts; and (3) the individual in a concrete situation can be represented mathematically.

In developing field theory, Lewin started by designating the individual person as an entity apart from everything else in the world. He then posited that each person is surrounded by his or her own "psychological environment." The combination of a person with his or her own psychological environment was labeled the "life space" of the individual. To describe his concepts, Lewin used a form of mathematics called topology, a method employed to describe spatial relationships in a nonmetrical manner. The life space was represented as shown in Figure 1.1. P represents the individual person, E represents the psychological environment, and all that is external to the life space is designated as nonpsychological aspects of the environment.

FIGURE 1.1: Representation of Lewin's Conception of Life Space

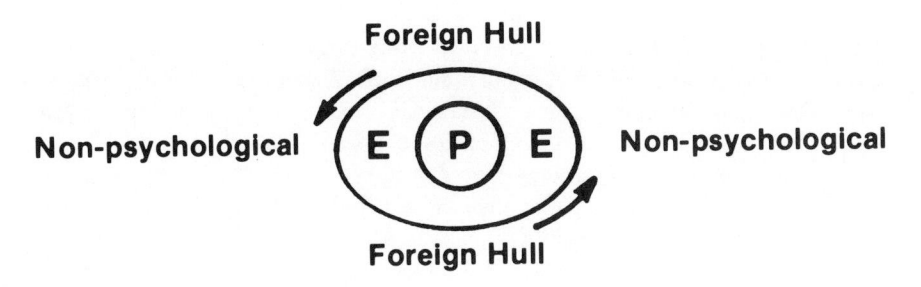

Foreign Hull

Non-psychological   (E (P) E)   **Non-psychological**

Foreign Hull

Source: Constructed by authors.

The life space represents all that can possibly influence the behavior of the person at any one point in time. Lewin, therefore, stated that behavior is a function of life space, $B = F(L)$, in that a permeable division between the person and the psychological environment allows them to interrelate and to influence each other.

Facts that exist in the area outside but immediately adjacent to the life space were called the "foreign hull of the life space" by Lewin, and these facts can significantly influence the psychological environment; that is, these facts can impinge upon the psychological environment in such ways and with such force as to change it. Facts in the psychological environment can also influence the nonpsychological environment. The division between the psychological and nonpsychological environments is once again described as permeable, and through this division facts from the physical world can enter the psychological environment and then influence the individual. Note, however, that Lewin maintains that nonpsychological facts may have no influence until they have moved into the psychological environment; that is, they are irrelevant until they become a part of the psychological environment. It was, however, because of this interactional effect that Lewin suggested that the study of facts in the foreign hull be called "psychological ecology" (1951).

Since the boundaries between the person and the psychological environment, and between the psychological environment and the foreign hull are permeable, this means that environmental facts can influence the person, $P = F(E)$, and that personal facts can influence the environment, $E = F(P)$.

Lewin held a major concern for humanitarian values and the application of democratic principles. Consequently, via the pragmatic implementation of field theory to social problems, he attempted to remove suffering and to improve human conditions. A principle prescribed by Lewin was that theory should always be applied in a research situation that was as near the real life situation as possible. Combining his theoretical formulations with his value set, he undertook the study of social conditions through "action research," a type of investigation aimed toward changing social conditions. Thus Lewin's work can be summarized as taking the environment as client, assessing it via action research, and then taking the results of the research and converting them into social change aimed at improving the lives of those residing in the environment of reference.

Lewin's formulations and work on social change serves as an appropriate foundation for the role of the applied behavioral scientist proposed here. Collaborative efforts for studying the environment through assessment methodologies and then modifying that environment to meet the needs and desires of its inhabitants, and implementing innovations through methods of planned change, certainly seem consistent with Lewinian theory and his model for change. Perhaps the conception of the environment set forth here is somewhat broader than Lewin's, and certainly methods for environmental assessment have proliferated and become more sophisticated in recent years; nevertheless, the idea remains the same.

Fritz Perls

Perhaps the best known current representative of the gestalt movement is the late Fritz Perls. His writing, in concert with Ralph Hefferline and Paul Goodman (1951), as well as his work at the Esalen Institute, have brought gestalt therapy and its underlying theoretical base to the forefront. Perls et al. (1951) noted that speaking of any organism as if it were by itself is simply an illusion. Every human function results from interaction in an organism/ environment field, consisting of sociocultural, animal, and physical aspects. For Perls, then, a person is always in an environmental context.

Carl Rogers

A differing phenomenological approach is represented by the works of Carl Rogers. His "self theory" (1951) presents a view of human behavior as innately good. He views people as being generally effective in dealing with their environment as long as certain conditions exist in that environment. Rogers (1961, p. 105) states that "if inappropriate learning conditions do not occur, man will develop as a kind, friendly, self-accepting, socialized human being although not always conventional and conforming." The environment Rogers favors for normal human development is the same as the one he proposes as being the necessary and sufficient climate to bring about change in therapy patients: a warm, accepting, nonjudgmental climate. Although Rogers seldom specifies the inclusive environment in his writing, it nevertheless appears obvious that it holds a prime position in terms of both human development and therapeutic procedures.

Abraham Maslow

Abraham Maslow gave to the phenomenological approach his conception of behavior being based upon a hierarchy of needs. He grouped (1954) these needs from lower to higher, stating that an individual must meet lower order needs prior to being able to turn attention to or fulfill those of a higher order. The hierarchy classifications include: physiological (primary survival such as food and water); safety (protection from physical and socioeconomic harm); belongingness (need for companionship); esteem (importance to self and others); and self-actualization (to reach one's human potential). The fulfillment of needs in all categories is dependent upon an individual's interaction with various components of the environment.

Existentialism

Existentialism, another form of phenomenology, grew out of a union of psychoanalysis and existential philosophy. The foremost contemporary proponents of the existential philosophy are Martin Heidegger, Martin Buber, and Jean Paul Sartre. European analysts including Medard Boss and Victor Frankl applied existential philosophy to their therapeutic work. Rollo May (1953), via his therapeutic work and writings, is most closely identified as the leader of the existential movement in the United States.

The major contributions the existentialists have made in regard to the place of environment in relation to human behavior include the following concepts. First is the notion that people and their environment are "all of a piece," that is, that separating people from environment is inapplicable in terms of explaining human behavior. Self-awareness always results from interactions with environmental events, situations and, especially, with others. Further, the existentialists maintain that behavior (existence) is always thought of as an attempt to cope successfully with immediate situations and present events. In other words, human self-awareness and existential awareness are discovered always in relationship to the environment. A person exists only in environmental context. Essence is always in the process of creation, emerging continuously from one's transactional struggle with the environment and its incessant challenges.

A MISSING LINK

Examination of the role attributed to the environment across the analytical, behavioral, and phenomenological personality theories clearly shows that when environmental influences are implied in personality development, emphasis has been placed on the social component and the psychosocial climate and, to a lesser extent, on institutional environmental units. The nonpsychological, physical environmental component has been the least understood and appreciated facet of environmental influences. Only Lewin attempted to address it with his fledgling concept of psychological ecology. Ironically, this formerly neglected environmental component is becoming a focus for contemporary efforts to understand and improve environmental influence on human behavior.

As shown previously in this chapter, approaches to improving the quality of human life have addressed the person apart from the environment. Even when environmental effects have been acknowledged, however, the physical component of the environment has been generally disregarded. In sum, the environment, while included in many personality theories and other applied behavioral science approaches, is frequently excluded from actual practice, treated like a forgotten stepchild.

And yet this situation shows signs of evolution. A growing awareness of environmental effects on people is emerging, with consequent development of practical action methodologies. Energy in support of this direction springs from a multitude of disciplines, professions, and movements, all of which are building on historical precursors. What can be said to explain the coalescence and rather sudden emergence of these energies in the decade of the 1970s, and where is all this leading those who are interested in developing change methodologies?

People Radicalism

The 1950s abruptly ushered in the civil rights movement, the 1960s extended "people radicalism" to college and university students, and the 1970s have seen the women's and the nascent men's liberation movement. The principal and paramount source of frustration for each of these "radical" movements can be viewed as an unhealthy environment that imposes rigidity of procedures, policies, programs, physical properties, and roles upon people. Each group in its own way decried this environmental condition by striking out against it and by seeking change. In turn, rallying cries became "Freedom Now!", "Power to the People!", and "Male Chauvinist Pig!" These slogans are captivating and directed at environmental conditions rather than at specific people. In essence, the common element can be seen as extreme dissatisfaction with the environmental status quo.

Radical Therapies

Jerome Agel's book, *The Radical Therapist* (1971), provides an example of how frustration with a part of the "system," the mental health delivery system, can be channeled into alternative approaches. Radical therapists see the environment as an oppressing agent, turning people into robots and controlling them through racist, sexist, and imperialist practices. In this view it is not the people who are sick but, rather, the environment. Radical therapy attempts to change the sick environment and its very practice is a political rather than a psychological act. Much of this approach owes allegiance to the past and ongoing works of R. D. Laing, Erving Goffman, and Thomas Szasz, each of whom has cogently criticized mental health practice as a system-serving, antihumanistic endeavor where the practitioner serves a population-control rather than a person-freeing function, with mental health treatment and its facilities unwittingly promoting a "maddening" environment.

Group-Oriented Modes

Dissatisfaction with sole reliance on individual psychotherapy and counseling as psychological treatment methods has been surfacing with some frequency in recent years (for example, Gazda 1971; Yalom 1975). Others have shown conceptually that individually focused methods of psychological remediation represent but one of 36 possible treatment modes (Morrill, Oetting, and Hurst

1974). This general perspective aids in partially explaining the sudden emergence of group experiences, all of which reached their apogee in the 1960s during the "encounter boom" of the human potential movement (Howard 1970). A virtual group "garden of earthly delights" blossomed then and it has matured considerably in the 1970s.

Gibb (1971) had developed a useful system that assists in organizing the plethora of group approaches into nine categories. Two group treatment approaches, milieu therapy and group psychotherapy, have been selected from this wide array for discussion in reference to their relative emphasis on environmental considerations in personal change efforts.

Milieu therapy (Jones 1953; Rapoport 1960) attempts to structure an entire mental health community into a healing climate. A premium is placed upon the creation of a permissive, communal, democratic atmosphere which is not only present in the hospital setting but is also extended to the patient's family and, hopefully, to society at large. The basic tenet of this treatment methodology is that individuals with psychological difficulties are best treated by placing them in a particular type of healthy environment. Thus, environmental manipulation (design) lies at the base of milieu therapy. In contrast, group psychotherapy generally tends to focus on one-to-one work in a group, where other members participate vicariously and are used to extend and apply an individual's learnings. Treatment is accomplished within a community of people, therefore, taking on the characteristics of an "Everyman drama" (Polster and Polster 1973, p. 286). Group members have an opportunity to confront themselves within the context of other members, providing a phenomenon that is credited with enhancing the whole therapeutic experience.

Thus, a comparison of these two group approaches reveals differing environmental emphases. Milieu therapy attempts to promote individual change through first creating and maintaining a conducive group climate, while group psychotherapy seeks to foster individual change directly within a supportive group context.

Sense of Community

The perceived feeling of being "at home" is what sense of community is all about. As society has become more differentiated, the sense of community has greatly diminished. Forces contributing to the diminution of this feeling are many, including the acceleration of change, technological advances such as television and the automobile, absentee ownership of property, low inner-city tax bases, the growth of bedroom communities and suburbs, conditions of overcrowding and overstimulation, the gradual decline of both the extended and the nuclear family, the proliferation of alternative value systems, and increasing numbers of the unemployed and underemployed resulting from an unstable economy. These separate but interrelated forces combine geometrically to produce massive and pervasive social disarray, resulting in fragmented personality structures and communities. Our communal connections are in serious jeopardy, severely shredding our sense of support, significance, and security, which have been identified as three primary attributes of a community (Klein 1968). And yet, perhaps the "times they are a changin." Bob Dylan, Joan Baez, Allen Ginzberg, and friends (Orth 1975), folk musicians who were very involved in the youth dissent of the 1960s, staged a concert tour for "fun; not ego," where they played in smaller, more intimate settings, forsaking the glitter, hype, and huge crowds characteristic of rock concerts these last 15 years. On another front, Hamer (1975) quotes from a recent interview with Milton Kotler, founder and director of the Institute for Neighborhood Studies: "Why shouldn't people be responsible for everything that affects their lives? Why should they say, 'Well, I didn't have anything to do with it'? Our object is always to increase people's responsibilities in their own communities. The people and the communities will both become better for it." This theme of "neighborhood power" is catching on across the country. In a tiny liberal arts college in the Midwest, the sense of community would seem to have been very strong indeed. Declared bankrupt, the college refused to die. Led by a dedicated group of students, administrators, townspeople, alumni, and faculty (who took a one-half pay cut), the college's fund-raising projects injected enough money and life back into the school for its doors once more to open. This is sense of community working at its best and its existence seems a positive sign for the quality of American life.

Community Mental Health and Community Psychology

Disenchantment with individual psychotherapy, counseling, and psychiatry as the primary mental health approaches in the country has been developing for years. Both the effectiveness (Eysenck 1952) and the scope of the mental health delivery system (Reiff 1967, 1975) have been directly questioned. On college campuses, for example, the adoption of a community-based, environmental-change approach to mental health has been suggested (Conyne 1975, 1978; Conyne and Clack 1975), the analysis indicating strongly that an intrapsychic mental health emphasis by itself is inadequate for the times. These authors are not alone. For example, Chu and Trotter in the *Nader Report on Community Mental Health* (1972) lend support to volunteers and paraprofessionals running their own agencies, with mental health professionals serving as trainers and supersivors. The *Report of the Midwest Subcommittee on Prevention* (1975) for the Division of Counseling Psychology of the American Psychological Association pictures the emerging purpose of counseling psychology to be "a community-based mental health approach with emphases upon skills in training, supervision, consultation, change agentry, and organizational development with a special focus upon minority and disadvantaged populations."

The intent of community mental health and its "cousin," community psychology, is to approach the community environment as the client. Community mental health centers, organized following the Community Mental

Health Act of 1963, were established through federal funds to offer five services: inpatient care, outpatient care, partial hospitalization, emergency care, and community education and consultation. Especially germane to the present discussion are the community education and consultation aspects of the Act. A particular focus was to create a "community of therapists" (Murrell 1973), where such "caretakers" (Caplan 1964) as teachers, bartenders, police, and so on would behave more therapeutically, thus serving to decrease the emergence of problems. A parallel community mental health goal of community-based care, coincidental with the right-to-treatment movement in mental health (for example, *O'Conner* v. *Donaldson*; *Wyatt* v. *Aderholt*), has resulted in a desired reduction of inpatients in mental institutions and a large influx of former patients into communities, along with considerable management problems that are as yet unresolved.

Community psychology began to develop an identity at the May 1965 Conference on the Education of Psychologists for Community Mental Health, held in Swampscott, Massachusetts, thereafter referred to as the Swampscott Conference. In its decade and a half of existence, community psychology has attempted to forge an emphasis away from the traditionally intrapsychic focus of clinical psychology and the community-care approach of community mental health, toward a social systems change focus. The National Training Conference on Community Psychology, held in August 1974 at Austin, Texas (the Austin Conference), further focused these directions and identified three broad community psychology models: community mental health/community psychology (Model I), systems and social change (Model II), and ecological community psychology (Model III) (Stenmark 1975). These models all approach the environment as the target for change—in fact, it can be said that the environment of an individual is the community psychology laboratory (Yolles 1966). Model III, ecological community psychology, most clearly approaches the emphasis we take in environmental assessment/design.

Architectual Design and User Behavior

Lawrence Haworth in his book *The Good City* (1963) has argued that the common cause unifying city inhabitants should be, simply, the city itself. For him, provisions must be made in the architectural style and planning of a city to allow a sense of community to develop and continue. Specifically, more parks, sidewalks, open spaces, more green areas, are needed. If architects and urban planners were to inquire, "What do people want to see in their cities?" they would probably obtain information of this kind. Ongoing campus environmental assessment data being obtained corroborates Haworth's position, as well. At the risk of overgeneralizing, the observation might be made that college students, too, want (or need) natural, open, green spaces on their campuses. Moreover, these spaces would seem to have important meaning to most people, regardless of setting.

The relationship of physical form and design to the functions people perform within physical space is one with which architects and applied behavioral scientists are only recently beginning to grapple. As Robert Sommer has observed in his book *Personal Space: The Behavioral Bases of Design* (1969), a shift in temporal perspective is needed from the analyses of the past and projections into the future to the study of the present, especially with regard to user behavior. Buildings and public spaces are planned and constructed to accommodate functions as well as to be aesthetically appealing. But are the end products satisfying to the consumers? Following completion, the architect usually leaves the project, never knowing of the impact on the people who actually use the structure. City planners and engineers create designs to maximize the efficient use of automobiles, resulting in people not only no longer wishing to walk, but being unable to find a place to walk if they so choose. This not only makes people flabby but cuts them off from each other (Hall 1969). User behavior is too often ignored, and therefore the same kinds of structures continue to be built, incorporating many of the same old problems! Louis Sauer (architect), Clare Cooper (urban geographer), Paul Gump (psychologist), and Aristide Esser (psychologist) have commented on the relationship between applied behavioral scientists and architects, and about user behavior in a paper by Sauer titled, "The Architect and User Needs" (1972). Bits and pieces of their conversation have been extracted to capture several important points (pp. 162-65):

Esser: Communication is the most important part of the total gap between the designers and the behavioral scientists, and of course, we need hard data.

Cooper: There is quite a bit of hard data available. It's just that it doesn't get into places where architects and other decision-makers see it or it is not written in such a way that they can comprehend it.

Sauer: By the time the architect is retained, the major most important decisions are made, which is [are]: where is it going to be, how many units, and how they are made. The architect is not a decisive actor in this scene.

Gump: (Regarding user behavior) . . . An architect and designer moves on. If one is going to follow up the effects of one's work and . . . make manipulations in terms of follow-up, we have to overcome what is now not a natural procedure in the way things go.

Sauer: The reason for that is time. When a doctor operates, it is within a certain time scale . . . but with an architect, that little project of 22 units, it's been four years since I began it and it's just being done. So from the time I began, when I started to factor some thoughts in, to the time I can run the test, is going to be from five to six years. That's why the architect moves on. There is a terrible time lag. It doesn't mean that we still can't do something about it.

And slowly concern for users of buildings and sites is developing. Paul Gapp reported in the *Chicago Tribune* (October 26, 1975) on a study of user behavior conducted by landscape architecture graduate students of the University of Illinois (Urbana). The First National Bank of Chicago plaza provided the behavioral setting for analysis. Through observational and interview techniques conducted during the spring and summer of 1975, these students were able to gather enough data to allow Professor Albert Rudledge to generate a 67-page summary of most interesting findings. In the words of the report, "The post-construction evaluation process can . . . be looked upon as never-ending, as lessons learned from the past leading to new assumptions to be tested in the future. Design has most often been looked upon as a linear process which expires upon the execution of the construction contract—whereas in reality, the end is not an absolute." This study of user behavior in physical settings serves to demonstrate one means for architects and others to obtain meaningful data—and from a source that has been too long neglected. Attention to user behavior can aid in designing and constructing environments more suitable for human behavior. Important, too, is that use behavior provides a bridge over which designers and applied behavioral scientists can walk together.

Ecology Movement

> My ears were hearing descriptions of the development of a problem almost incomprehensible in its enormity, with prediction of starving millions, violent revolutions, and wars directly fostered by population pressures, while my eyes looked out over a group of very satisfied and comfortable people who had just finished wining and dining at the area's finest restaurant, their clothing stylish, their late-model, often expensive cars parked outside waiting to whisk them away to their comfortable upper-middle class homes. And sure enough, there among the audience were a few individuals dozing off for a nice, full-stomach, after-dinner nap, while the speaker at times perhaps slightly irritated their slumber with strong words about empty bloated stomachs, skeletal children, and the borrowed time for America's way of life. (Bartz 1971)

Rachel Carson's *The Sea Around Us* (1951), and *Silent Spring* (1962), John Steinbeck's *The Grapes of Wrath* (1939), William and Paul Paddock's *Famine 1975!* (1967), Paul Ehrlich's *The Population Bomb* (1968), Garrett DeBell's *The Environmental Handbook* (1970), and Ruth Moore's *Man in the Environment* (1975), each in its own way extrapolates on Thomas Malthus's nineteenth-century economic theory that population would increase geometrically while the food supply would outstrip the earth's resources, with starvation, war, and pestilence resulting.

The above sources are in the spirit of the ecology movement that advocates the recognition of the earth as a finite ecosystem. This earth-view holds that all living creatures are intimately interrelated, with total known resources approaching rapid and irreversible depletion. Many attempts at attitude and behavior change and some policy changes have arisen from this perspective. Primary among these have been attempts at population control, clean air legislation, development of alternative power technologies, recycling efforts, and so on, each of which carries political arguments both pro and con. (For a cogent article highly critical of the ecology movement, see "Ecology is a Racist Shuck," by Robert Chrisman, 1970). Neither the ecology proponents nor its critics can be accused of understating their positions.

The position taken here is not to side politically, but to underscore the ecology movement as an important contemporary force that has contributed to the development of an environmental perspective on the human condition. Bartz (1971) has wondered about Maslow's (1969) contention that the first and overarching big problem is to make the good person. Bartz (p. 383) believes it is not; rather, it is to first insure that there are *living* people, with enough to eat, room to live, and environments that are worth living in. "To the man who is starving in the street, who has watched his children die of disease and malnutrition and his country collapse in anarchy, questions of what makes a 'good person,' self-actualization, psychotherapy, interpersonal relations . . . are just so much bull." This position, taken by a psychologist, prods all applied behavioral scientists to examine closely their working assumptions and how they expend their time and expertise.

Applied Behavioral Science

The applied behavioral scientist attempts to foster planned change, with an individual, group, organization, system, or environmental focus. The term, "applied behavioral science," is an embracing one, including professionals whose raison d'être is the application of scientific principles to improve the human condition and to influence positively interpersonal behavior, organizational functioning, and environmental climate. Kurt Lewin, perhaps more than any other single person, may be seen as its founder and the National Training Laboratories (NTL) as the organization that gave needed impetus and nurturance to its development.

Many of the change interventions that are now available will be reviewed in Chapter 4. The range and depth of possible interventions, with alternative foci on individuals, groups, organizations, and environments, is rapidly growing. Gaining increased importance among applied behavioral scientists is what has been labeled a meta-direction for interventions (Conyne and Clack 1975) with efforts aimed at environmental change and design. Related professional work in organizational assessment and development, ecological community psychology and sociology, social ecology, ecosystems, and environmental-ecological psychology have all combined to suggest that this meta-direction is an emerging emphasis spreading throughout the applied behavioral sciences.

As this chapter has pointed out, the influence of the environment on human functioning (and its reciprocal) has remained largely an untapped resource for change projects, although a person-environmental emphasis is emerging within the applied behavioral sciences, integrating these heretofore separate components.

SUMMARY

The environment is an important influencer of human behavior. One need only examine everyday experience to sense the truth of this statement. Yet the primary emphasis of the applied behavioral sciences, and especially of psychology, has been on people apart from their environment.

This chapter has examined in some detail the underdeveloped role attributed to the environment by personality theorists. Though not explicitly stated, however, most analytic, behavioral, and phenomenological personality theorists give implicit importance to the environment as a shaper of personality, while a few are explicit in their extrapolations of environmental effects.

More contemporary forces leading to a new environmental awareness were discussed, including people radicalism, the radical therapists, group experiences, sense of community, community mental health and community psychology, architectural design and user behavior, the ecology movement, and meta-directions in the applied behavioral services.

All of these forces, in sum, have led to current interest in the transactions between people and their environment. This interest underlies the topic of this book, environmental design, an innovative model for use in improving human functioning by positively modifying environmental settings and structures.

2

ENVIRONMENTAL CLASSIFICATION: UNDERSTANDING THE HUMAN ENVIRONMENT

It may be recalled that in *The Music Man* (Willson 1950) it was critical for "Professor" Hill to "know the territory" of River City. In his case, this knowledge was necessary for him to successfully select a piece of it to "con." In environmental design, the central focus of this book, getting to know the territory is termed "environmental classification." Several methods have been developed to accomplish this task. The Music Man would be interested in them, but then he might object to the complexity used in what for him appeared to be a natural and relatively efficient approach: one comes to know the territory by sharpening one's senses and getting to know the lay of the land and the people who live there. Actually, these are still basic methods that characterize many environmental classification approaches.

And yet, as with the varieties and vicissitudes of life itself, environmental classification has grown more sophisticated and complex; however, it is perhaps not more effective because the methodology is still in its empirical infancy (Moos 1979b). Beginning with the primary question of what an environment is, classification moves toward examining and trying to understand various slices or elements of a particular environment. Environmental classification is conducted to help in describing and understanding an environment. It is a critical first step in environmental design, the "evaluated, planned, collaborative change of human environments," which will be elaborated in subsequent chapters. At this point an environment needs to be defined.

WHAT IS THE ENVIRONMENT?

Steele (1973) has presented a useful definition of environment in which he has stressed the importance of four successive environmental levels: geophysical environment, containing the weather, terrain, seasons, and the largest built products of humanity (roads, bridges, building complexes, and the like); techno-physical environment, the built physical objects, on a smaller scale, that are in a person's or a group's immediate surroundings (furniture, machines, art work, and so on); social environment, the immediate psychosocial climate that surrounds a person or a group (opinions, norms, values, and so forth); and surrounding these three levels is the culture in which the person or group is located, including shared history and customs, accumulated knowledge and common language, and the totality of people over time.

While environmental psychology (for example, Hiemstra and McFarling 1978; Ittelson et al. 1974; Proshansky, Ittelson, and Rivlin 1970) and ecological psychology (Barker 1968) have provided the impetus and synthesizing forces for applied behavioral scientists, their combined emphasis has been primarily on the physical or nonpsychological environment, from a research and theoretical stance. This focus represents a major divergence from previous neglect of the physical environment, and therefore it represents a significant contribution. Along with Moos (1973), however, the authors of this book find subscribing to this approach alone too limited. Thus the approach taken here is both interactive and integrative. It involves assessing the transactions of people with the physical, social, institutional, and ecological climate units of an environment. A further departure is that this practical approach to the environment is rooted in environmental design rather than in theory and research alone.

Further, a distinction is made between "environment" and "environment of reference," designated as E_r. An environment can be infinite in scope unless it is bounded in some way. The term E_r provides a label necessary for specifying the setting that is selected for design; for example, that the E_r is Sunnyside Park rather than a whole city. Therefore, the term E_r will be used throughout this book to refer to a designated portion of a total environment, a bounded setting.

Environmental Components

An E_r is viewed as consisting of three primary components, three interactive effects components, a collective impression dimension, and a contextual factor. The three major components are termed physical, social, and institutional, while the three interactive effects components are labeled physical-social, social-institutional, and institutional-physical. The ecological climate is the E_r constituents' aggregate impression, emanating from an accumulation of the values, attitudes, and opinions toward all components of the E_r. These seven environmental units are always imbedded within the contexts of the larger environment. An E_r is depicted in Figure 2.1, and each environmental unit described is subsequently discussed in more detail.

The physical component of an E_r subsumes both natural and built features including weather and climate, terrain, and built objects from the largest to the

FIGURE 2.1: An Environment of Reference (E_r)

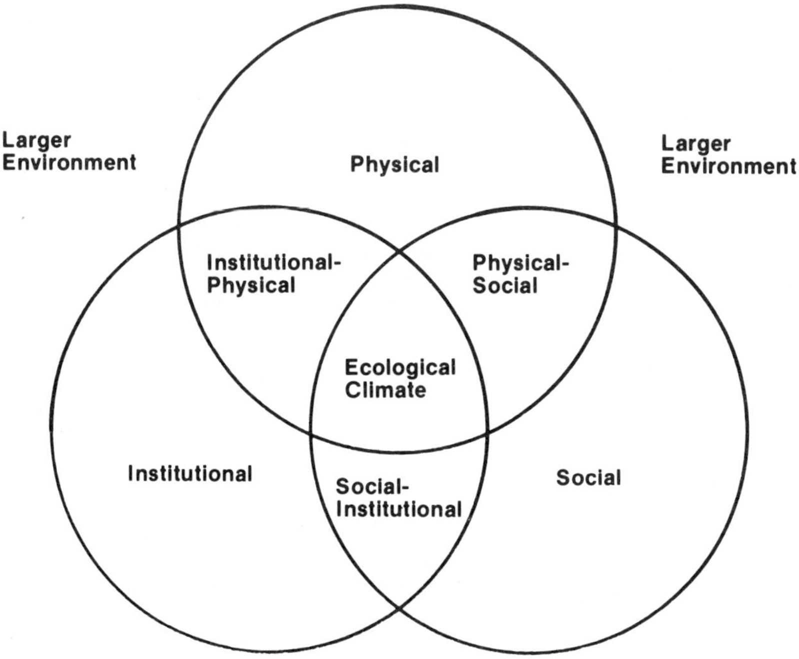

[Venn diagram with three overlapping circles labeled Physical, Institutional, and Social. Overlaps are labeled Institutional-Physical, Physical-Social, Social-Institutional, and the center is Ecological Climate. Outside the circles on left and right: Larger Environment.]

Source: Constructed by the authors.

smallest scale. The social component contains the demographic and personal characteristics of people and their behavior. The institutional component is comprised of both written and unwritten and formal and informal laws, codes, policies, procedures, and mores; in sum, all policies and procedures that implicitly or explicitly govern human behavior in the E_r.

The three interactive components have heuristic value in that they serve to show relationships among the physical, social, and institutional components of an E_r. The physical-social component represents an interaction of natural or built environmental elements with the characteristics and relationships of people. A sudden thunderstorm intervening during a family picnic may result in a change from a lazy, congenial social atmosphere to one of frenzy and aggravation; or the social interactions of a group of people may turn a street corner into a regular meeting place. The interactive social-institutional component can be illustrated by the development of "grapevine" communication to overcome the lack of formal channels of communication in some work place (E_r), or the effects of the 55-mile-per-hour speed limit on the bahavior of a cross-country truck driver. The institutional-physical component is typified by a zoning change that would replace a green belt with a housing development, or the protection by law of the grandeur of a natural phenomenon as a wildlife preserve. Due to the newness of assessment methodologies in use at this time, little has been done to isolate these interactive effects; nevertheless their existence is apparent.

The ecological climate dimension is the summary judgment that constituents give to an E_r. It is defined as the predominant, molar evaluation of an E_r that reflects all its components. Everyday expressions that characterize the workings of the ecological climate dimension might be, "Austin is a good place to live," or "This is a lousy place to work." That is, the ecological climate is a global, shared reaction to an E_r. This dimension exists as an attribute of an E_r and it serves, also, as a mediator in the ways individuals perceive a particular environment. If "everybody" is saying Austin is a good place to live or the Smith Company is a lousy place to work, credence is given to these general shared perceptions, and there is a tendency to view an E_r from this base. In sum, the ecological climate exists as an entity in an environment and it serves to temper perceptions of all other environmental components (Moos 1979a, 1979b). It is an amalgamation of individual global perceptions. Further, all individuals have their own individual perceptions of an E_r, which may or may not be consonant with the ecological climate. To illustrate a discrepant situation, some residents may regard Austin as an unfriendly city (contrary to shared perceptions) and the president of the Smith Company might view his organization as being top-notch (again, contrary to shared perceptions).

Examples of E_rs

Perhaps some extended examples will further clarify the definition of E_r.

Twenty behavioral scientists from throughout the United States have been carefully screened in terms of their academic credentials and work experiences for acceptance into a human dynamics workshop being conducted by a small group of eminent leaders in their field. As the participants arrive at the social sciences building of the prestigious eastern university, the site of the workshop, they note that the ivy-covered building nestled in the sprawling urban campus projects the essence of academia. Upon entering the seminar room, participants find exactly 20 desks spaced some distance from each other, all facing a slightly elevated platform on which stands a well-polished lectern. Similarly located on each desk are a pad of paper, a ball-point pen, an ash tray, and a packet of printed material. Closer examination indicates that the top sheet of the material is an hour-by-hour agenda of the workshop's activities, including structured breaks. A notation at the bottom of the sheet reminds all participants that all workshop activities will begin promptly at the appointed hour so that adjournment can likewise occur on time. A few of the participants nod to or formally introduce themselves to those near them; but the room becomes silent as the organizer and main speaker of the conference enters, followed single file by the other workshop staff. The leader wears a stylish three-piece plaid suit, is well groomed, and strides purposefully to the lectern. He turns and faces the participants and states, "Gentlemen, we are here to further your understanding. Since this is a short workshop, I suggest that you apply yourselves to the fullest in order that you may gain the most from the distinguished presenters that have been assembled for your benefit. Without further ado it is my pleasure to introduce Dr. Upright, who will present the opening lecture—Dr. Upright."

Before analyzing the E_r in the above example, it may be useful to view a second example of an E_r and then examine their differences by applying the definition of E_r discussed previously in this chapter.

Twenty people from many walks of life have applied and been selected for participation in a weekend personal growth workshop. As the participants arrive at the oceanside location of the well-known Growth Center they are aware of the lush grounds, the breaking surf at a distance, and the artistic, natural landscaping. Reporting to a large room, they note the comfortable-looking overstuffed chairs and sofas and the many colorful pillows and cushions scattered about the floor. Two very casually dressed people who identify themselves as the group's leaders mill about the room warmly greeting the arriving participants, inviting them to meet their fellow participants and to make themselves comfortable. Shortly after the scheduled starting time one of the leaders asks the participants to gather themselves so that all can hear. She notes that few activities other than meals are scheduled, and that the learning that will occur during the workshop will come primarily out of the resources found within and among themselves. And with that she suggests that members share their personal goals as a way of giving direction to the total experience.

For purposes of demonstration, the E_rs in the examples above will be described and contrasted by identifying factors in the physical, social, and institutional components of each E_r and then the ecological climate will be extrapolated from these descriptions. Interactive components in these examples will not be identified, but the reader is encouraged to try to do so.

Table 2.1 presents a way to examine each E_r previously discussed. Reviewing this chart makes it possible to quickly notice differences in the two workshops (E_rs) even though they contain highly similar contents of human dynamics and personal growth. To say this in another way, it would be expected that these E_rs would have differential effects on participants, an expectation that evolves from the definition of an E_r. Applied to the two workshop examples, the expectation is that the E_rs will affect participants unequally because their physical, social, and institutional components and their resulting ecological climate dimensions are distinctly dissimilar.

Each E_r, then, would be expected to exert immediate and powerful impact on participants. In the first E_r (human dynamics workshop), those who attend will probably be primarily recipients who take notes, meet on time, and interact cognitively in a quite formal atmosphere. In the second E_r (personal growth workshop), members will probably be actively involved in the entire experience,

TABLE 2.1: Two Environments of Reference (E_r)

Environmental Component	Human Dynamics Workshop	Personal Growth Workshop
Physical	Large, sprawling urban campus	Oceanside Growth Center
	Ivy-covered buildings	Lush and natural surroundings
	Exactly spaced desks	Breaking surf
	Elevated platform	Artistic landscaping
	Polished lectern	Overstuffed furniture
	Arrangement and type of materials on desk	Pillows on floor
Social	Participants nod and formally introduce themselves	Casual dress of leaders
	Leaders enter single file	Leaders mill about room greeting participants
	Clothing of leader is stylish, three-piece plaid suit	Participants are encouraged to make themselves comfortable
	Leader is well groomed	Leaders encourage inter-participant introductions
	Leader strides purposefully	Leader "suggests" activities
	Leader's greeting is formal and has a high task orientation	
Institutional	Meeting held at university	Few activities scheduled
	Scholarly reputation of university	Resources of workshop located within participants
	Printed material stating rules	Participants invited to share their personal goals
Ecological Climate	Stuffy	Fluid
	Formal	Natural
	High-powered	Open
	Impersonal	Personal
	Cold	Warm
	Intellectual emphasis	People emphasis
	In the "midst of greatness"	"Among friends"

Source: Compiled by authors.

following a loose time schedule, while sharing many personal feelings in a highly informal atmosphere. The point is not that one E_r is better than the other, that one is good and the other bad, but rather that each E_r has strong and differential effect upon participants. Implied in the examples is the position that an E_r is to a large extent selected and/or created by humans, giving rise to the possibility that its impact can be made more positive on humans through environmental design. This point, implicit now, will become explicit in subsequent chapters.

Having a general definition of what an environment is provides a background for conducting environmental design. Needed next, therefore, is information to use in classifying environments. Classification approaches are important because they make it possible to describe and understand a variety of environments. Several environmental classification approaches have been developed over the past decade or so. Six general approaches to environmental classification that tap much of this wide range of existing approaches will be overviewed in this chapter. Data sources typically used in these classification approaches will then be discussed. This combination of classification approaches and data sources yields a matrix that is presented both to summarize the overview section, and to provide guidance for those interested in environmental design.

Following this overview section, five environmental classification models, which can be seen in relation to the matrix already developed will be examined. These models (social ecology, ecosystem, open-system, functions of physical settings, and mapping) receive attention because of their implicit usefulness for change agents interested in environmental design.

CATEGORIES IN ENVIRONMENTAL CLASSIFICATION

Rudolph Moos's work in his Social Ecology Laboratory at Stanford University has contributed strongly to environmental classification and to environmental assessment research methodologies. One example is his helpful categorization of the variety of human environment classification approaches available into six broad categories. Because this work is so useful conceptually, the overview of environmental classification draws heavily from it.

Moos (1973) has presented six categories of human environments that he views as having relationship to human functioning: ecological, behavior setting, organizational structure, inhabitant's behavior and characteristics, psychosocial climate, and functional reinforcement analysis. Each of these classification strategies is discussed below. These often overlapping categories were hewn out of the broad, cluttered environmental classification panorama, and they help to sort out the complexity.

Moos constructed the six categories in order to identify initial directions for organizing the nascent environmental assessment field. He stresses that accomplishment of this task is necessary to provide a common lexicon for change agents as they begin contributing to the humanistic design of physical and social systems.

General Approaches

Ecological

In the ecological perspective, society is viewed as being shaped by geographical, meteorological, and physical design dimensions of the environment. Such factors as terrain, weather, and buildings serve as classifiers. Environmental determinists have maintained that environmental elements and characteristics are directly connected with emerging personality traits, giving rise to such notions, for example, as hot, humid weather being paired often with inactivity, and cooler, drier weather associated with productivity. Ecological and environmental psychology, architectural design, and urban planning owe much of their professional development to the ecological perspective, which emphasizes the effect of the natural elements and of the larger built environment on human perceptions and behavior.

The world of the applied behavioral scientist, architect, and urban planner is centered more directly on the human effects of the built environment, consisting of architectural and physical design variables. Important work in the area has been done by Craik (1970), Holahan (1980), Ittelson et al. (1974), and Proshansky, Ittelson, and Rivlin (1970). Sommer (1969) offers a very interesting analysis of how designers and applied behavioral scientists can merge their respective disciplines through a focus on user behavior in built environments. Steele (1971, 1973) has provided an interesting and useful physical environment assessment approach that will be explored later in subsequent chapters.

Innovative experimental projects are occurring in physical design. For instance, Paolo Soleri, the architect, is planning to test the effect of ultra-high density on humans through Arcosanti, his current architectural endeavor that is located 70 miles north of Scottsdale, Arizona. This project is a mini-arcology, combining architecture and ecology, and it is comprised of modules stacked 30 stories high, housing 3,000 people on seven acres of land. Soleri reports viewing the effort as "earth's first self-contained urban structure, the preliminary test of maximum density in the only way possible—pragmatically" (Schaar 1975, p. 7).

On the other hand, Hall (1969) points to some of the dangers inherent in architectural projects such as Soleri's Arcosanti. Addressing urban renewal, he notes that while high-rise apartments are more attractive than the slums they replace, they are more disturbing places in which to live. The high-rise fails to meet human needs such as security and the desire of parents to observe and supervise their children at play. Hall proceeds to describe the necessity for considering ethnic and social class dimensions in urban architectural projects, suggesting that high-rises may be an effective way for maximizing the use of space but detrimental in terms of family, neighborhood, and social ramifications.

Effects of the built environment on humans is a growing area of interest that attracts a diverse range of investigators drawn from a variety of disciplines including psychology, sociology, urban planning, architecture, and geography (Holahan 1980). As a testimony to the current high interest in this area, environmental and ecological psychology programs have emerged in universities, the Environmental Design Research Association (EDRA) was established to attract the broad group of researchers interested in ecological matters, and a new journal (*Environmental and Behavior*) has been initiated to provide an outlet for this new research area.

Behavioral Settings

The behavioral setting approach (Barker 1968; Barker and Associates 1978; Barker and Gump 1964) and others (for example, Wicker 1979a, 1979b) has contributed significantly to behavioral ecology, the description of molar behavior and functions performed in specific ecological contexts. These contexts, called behavior settings, occur naturally. They are neither created nor controlled by experimenters. Behavior settings contain two interacting components, the specific behaviors actually occurring and the nonpsychological environmental objects with which the behavior is transacted. Thus, they have both an environmental and a behavioral aspect, the combination commanding pervasive impact on individuals. Behavioral settings, such as an office, locker room, church, brothel, or classroom, are stable units that themselves exercise considerable "demand" for certain behaviors to be performed in each of them. For example, people almost never worship in a brothel nor do they generally have sexual intercourse in a church, although under unique circumstances (such as war) these unexpected behaviors could occur. The behavior setting itself, then, enforces strong behavioral sanctions that would seem to apply across like situations. Behavior at a football game in Stanford, Connecticut would be very much like behavior at a football game in Las Cruces, New Mexico; the name of the game is essentially the same.

In the traditional behavior setting approach to environmental classification, particular real-world settings are identified for making detailed, unobtrusive observations of naturally occurring behaviors. The observer is a transducer of data rather than a manipulator. Wicker (1979b), however, has recently challenged this approach by proposing that technologies be developed that would allow deliberate intervention within behavior settings in order to improve setting functioning and to enhance the well-being of people who occupy them.

Underlying Barker's behavioral setting approach is the work of Egon Brunswik (1955). He proposed the Environment-Environment Unit (E-E Unit), the so-called "macro unit" of psychological attention. This unit, which Barker

(1960) has called the "true vein of psychological ore," extends from the afferent ecological environment physical stimuli (what acts on the organism), through the organism (intrapersonal action), to the efferent ecological environment (what the organism acts on), or:

Afferent Ecological Environment → Organism → Efferent Ecological Environment

In this psychological unit, the environment, the organism, and behavior are all interdependent. In a simple example, loud music from a neighbor's stereo (afferent ecological environment) influences George to decide to ask the neighbor to please lower the volume on her stereo (organism), which she does (efferent ecological environment). Barker's behavior settings approach emphasizes the E-E Unit by minutely observing the interface of environment, person, and environment in a setting. In such a manner every detailed descriptive classification of the setting evolves, producing specific data that can guide subsequent environment design.

Organization Structure

Environments can be classified according to organizational structure variables, arising from demographic, behavioral, and/or perceptual data sources. Descriptive analyses of organizations, based on relevant demographic data such as size, organizational chart, staff educational background, salaries, and so on, yield relatively objective data. This demographic approach allows for a description of one organization as well as for comparisons of organizations with each other. For example, on the basis of these criteria the environment of college A can be compared with that of college B, or business A with business B.

This is a rather static approach, however, providing few environmental data of psychological or behavioral interest. A more dynamic approach is found in exploring relationships between demographic variables and selected attitudes and behaviors. Astin (1968), for instance, has investigated the effects of selected college and university variables, such as faculty-student ratio and total undergraduate enrollment, on undergraduate achievement. He concludes that these traditional indexes contribute little to student academic achievement. The study of crowding behavior also well illustrates this more dynamic method. Altman, Taylor, and Wheeler (1971), Barker and Gump (1964), Duhl (1963), Freedman (1975), Freedman, Klevansky, and Ehrlich (1971), Hall (1969), Milgram (1970), and Sommer (1969) have all studied the relationships of the effects of crowding, size, and social isolation on humans, with generally inconclusive results. Clearer are the negative outcomes emanating from experimental laboratory studies of animals in crowded conditions.

Part of the authors' own focus in environmental classification has been to conceptualize organizational structure variables, such as size and procedures used, in relation to their impact on an organization's client-consumers. This framework evolves from an open-system model (Katz and Kahn 1966), to be discussed in the next section. Such an extended view has been found to open new territory for design projects.

Inhabitants' Behavior and Characteristics

The work of Astin (1968), Astin and Holland (1961), and Holland (1970, 1973) illustrates this fourth environmental classification method. In general, their positions maintain that an environment reflects, in large part, the personal characteristics and perceived behavior of its inhabitants. This view is analogous to "You are what you eat": the form of an environment results from the people it contains.

The earlier work of Henry Murray (1938), in which he first articulated study of behavior as an interaction between personality needs and environmental press, has contributed to this environmental classification view as well as to the climate view to be discussed next. Murray's work was of seminal importance to development of the person-environmental perspective.

In the present classification approach, objective demographic data about the environment and the people in it are obtained. Specific attention is then given to the degree of congruence that is found to exist between people and the environment.

Holland's (1970, 1973) Self-Directed Search (SDS), a vocational interest inventory growing out of his assumptions regarding personality and work environments, serves as an adequate example of this environmental classification approach. Holland has identified six personality types and the same six environment types: realistic, intellectual, social, conventional, enterprising, and artistic. The congruence between environment and personality type is assessed through the SDS to suggest appropriate career choices. The assumption that Holland makes, which characterizes this strategy, is that the match between people and environment is the crucial variable for classification purposes. A congruent people-environment match, for example, would be an artistic environment resulting from a predominance of the artistic personality types creating it.

Psychosocial Climate

Early work in this classification area has drawn from demographic and behavioral data sources. Moos (1973) points out that most recent work relates to the development and use of perceptual data regarding the psychosocial climate of institutions. Pace and Stern (1958) extended Murray's concept of environmental press to the perceived environmental climate of colleges and universities, adding that his perceived climate dimension strongly influences people's behavior. Stern (1970) comprehensively presents the need-press theory, its empirical procedures, and research. Most of the need-press climate orientation developed from operationalizing Lewin's (1936) concept of behavior as resulting from an interaction of people with their environment [B = f (P, E)], and from Murray's personality theory.

Several kinds of measures are available in this fifth classification approach. For example, ten perceived social climate scales have been developed by Moos (1979a) in the Social Ecology Laboratory at Stanford University. Each scale is specific to an environment and belongs to any of four broad types: treatment environments (three scales), total institutions (two scales), educational environments (two scales), and primary settings (three scales). Moos (1973, 1979a, 1979b) has identified three basic psychosocial climate dimensions that he claims "characterize and discriminate among different sub-units within each of these . . . environments" (1973, p. 657): a relationship dimension, which assesses the involvement of people with their environment and the degree of interpersonal support and expressiveness present; a personal development dimension, which assesses the opportunities that the environment affords for personal growth and enhancement of self-esteem; and a system maintenance and system change dimension, which assesses the environment's orderliness, clarity, control, and responsiveness to change.

Other psychosocial climate scales contain dimensions that are similar to those mentioned above. In all, these scales are used to classify an environment according to its perceived climate. The scales have been proved useful also in environmental assessment, with resulting data used in environmental design.

Functional Reinforcements

The stimulus variables contained in particular environments serve to shape the range and expression of human behavior. The reinforcement consequences present in specific social and physical environments are influenceable determinants of the variety of human behavior to be expected (Bandura, 1974). The functional analysis of these environmental stimuli and reinforcements is an environmental classification methodology whose origins lie in the social learning approach to behavior therapy (Bandura 1969; Mischel 1979). This classification approach seeks to specify the environmental conditions that influence, support, and maintain particular behaviors of selected individuals.

The functional reinforcement analysis approach shares much in common with the behavior setting method of Barker, discussed earlier in this chapter. Both are focused on specific environmental settings with reference to identifying and describing salient environmental influences on behavior. A functional reinforcement analysis differs from the behavior setting approach, however, in its idiographic rather than molar emphasis. Also different is its attempt precisely to assess the relationship between behavior elicited and the exact controlling stimuli, discriminative stimuli, and substantive reinforcers directly associated with the behavior. This classification strategy seeks to delineate specific environmental stimuli and reinforcers surrounding one individual's behavior, through participants' perceptions and from behavioral ratings made by independent observers. Such an analysis could be conducted, for example, to identify the environmental conditions sustaining Johnny's ability to ask questions in English class but his failure to do so in history class.

The goal is to discover what conditions in specific environments stimulate, maintain, and reinforce precise bahaviors of individuals. Once these environmental conditions associated with certain behaviors are identified, then behavior change can be approached from an environmental design perspective. Farson (1969) has captured this perspective when he suggests that, "instead of trying to improve people, improve environments. . . . People, fundamentally, change little in their personalities and attitudes. They can, however, change markedly in their responses to different environments, situations, and conditions" (p. 21).

Trying to enhance people's behaviors, and thus their lives, cannot be approached willy-nilly through environmental design. Functional reinforcement analyses of environments can provide a large amount of necessary data about an individual's behaviors, related environmental stimuli, and reinforcers. Needed as well is an accompanying value system for environmental design. Practitioners need to come to grips seriously with guidelines for deciding what behaviors are to be increased or decreased through environmental design. The functional reinforcement classification approach serves to bring to the fore questions and issues regarding the relationship between environmental design and human values. This relationship will be addressed in the discussion of the implications of environmental design in Chapter 6.

Environmental Classification Data Sources

Menne (1967) has suggested three environmental classification data sources, labeling them demographic, perceptual, and behavioral; Hyne (1976) has added a fourth, multimethod. A discussion of each source follows.

Demographic data include descriptive indexes of an environment, such as number of faculty members, institutional size, racial and sexual indexes, course registration data, economic indexes, residence patterns, and the like. These variables are specific, verifiable, and lend themselves to manipulation. They are relatively stable over time however, and thus tend to be generally unresponsive to environmental changes. A city's telephone directory provides an everyday example of a readily available source containing useful demographic data about a city, its services, and its residents.

Perceptual data for environmental classification arise from the feelings, attitudes, opinions, and impressions of specific people (target groups) in a population. As Pace (1969) observes, the use of collective perceptions as a data source rests on the cliché that "fifty million Frenchmen can't be wrong." The argument here is essentially from phenomenological psychology, and it embraces the position of the gestaltist Koffka (1922), who asserted the importance of the perceived environment over the actual environment. In this view, what people think is true is true for them, and that is reality. Thus, a civic center may offer many valuable and entertaining programs, but if a large number of people perceive its physical structure to be cold and uninviting, this perceived reality may influence them to stay away. In this view, people act on their own unique perceptions of reality. As a data source for environmental classification, perceptions are quite responsive to environmental design, yet the question persists as to whether or not perceptual reports may be biased (Centra 1968), or reflect a too limited perspective. Many instruments are currently available however, to provide perceptual data for environmental classification, including the Institutional Functioning Inventory (Peterson et al. 1970), the College and University Environment Scale (Pace 1969), and the Social Climate Scales (Moos and Humphrey 1974).

The behavioral approach to environmental classification represents a third data base. Behavioral data used for this purpose stem from the influence of experimental psychophysics and Watsonian behaviorism, where the environment is what it is, not how it is perceived to be or experienced. Of relevance in our civic center example would be the specific uses people make of the center, rather than their individual or collective perceptions of it. Data for environmental classification are generated from the careful observations of specific behaviors and events in selected behavior settings. This focus is best expressed through environmental psychology (for example, Proshanky, Ittelson, and Rivlin 1970), and from ecological psychology (Barker 1968), with their emphases on the objective relationship between the physical environment and specific functional behaviors. Behavior mapping in environmental psychology well represents a procedure for gathering this kind of data.

Behavior as the data source includes not only specific behaviors but also nonpsychological objects with which behavior is associated. Thus, behavioral data in a classroom might include talking and sitting (specific behaviors) in relation to seat, wall, and blackboards (associated nonpsychological objects). Also, it might include geographic references such as location and spatial relationships. Specificity and objectivity are important criteria that offer advantages for later environmental change efforts. Minimized or excluded in this approach are subjective perceptions and, perhaps, the added richness associated with felt experience.

The fourth data source is a combination of the previous three, and it can be termed multimethod. In this shotgun or comprehensive approach (depending on one's biases), the demographic, perceptual, and behavioral sources of data are all used in combination. The College Student Experiences questionnaire (Pace 1979) illustrates this method. The multimethod approach to environmental classification allows for broadness and quantity in data collection, the capacity to approach a question from several perspectives, and it can lead to subsequent opportunities for more defined and focused study. Its limitations include the relative superficiality and nonspecificity of analysis which, when present, results in problems of interpretation and of immediate action. A very real danger is that a researcher or practitioner may simply be overwhelmed by the complexity of the data, thus thwarting action.

ENVIRONMENTAL CLASSIFICATION MATRIX: A CONCEPTUAL TOOL

The environmental classification matrix depicts the interrelation between the environmental categories adapted from Moos (1973) and data sources adapted from Hyne (1976). Each of the six environmental categories is related to the relevant data source(s). Classifications result from this combination. For instance, referring to Figure 2.2, an organizational environment can be understood from the standpoint of its structure, in which case relevant data sources for classification would be demographic, perceptual, behavioral, and a combination of these sources (multi).

This matrix may appear nice and neat, with no "slop." Let the reader be assured that it contains considerable overlap and some guessing: an attempt has been made to provide an organization that makes sense, while being as true to each dimension as possible. The chart can be seen as a snapshot capturing a fast moving target with a relatively unsophisticated camera, but this represents the current state of the art. Figure 2.2 presents the matrix.

The combined data source and category approach to environmental classification responds to two significant questions: What do we assess (categories)? and how do we obtain useful information (data source)? The environmental classification matrix provides direction for conceptualizing an E_r and it can be used to guide preliminary efforts in the subsequent environmental design activities.

FIVE ENVIRONMENTAL CLASSIFICATION MODELS

Now that several general environmental classification approaches have been overviewed, five models will be explored in greater detail. Each of these models generally endorses an ecological perspective (person-by-environment); yet each emphasizes a unique aspect of that view. Incidentally, these five models will be followed beyond this chapter to examine each of their approaches to assessment (Chapter 3) and to design (Chapter 4). The models are the social ecology model of Rudolf Moos (for example, 1979a), which takes a social ecological perspective; the ecosystem model of campus design (for example, WICHE 1973), which takes a transactional perspective; the open-system model (Katz and Kahn 1966), which takes a sociotechnical perspective; the functions of physical settings model (Steele 1973), which takes a sociophysical perspective; and cognitive (Downs and Stea 1973) and geographic models (for example, Smith 1979), which take a mapping perspective.

FIGURE 2.2: Environmental Classification Matrix

Data Sources   Category

	Demographic	Perceptual	Behavior	Multi
Ecological	X	XX	XXXX	
Behavior Setting			XXXX	
Organizational Structure	XXXX	XX	XX	X
Inhabitants Characteristics	XXX	XXXX		
Climate	X	XXXX	X	X
Functional Reinforcements			XXXX	

Note: XXXX = Most frequently used data source, XXX = Frequently used data source, XX = Somewhat frequently used data source, X = Occasionally used data source
Source: Constructed by the authors.

Social Ecological

Social ecology has emerged from ecology and human ecology. With these roots, it is concerned with the interactions of humans with their environment. Social ecology retains a focus on the ongoing adaptation of humans with physical characteristics of environments (for example, buildings, weather, temperature, and so on), yet, in addition, focuses on the social environment and its interaction with a physical milieu. A further distinguishing aspect of social ecology is its explicit value orientation that supports the promotion of optimal human functioning (Insel and Moos 1974).

Rudolf Moos is a leader in the field of social ecology, certainly so in the development of environmental classification and assessment. His work was mentioned in the earlier section on psychosocial climate. He and his colleagues' recent efforts have been to both broaden and consolidate their social ecological work.

In an interview with Lonnie Snowden, Moos (1979b) talks about these emerging directions. He identifies three general areas that it is important to examine. The first of these areas pushes the social ecology model beyond an emphasis on social climate measurement and change efforts only to include physical and architectural variables, organizational factors, and the aggregate characteristics of people in a setting. Next, he discusses the importance of developing a conceptual framework that sufficiently interrelates these environmental variables so that the "reciprocal causation" (p. 180) that exists between people and environments can be explained. Last, Moos is interested in the cognitive processes and the coping responses that people use to mediate the influence of an environment on them. In that regard, he echoes the emphasis of Bem and Allen (1974) and Mischel (1973, 1979) who have observed that the study of environments balances and should not displace the study of individuals. Mischel (1979), in fact, wants to move beyond the whole person-situation debate that has surrounded this phenomenon. He suggests that person and situation are interactive entities, and that greater attention needs to be paid to the role of cognition in personal functioning. It should be observed that the mediator phenomenon, as evidenced in cognitive appraisal, coping, social support, and so on, is currently gaining considerable favor as a critical factor in the person-situation interaction (for example, Fowler et al. 1979).

What emerges from these future directions is an integrative, social ecological, conceptual framework for understanding person-situation interaction. It includes social-environmental (for example, social climate), physical-environmental (ecological), and mediating processes in relation to outcomes. Figure 2.3 portrays this framework.

As can be seen by examining this figure, an objective environmental variable (such as a cold day) cannot be related directly to an outcome variable (such as boredom). Although environments and people are interactive, the nature of this activity is mediated (or moderated or buffered) by cognitive

FIGURE 2.3: A Framework Relating Environmental and Personal Variables with Outcomes

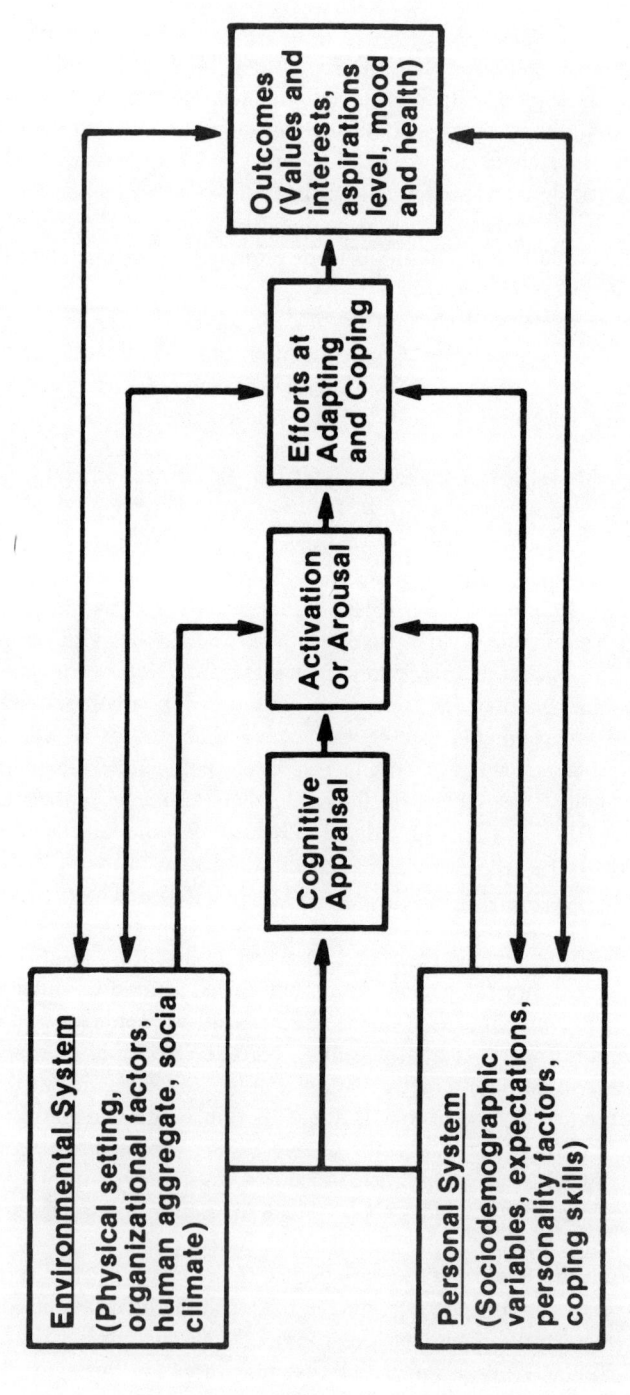

Environmental System
(Physical setting, organizational factors, human aggregate, social climate)

Personal System
(Sociodemographic variables, expectations, personality factors, coping skills)

Cognitive Appraisal → Activation or Arousal → Efforts at Adapting and Coping → Outcomes (Values and interests, aspirations level, mood and health)

Source: Adapted from Rudolf Moos, *Evaluating Educational Environments* (San Francisco: Jossey-Bass, 1979) Figure 1, p. 5. Reprinted with permission.

appraisal (an individual's evaluation of the environment), and when the environment is perceived as requiring a response, by coping and adaptation techniques. Thus, a cold day could be appraised by John as a good opportunity to stay inside and watch a basketball game (coping), leading to a feeling of contentment (outcome); while Sue could evaluate the cold day as foreboding, leading her to sleep (coping) and to feel guilty (outcome). Of course, many other variations are also possible, illustrating the importance of the mediating processes. Further, when the conceptual framework in Figure 2.3 is examined, it can be seen by the directionality of the arrows that adapting/coping efforts and outcomes realized both exert direct influence on the environmental and personal systems that, in turn, directly influence one another.

Ecosystem

This model is based on the person-environment paradigm as applied to the higher education setting (Banning 1978; Banning and Kaiser 1974; Huebner 1979; WICHE 1973). The ecosystem model is used to view the campus community as a series of transactions occurring among its various environments and campus members. Methodologically, the ecosystem model involves the continuous study of campus systems and how they interrelate with one another to create a range of environmental conditions for students. Action resulting from such study is taken to reduce student problems not by treating the student but by designing or modifying the environment that shapes student behavior.

The following assumptions are basic to the design philosophy of the ecosystem model (WICHE 1973, p. 6):

1. The campus environment consists of all the stimuli that impinge upon the students' sensory modalities and includes physical, chemical, and social stimuli.
2. A transactional relationship exists between college students and their campus environment, i.e., the students shape the environment and are shaped by it.
3. For purposes of environmental design, the shaping properties of the campus environment are focused upon; however, the students are still viewed as active, choice-making agents who may resist, transform, or nullify environmental influences.
4. Every student possesses a capacity for a wide spectrum of possible bahaviors. A given campus environment may facilitate or inhibit any one or more of these bahaviors. The campus should be intentionally designed to offer opportunities, incentives, and reinforcements for growth and development.
5. Students will attempt to cope with any educational environment in which they are placed. If the environment is not compatible with the students, the students may react negatively or fail to develop desirable qualities.
6. Because of the wide range of individual differences among

students, fitting the campus environment to the students requires the creation of a variety of campus subenvironments. There must be an attempt to design for the wide range of individual characteristics found among students.
7. Every campus has a design, even if the administration, faculty, and students have not planned it or are not consciously aware of it. A design technology for campus environments, therefore, is useful both for the analysis of existing campus environments and the design of new ones.
8. Successful campus design is dependent upon participation of all campus members including students, faculty, staff, administration, and trustees or regents. In order to make campus design a reality, the ecosystem model identifies environmental shaping properties, those things in the environment that either help or hinder student growth, help or hinder a school in attaining its objectives. This information is used to design out dysfunctional features in the environment or design in environmental features which improve the quality of educational life.

Fawcett, Huebner, and Banning (1978) have attempted to translate these assumptions into a conceptual framework that could be used to classify a campus environment for subsequent assessment and design activities. The framework dimensions include design levels (individual, group, all students), student development targets (mental, physical, social), and campus environmental settings (academic programs, student activities and services, student living). Each of the resulting 27 cells is thought to represent the transaction between a student (or collective of students) and a class of environmental settings in relation to mental, physical, or social development. The methodological implementation of campus ecosystem design will be elaborate in Chapter 3.

Open-System

The open-system model, developed by Katz and Kahn (1966) and discussed by others (for example, Kast and Rosenzweig 1970), is directed at the organizational level of social systems. It classifies organizations as sociotechnical systems that are constantly interacting with other external environments. Related models that contribute to the environmental classification of organizations include the Tavistock approach, which focuses on internal and external organizational boundary conditions, the consulcube (Blake and Mouton 1976), and process consultation (Schein 1969), which are focused on human process conceptions of organizations and the differentration-integration model (Lawrence and Lorsch, 1969), which is concerned with task-function specialization and coordination. (See Goodstein, 1978, for a review of each of these models.) It was decided to discuss the open-systems model because it provides both a basic and an elegant framework for classifying organizations, and because it is capable of serving as a heuristic for generating environmental design projects in organizations.

The open-system framework emerges from the application to organizations of system theory (von Bertalanffy 1956), which is based on biological science rather than physical science principles. In this approach organizations are viewed as open to and dependent on their environments. Thus, an organization can be seen as engaging in a continued cycle of input-transformation-output and renewed input processes, similar to those in which a green plant engages in the process of photosynthesis. Organizations import energy from their environment (for example, raw materials, people, grants), and transform the imported energy into products that are related to the organization (for example, a mental health unit develops prevention programs), exports the product to the environment (the prevention programs are carried out in the community), and the organization is then reenergized and receives feedback from environmental sources (for example, consumers of the program do not suffer problems). In this process, an organization has its own system of internal functioning (inputs, transformations, outputs) that is continually dependent on the larger environmental system of which it is a part.

The boundary between an organization and its environment is typified by mutual permeation. This condition demands that organizations cannot be conceived of as static independent entities, without reference to their external environment (a "closed system view"). Rather, the open system's view of organizational functioning provides a classification approach that is dynamic and transactional with regard to external environments. This organization-environment interface perspective (Lawrence and Lorsch 1969) shares much in common with the person-environment interface perspective discussed earlier (for example, Brunswik 1955; Moos 1979a).

Functions of Physical Settings

Steele (1971, 1973) makes a case that organization consultants and architects have been mutually deficient in understanding each other's professional worlds. He maintains that organization consultants have not given enough credence to the effects of physical environment on users and, conversely, architects and space planners have failed sufficiently to understand behavior when they design physical structures. To better acquaint these often disparate groups with the relationship between physical settings and behavior, Steele proposed the functions-of-physical-settings model that classifies human environment along sociophysical lines. Steele sees this sociophysical approach as complementing characteristic change effort foci (such as in most organization development efforts) and as supplementing the sociotechnical approach that typifies the open-system model just examined. Although Steele envisions the "social architecture" of norms, communication patterns, decision-making processes, and so on to be the dominant factor in most systems, he suggests that the physical environment generally exerts an important reinforcing or canceling role. Further, in some cases the physical environment can be a major force in determining developments in a social system. (For example, compare a decentralized counseling service, where outreach offices of the same agency are scattered throughout a community, with an agency located centrally in one small building.)

Therefore, the sociophysical classification approach is concerned with the effects of physical settings on social functioning. What is being referred to by physical setting effects? Here are some examples (Steele 1971, cited in French, Bell, and Zawicki 1978, p. 309).

> In general, these effects run the gamut from making it difficult or easy to interact face-to-face (our offices are 2,500 feet apart or 10 feet apart; there is a wall with no opening between us, or a door or no wall at all) to influencing the mood of people who are in a particular place (all our walls are lime-green and the place "feels" like the early years of the depression), to creating an interpersonal climate (when I am in your office, all your furniture is arranged so that it separates you and me, and I feel like an unwanted intruder who is looked on as somewhat unpredictable and dangerous).

A sociophysical classification of an environment contains the following dimensions (Steele 1973, p. 25):

(1) *Security and Shelter* refers to protection from harmful or unwanted stimuli in one's surroundings, such as a roof keeping out the rain or a thick wall keeping sounds out of the bedroom.
(2) *Social Contact* refers to the arrangements of facilities and spaces that permit or promote social interaction, such as a garden apartment's central bank of mail-boxes where people accidentally come face-to-face with one another.
(3) *Symbolic Identification* refers to the messages sent by settings which tell someone what a person, group, or organization is like, such as the things a person exhibits in his/her office.
(4) *Task Instrumentality* refers to the facilities and layouts appropriate for carrying out tasks in a particular setting, such as a sound-proof room for taping records.
(5) *Pleasure* refers to the pleasure or gratification the place gives to those who use it, such as the views hikers enjoy while visiting the Olympic Peninsula in Washington.
(6) *Growth* refers to the stimulus for growth the setting gives the user, such as when a person learns something new about himself (herself) from his (her) feelings while lost in a dark woods overnight.

Conceptualizing environments from the sociophysical perspective demanded by the functions-of-physical-settings model provides yet another approach to understanding environment and behavior transactions. It opens many new areas for change agents who tend, by training and orientation, to turn nearly automatically to understanding behavior in environments in terms of human processes. Environmental psychologists may represent a notable exception because they are attempting to focus directly on the physical (built) environment-behavior transaction (for instance, see Holahan 1979).

Mapping

Environments can be classified through the production of spatial relationship maps that are thought to organize or to represent behavior. Perhaps lumping together cognitive and geographic maps in one brief discussion does a disservice to both kinds of maps due to the brevity of the discussion possible and to the fact that the maps themselves differ qualitatively. Because they share enough similarities, however, they will be considered together.

Cognitive maps (Downs and Stea 1973) are really functional analogies that are used to represent categorically the mental picture that individuals have of environments, whereas geographic maps are spatial illustrations of actual physical objects. Cognitive mapping is a "process comprised of a series of psychological transformations by which an individual acquires, codes, stores, recalls, and decodes information about the relative locations and attributes of phenomena in his everyday spatial environment" (Downs and Stea 1973, p. 9). These convenient sets of shorthand symbols vary across individuals and groups and are thought to influence behavior in and use of environments. The cognitive map itself, however, is an analogy to be used, not an object that exists in and of itself.

Cognitive maps are made, for instance, by asking residents of a neighborhood how much stress they feel when walking on certain unsafe streets (Panati 1976). Responses are tallied and then contour lines are drawn over a physical map of the neighborhood. These resulting maps look very much like the high- and low-pressure zones of a meteorological map seen on any television weather show, yielding pockets of high and low perceived stress. Panati reports that one researcher who used this approach was able to demonstrate that a school-bus route in a section of Philadelphia contributed to an increase in school truancy because many of its stops were at corners where children were afraid of being attacked and beaten. In such a manner cognitive mapping can be used to discover how people organize various aspects of their environments; these maps provide classifications of the environment.

Geographic maps (for example, Smith 1979; Struening 1975) are actual spatial representations of existing physical phenomena. They are useful (but underused) in classifying environments when questions of interest concern the distribution of people, events, or conditions over a specified geographic area. For instance, one might wish to understand an environment in relation to any of the following questions: Where do senior citizens reside in relation to public transportation accessibility? What is the relationship between rapes and the distribution of police protection? Where do high academic achievers live both on- and off-campus? What is the relationship between voting and geographic accessibility to polling places? Geographic maps for these questions can be produced by assigning a location to each piece of data. Spatial relationships are yielded, again similar to contour maps in atlases or in meteorological maps, and subsequent analytic procedures can be used to study relationships between locations displayed on the maps.

Geographic and cognitive maps approach environmental classification in ways that are different from those used in the other models that have been discussed. They capture highly useful perspectives of environments that hold great potential for environmental design. This potential will be examined in detail in the next two chapters as the assessment and change function of all five models is considered.

SUMMARY

Environmental classification is a preliminary and important step in environmental design. This chapter has sought to present approaches and models that can be used to classify and thus to understand human environments. An environment was defined in general terms and six categories for classifying human environments were presented: ecological, behavior setting, organizational structure, inhabitants' personal characteristics, psychosocial climate, and functional reinforcement analysis (Moos 1973). Four sources for offering data necessary for describing environments were discussed (Hyne 1976): demographic, perceptual, behavioral, and a combination form. The categories and data sources were organized into an environmental classification matrix. Most of this chapter was devoted to an examination of five environmental classification models that emphasize different aspects of an ecological orientation: social ecological, ecosystem, open-system, functions of physical settings, and mapping (cognitive and geographic). Assessment and change functions for each of these models are the focus of Chapters 3 and 4 to follow.

3

ENVIRONMENTAL ASSESSMENT: CHARTING THE PERSON-ENVIRONMENT INTERFACE

Environmental assessment is the data-gathering, diagnostic phase of environmental design. This chapter will define environmental assessment and consider several environmental assessment instruments and procedures. There will be an overview of several instruments being used in higher education and business and industry, and particular attention will be given to procedures associated with the social ecology, ecosystem, open-system, functions-of-physical-setting, and cognitive and geographic mapping models. Through this chapter, the reader will become acquainted with a variety of both specific instruments and general procedures that are useful for assessing the people-environment relationship.

WHAT IS ENVIRONMENTAL ASSESSMENT?

Assessment, diagnosis, testing, psychometrics—these have been staples of psychologists. Usually, however, these measurement approaches have been centered on intrapsychic phenomena such as intelligence, personality, achievement, interests, attitude, needs, and so on; these areas have constituted most of the world of psychological assessment. It has been different, of course, for sociologists. Their assessment approaches have been focused on group, organizational, and societal levels of analysis, rather than the individual level.

Environmental assessment can be seen as a new form of appraisal that calls for a rapprochement between traditional psychological and sociological approaches. It is used to identify the relationships that exist between people and their environment. As such, it includes but extends beyond needs assessment (for example, Aubrey and McKenzie 1978; Bell, Warheit, and Schwab 1977; Hays and Linn 1975), which retains a person emphasis, to focus on the environmental conditions that meet or fail to meet assessed needs. Therefore, it is used to describe persons, settings, and their relationship, attempting to respond to Price's (1976) observations that "substantial interactions exist between the type of person inhabiting a particular kind of setting and the characteristics of the setting itself" (p. 296).

Environmental assessment is undertaken to measure "person-environment fit" (French, Rogers, and Cobb 1974) and thus the degree of adjustment that an individual experiences in an environment. Murrell (1973) has termed this same dynamic "psychosocial accord," or the degree of "harmony" existing between a person's requirements and those available in his or her social system. Others have referred to the process as degree of "match or mismatch" (congruence or incongruence) between the supplies of individuals and the demands of an environment. The concept of "optimal mismatch" has been offered (Huebner in press) as an ideal person-environment state, where demands exist beyond supplies to such an extent that individuals are challenged to proceed, but yet perceive sufficient support so as not to be overwhelmed in the process.

Environments, of course, can be terribly frustrating places where demands can outweigh supplies. Katsarelas (1980) provides a humorous but painful illustration:

> A good friend of mine was planning on graduating this April and going to medical school. Despite the fact that no one else was planning on his going to medical school, he insisted on going, maintaining that the rejection letters were a prank and that the acceptance letters were forthcoming. But his hopes were darker the other day when he received a letter from the Academic Admissions Board informing him he cannot graduate.
>
> It happens that Fred (his real name) failed to meet all the criteria for graduation and will have to attend summer school. The letter is a good warning to those of you who believe you are headed smoothly down the road to commencement exercises.
> Dear Mr. McZinsky:
>
> We regret to inform you that you will not be allowed to graduate Saturday, May 3, 1980. After reviewing your transcript, the Audit Council and the Academic Admissions Board of the College of LS&A have discovered you have not yet completed the necessary work required for graduation.
>
> The University takes pride in explaining its regulations clearly and coherently, and it is a shame you have not been able to follow simple instructions.
>
> According to our evaluation, Mr. McZinsky, you have first of all not finished your four 400-level cognates required for successful completion of your biology/zoology major/concentration. You filed for Distribution Pattern II (Plan C under the old format) and according to the University of Michigan Bulletin, 1977-1978, Pattern II

encompasses only 300-level cognates of humanities and social sciences under the new plan, with qualified exceptions to dual BA and BS graduates of the College of LS&A and the School of Nursing. Biology concentrators must complete 24 hours of C or better work in Plan A or C (under the old plan) or Pattern I or II (under the new plan). Or, the student must complete 13-23 credit hours of class inside or outside his or her field of study, while being certain to fill out Form J (see Bulletin, p. 18) or Form X (see Bulletin, p. 48). Ten credit hours of work must be completed within non-cognates, but only with counselor's permission, bladder disruption, and proper completion of Document 3DXZ (file No. 42).

Also, Mr. McZinksy, your 432 "Behavior Modification of Hari Krishna" cannot count towards a humanities cognate, for only 17-24 credit hours under Distribution Plan W (old format) or 12-16 credit hours under Pattern II may be counted toward successful completion of a BA, BS, or BGS in 7 semesters of 2.0 work or better, not including social and/or natural science courses, under new plan C83XZ (see Bulletin, p. 98) or old plan (see Bulletin, p. 23).

If you have any questions, feel free to contact me in 1230 Angell Hall on odd and/or rainy days, or Room 384 Student Activities Building on even and/or sunny or partly sunny days, unless there has been more than three inches of precipitation for the month.
Signed, Elton Gullett, Assistant Associate Director, Academic Admissions

Extending this example, an environmental assessment of the university's academic admissions procedures might reveal discrepancies between university administrators' perceptions of their clarity and how clearly they are perceived by at least one student (Fred McZinsky).

Environmental assessment is conducted by investigators in order to quantify and describe the existing and/or ideal relationships between humans and their environments. It is associated with the Lewinian paradigm discussed in Chapter 1, where behavior is considered to be a function of persons interacting with their environment $[B = f(p \times e)]$. As such, both psychological and sociological perspectives are demanded of the investigator, as well as of those in architecture and planning. The investigator needs to be able to assess the p x e transaction from an ecological view, where psychological, sociological, and physical environmental considerations are important as they interrelate with one another. Actually, environmental assessment might more accurately be termed ecological assessment (in fact, some have referred to the process as "eco-mapping"), because the label "ecological" connotes more clearly the transactional focus of the assessment.

Moos (1979b) has discussed general criteria he and his associates have followed in constructing environmental assessment procedures. These criteria are useful for orienting practitioners to issues that usually need to be considered in instrument construction:

The environmental assessment procedure should be consistent with a conceptual approach, such as one or several of the classifications of human environments that were examined in Chapter 2. Methodologically, an environmental assessment procedure should be able to discriminate empirically among environments, must be internally consistent, must be amenable to reliable observation or judgment, and so on. The procedure must be pertinent to people in the setting. Its items should tap environmental dimensions that are meaningful to respondents, and the items should be understandable. Aulepp and Delworth (1978) have offered many useful practical tips that the reader is encouraged to examine; some of these will be discussed later in this chapter under ecosystem methodology. Moos expands on each of these criteria. Especially useful is the discussion of methodological issues and of ways to handle conflicts that typically recur among the construction criteria (Moos 1979b, pp. 148-51).

ENVIRONMENTAL ASSESSMENT APPROACHES

Examples of Instrumentation

A large number of environmental assessment approaches (instruments, procedures, models) exist. Following Moos, several of these approaches were organized (in Chapter 2) within categories (for example, the Environmental Assessment Technique of Astin and Holland (1961) is organized within the inhabitant's personal characteristics category). Others have approached this task in different ways. Walsh (1973, 1978) has placed a range of person/environment interaction approaches into what he terms "theoretical viewpoints": Barker's behavior setting theory, the subcultural approach, Holland's theory, Stern's theory of need x press = culture, Moos's social ecological approach, and Pervin's transaction approach. Drum and Figler (1973) have assembled a collection of environmental assessment instruments used by schools and colleges.

Keating (1976) has provided brief descriptions of several environmental assessment instruments that are especially of import for campus administrators. An abstract of Keating's summary is presented in Table 3.1 to give an overview of several instruments.

This summary of some environmental assessment instruments for use in higher education is included for two reasons: first, to acquaint the reader quickly with some existing instruments to give a sense of what they are like; second, environmental assessment instrumentation has been developed quite extensively in reference to higher education environments, so it is a natural focus for exploring such instrumentation.

Of course, it is the case that other environments are associated with considerable work in environmental assessment approaches. Business and industry is a good example. Here, organizational surveys have enjoyed an extended history. Two of several exemplary instruments are *The Survey of*

Organizations (Taylor and Bowers, 1972), which measures organizational functioning through climate, supervisory leadership, supervisory-needs indexes, peer leadership, and other factors (see Hausser, Pecorell, and Wissler 1977); and the *Index of Organizational Reactions* (Smith 1976), which measures job satisfaction through supervision, kind of work, amount of work, financial situation, career future, company identification, coworkers, and physical conditions (see also Dunham and Smith 1979).

Other sources containing summaries of relevant instrumentation exist also. For example, Lake, Miles, and Earle (1973) provide a helpful, systematic review of 84 different instruments related to social functioning. This review considers instruments that are personal in nature (about one-half of the instruments), interpersonal (about one-quarter), and those that are group or organizational in focus (about one-quarter). It is a valuable addition to the standard review of social psychological attitude measures (Robinson and Shaver 1969, 1978), which has been available for several years prior to the Lake et al. resource.

Environmental Assessment Procedures

The preceding section attempted to familiarize the reader with environmental assessment from a definitional standpoint. It pointed to a range of existing environmental assessment instruments that have been developed in reference to college or organizational environments in business and industry. This section turns to an examination of environmental assessment procedures, methods, or techniques that evolve from the five environmental classification models discussed toward the end of Chapter 2: social ecological, ecosystem, open-system, functions of physical settings, and cognitive and geographical mapping.

Social Ecological

Rudolf Moos and his associates in the Social Ecology Laboratory at Stanford University have contributed significantly to the social ecological approach that was described in Chapter 2. It will be recalled that their emphasis has been primarily on the social climate of a range of environments; they have developed ten social climate scales that will be examined in some detail. Recent work in their sheltered care project has led to the development of new environmental assessment techniques (*Multiphasic Environmental Assessment Procedure*, MEAP: Lemke et al. 1979) that are designed to measure not only the social climate of sheltered care settings but also environmental system domains of physical settings (for example, architecture and physical design), organization factors (for example, size, staffing, structure), and the human aggregate (the collective personal characteristics of people in a setting). The MEAP represents an extended assessment focus for this social ecology group, one that incorporates several of the classification approaches discussed in the previous chapter. The MEAP environmental assessment instruments will be described following an examination of the various social climate scales that preceded them.

TABLE 3.1: Some Environmental Assessment Instruments for Campus Administrators

Instrument	Author	Environment	Target	Focus
College and University Environmental Scales (*CUES*, 2nd Edition)	Pace	Total university	Students in attendance at least 3 semesters	Practicality, Community, Awareness, Propriety, Scholarship, Campus morale, Quality of teaching and Faculty-Student Relationships
College Student Questionnaire (*CSQ I*, *CSQ II*)	Peterson	Attitudinal and biographical information	CSQ I: Entering freshmen & transfer students; CSQ II: enrolled undergraduates	CSQ I: Educational and vocational plans, secondary school information, family background, attitudes; CSQ II: Educational and vocational plans, college activities, attitudes
Institutional Functioning Inventory (*IFI*)	Peterson, Centra, Hartnett, and Linn	Total university	Faculty, administrators, staff; (students may complete first half)	Intellectual-aesthetic extracurriculum, freedom, human diversity, concern for improvement of society, concern for undergraduate learning, democratic governance, meeting local needs, self-study and planning, concern for advancing knowledge, concern for innovation, institutional esprit
Institutional Goals Inventory (*IGI*)	Peterson	Total university	Faculty, administrators, students	Output goals: Academic development, intellectual orientation, individual/personal development, humanism/altruism, cultural/aesthetic awareness, traditional

50

Instrument	Author	Environment	Target	Focus
				religiousness, vocational preparation, advanced training, research, meeting local needs, public service, social egalitarianism, social criticism/activism. Process goals: Freedom, democratic governance, community, intellectual/aesthetic environment, innovation, off-campus learning, accountability/efficiency.
Student Reactions to College	Warren and Roelfs	Total environment of community and junior college	Students with minimum of one term's experience at the college	Quality of instruction, student-centered instruction, academic performance, studying problems, instructor accessibility, involvement with faculty and staff, certainty of plans, active involvement in planning, programming problems, problems of registration and scheduling, administrative control of students, desire for help with living problems, financial and related problems.
University Residence Environment Scale (URES)	Moos and Gerst	Residence halls, Greek houses, religious and other special-interest groups	Residents and staff members	Relationships, personal growth, system maintenance and system change.

Source: Reprinted, by permission from Keating, "Assessment Instruments and Techniques." In *Training Manual for an Ecosystem Model*, edited by Lou Ann Aulepp and Ursula Delworth, pp. 99-111 (Technical Appendix B). Boulder: WICHE, 1976.

A set of ten scales has been developed that assess similar underlying patterns of social environments across settings (Moos 1979a, 1979b). Chapter 2 discussed these three underlying dimensions of social climate: relationship, personal growth, and system maintenance and system change. The ten social climate scales, all of which are based on the three dimensions just listed, are presented below in relation to the environmental setting they are designed to assess:

Scale	Setting
University Residence Environment Scale (URES)	Educational: living group
Classroom Environment Scale (CES)	Educational: junior/senior high school classrooms
Family Environment Scale (FES)	Primary: family
Work Environment Scale (WES)	Primary: work milieu
Group Environment Scale (GES)	Primary: social and task-oriented group
Work Atmosphere Scale (WAS)	Treatment: hospital
Community-Oriented Programs Environment Scale (COPES)	Treatment: community-based psychiatric treatment programs
Sheltered Care Environment Scale	Treatment: sheltered care settings
Correctional Institutions Environment Scale (CIES)	Total institution: correctional institutions
Military Company Environment Scale (MCES)	Total institution: military basic training companies

Table 3.2 shows examples of the relationship between the three underlying dimensions of social climate and selected social climate subscales.

In examining the contents of Table 3.2, it is useful to try to sense the quality of each dimension. For instance, involvement and cohesion characterize the relationship dimensions; independence, autonomy, and task orientation typify the personal growth dimension; and order, clarity, and innovation reflect the system maintenance and system change dimension.

Table 3.3 briefly describes the ten subscales (Moos and Humphrey 1974), organized by dimension. Examination of this table should give you a good idea of the person-environment "content" that the GES seeks to obtain. Further, with some qualifications, one can generalize from the GES orientation to other social climate scales to understand generally their focus.

The format of the scales is generally consistent. With the exception of the *Sheltered Care Environment Scale*, which uses a Yes/No response format, the other nine scales are based on a true/false response format. Each scale has three forms: Form R (Realistic), which is used to assess the perceived actual state of a setting; Form I (Ideal), which is used to assess perceptions of an ideal setting;

TABLE 3.2 Group Environment Scale Subscale Descriptions

Subscales	Relationship Dimensions
1. Cohesion	Extent of members' involvement and participation in the group; of their affiliations and commitment to the group; of the help, manifest concern, and friendship displayed to each other.
2. Leader Support	Amount of help, manifest concern and friendship displayed by the leader to members.
3. Expressiveness	Extent to which freedom of action and expression of feelings are encouraged.

	Personal Growth Dimensions
4. Independence	Extent to which the group tolerates and/or encourages independent action and expression in its members.
5. Task Orientation	Degree of emphasis in practical, concrete, "down-to-earth" tasks, decision-making, or training.
6. Self-Discovery	Extent to which the group tolerates and/or encourages members' revelation and discussion of personal detail.
7. Anger and Aggressiveness	Extent to which the group tolerates and/or encourages open expression of negative feelings and inter-member disagreement.

	System Maintenance and System Change Dimensions
8. Order and Organization	Degree to which the activities of the group are formalized and structured; the degree of explicitness of group roles, norms, and sanctions.
9. Leader Control	Extent to which the tasks of directing the group, making decisions, and enforcing rules are assigned to the leader.
10. Innovation	Extent to which the group tolerates and/or facilitates diversity and change in its own function and activities.

Source: Reproduced by special permission from *Manual for the Group Environment Scale*, Form R, p. 27, by Rudolf Moos, PhD., and Barrie Humphrey, MD. Copyright 1974. Published by Consulting Psychologists Press Inc., Palo Alto, CA 94306.

TABLE 3.3: Examples of GES Items for Its Subscales

Subscale	Dimension	Example Items
1. Cohesion	Relationship	There is a feeling of unity in this group.
2. Leader Support	Relationship	The leader spends very little time encouraging members.
3. Expressiveness	Relationship	When members disagree with each other, they usually say so.
4. Independence	Personal Growth	Individual talents are recognized and encouraged in this group.
5. Task Orientation	Personal Growth	There is very little emphasis on practical tasks in this group.
6. Self-Discovery	Personal Growth	Personal problems are openly talked about.
7. Anger and Aggression	Personal Growth	Members are often critical of other members.
8. Order and Organization	System Maintenance and System Change	The activities of the group are carefully planned.
9. Leader Control	System Maintenance and System Change	This group is run in a pretty loose way.
10. Innovation	System Maintenance	Things are pretty routine in this group most of the time.

Source: Reproduced by special permission from *The Group Environment Scale,* Form R, by Rudolf Moos, PhD., and Barrie Humphrey, MD. Copyright 1974. Published by Consulting Psychologists Press Inc., Palo Alto, CA 94306.

and Form E (Expectations), which is used to assess new members' anticipations of a setting or expectations about a new setting. In general, the separate forms of each of these scales include from 70 to 100 items.

As can be imagined, use of the separate forms allows for interesting comparisons of environmental descriptions: for example, how members actually see the social climate of their group versus how they would like it to be, or how the group leaders view the group as compared with members' perceptions. Chapter 4 will examine the kind of environmental assessment data produced from this methodology, when design programs are considered.

Items used in the social climate scales are stated in a straightforward manner and in such a way as to be answerable in a True/False (or Yes/No for the SCES) format. The GES focus and format reflect the family of social climate scales referred to earlier. As was pointed out, however, the most recent work in the sheltered care project has produced an expanded set of environmental assessment procedures that include, but go beyond, the measurement of social climate. These sheltered care assessment procedures will be discussed briefly.

Chapter 2 presented the social ecological comprehensive model for classifying human environments. Of interest here is the component called "environmental system," consisting of physical setting, organizational factors, the human aggregate, and social climate. Social climate is conceptualized as an independent domain within these environmental variables and as the main mediator of the influences of the other three variables (Moos 1979a, 1979b).

The *Multiphasic Environmental Assessment Procedure* (MEAP) is an attempt to measure these separate environmental variables. This procedure provides "the ability to describe . . . environments multidimensionally [making] it possible to monitor the quality of the environment, to assess the impact of specific features or programs, and to examine the interaction between resident and environmental characteristics" (Lemke et al. 1979, p. 1).

The MEAP instruments are briefly described below.

Physical and Architectural Features Checklist (PAF). The PAF is comprised of questions about various aspects of the physical environment, both inside and outside the facility, and of its neighborhood context. It is completed by using direct observation and measurement, supplemented by information supplied by the administrator or another staff member who is familiar with the facility.

Policy and Program Information Form (POLIF). The POLIF covers information on organizational policies, procedures, and services. Questions address financial and entrance arrangements, the types of rooms or apartments in the facility, the way the facility is organized, and services provided for residents. The POLIF is completed through interviews with the administrator (or with another who is familiar with the administrative aspects of the facility), and through tabulating information from staff service utilization forms.

Resident and Staff Information Form (RESIF). The RESIF focuses on the personal characteristics of facility residents, their current functioning, and their involvement in activities. Questions about staff are also included. The RESIF is completed primarily through tabulating information from social histories, medical records, activity records, staff records, and interviews.

Rating Scale (RS). The RS taps observers' personal impressions of the total facility, the cleanliness and condition of the physical environment, and resident and resident-staff interaction. It is completed through observation.

Sheltered Care Environmental Scale (SCES, Forms R, I, and E). The SCES is a 63-item social climate scale with a Yes/No reponse format that is designed to measure the dimensions of relationship, personal growth, and system maintenance and system change. It is a perceptual instrument that can be completed by residents and staff.

As can be seen, the MEAP is a multidimensional environmental assessment approach in social ecology that utilizes a variety of data collection modes (for example, survey, archival, observation, interview). It retains the long-standing social climate measurement in social ecology, but it obviously adds other foci. For example, in its use of observational ratings and interviews, the MEAP can be likened to aspects of behavioral mapping in environmental psychology (Proshansky, Rivlin, and Ittelson 1970), the sociophysical approach used in rating the functions of physical settings (Steele 1973), and the evaluation of human services methodology used in the *Program Analysis of Service Systems* (PASS) (Wolfensberger and Glenn 1975).

The discussion of the social ecological approach to environmental assessment will be resumed in the next chapter, which will emphasize the kind of data obtained and how these data are converted to environmental design. First, there are several other environmental assessment procedures to be examined.

Ecosystem

As mentioned in the discussion in Chapter 2, the ecosystem model is a higher-education-oriented environmental design approach that is based on a transactional perspective. It is used "to identify environmental-shaping properties in order to eliminate dysfunctional features and to incorporate features that facilitate student academic and personal growth" (Aulepp and Delworth 1978, p. ix). The ecosystem model provides a methodology for the assessment of campus environments and for the design of environments to produce more optimal person-environment fits (Banning and Kaiser 1974; WICHE 1973).

Aulepp and Delworth (1978) indicate that the ecosystem model requires the participation of a collaborative planning team in the environmental assessment process. The team uses a two-phase assessment technique (Aulepp and Delworth 1978) to gain the necessary information for the later design of environmental conditions.

In the first phase, respondents are queried about their perceptions of the campus environment or of behavior in the environment. Typical testing approaches are used in this phase. For example, the team might use a standardized commercial environmental assessment instrument, modify an existing instrument in some acceptable way, or develop its own instrument. Frequently, one of the latter two options is followed because existing instruments fail to capture fully the uniqueness of any single environment.

The second phase of environmental assessment in the ecosystem approach is developed by the team. The purpose of this phase of assessment is to supplement the quantitative information yielded as a result of phase one with qualitative, descriptive, subjective information from the respondents. In ecosystem terminology, phase two provides "environmental referents" (WICHE 1973), the specific features in the environment that are associated with respondent perceptions. These environmental referents (ERs) are considered critical for subsequent design efforts. Interrelating information acquired from respondents in both environmental assessment phases (quantitative and qualitative information) provides a detailed picture of the person-environmental interface.

The discussion of ecosystem environmental assessment that follows will concentrate on instrument development in phase one and on the creation of environmental referent forms in phase two. The reader is referred to Aulepp and Delworth (1978) for treatment of other matters such as the selection or modification of existing instruments.

Developing a Quantitative Instrument. Development of a quantitative instrument is time-consuming and should be engaged in only if satisfactory environmental assessment instruments are unavailable. An obvious advantage to instrument development, however, is that resulting products usually have substantial "face validity" for respondents, one reason being that local terms can be used.

Four steps need to be considered in instrument development during phase one: determining the assessment focus, selecting the assessment scope, reviewing and selecting response formats, and writing items. Each of these steps will be discussed, beginning with the assessment focus.

One of the authors (Conyne) directed a university planning team that intended to focus on the relationship of new off-campus students with the university and the larger community. Team members felt that these students were largely ignored by both the institution and the city and that, in turn, they probably felt disconnected and uninvolved. But the initial issue related to discovering if these impressions were accurate. Therefore, the team was faced immediately with the question of what to assess? For instance, should they simply review the past academic performance of this group of students and assume that they could infer from it what they needed to know about involvement? Should they ask a key informant, such as the president of the Transfer Students' Union, about her knowledge of what these students face? Should they investigate the participation of this group of students in social activities? Should they interview these students? Should they gather baseline data about current usage of campus and community facilities by these students? Did they need to assess the experience of these students compared with, say, new students who live *on* campus? Many other questions could be asked, also. The point here is that a team just cannot reasonably begin to develop environmental assessment instrumentation without giving serious consideration to what (or whom) they should be assessing. This issue needs to be addressed within the context of project goals. In this case, the team administered a sample survey to both on- and off-campus students to gather comparative data regarding their perceptions and use of a range of campus and community resources.

The second step, selecting the assessment scope, is intimately related to what to assess. In fact, scope needs to be considered in tandem with assessment focus. Where assessment focus is concerned with content, scope is concerned

58 / ENVIRONMENTAL ASSESSMENT AND DESIGN

with how much to assess. If the team decides on a focus for assessment (for example, to ask new, off-campus students about their "involvement satisfaction"), assessment scope could be restricted to one of three levels (WICHE 1973): life space level (for example, one student only); micro level (for example, students in one off-campus neighborhood only); and macro level (for example, all students who are new to the university and who live off-campus). Further, assessment scope is concerned with the breadth of assessment approaches to use (that is, how much assessment). One approach, such as a questionnaire, could be used, or a battery of approaches including interviews, archival data, observation, and so on could be used. Scope must be bounded in some way. This decision is a strategic one that must be based on a combination of goals and feasibility.

For Step 3, reviewing and selecting response formats, there are four main item response formats that can be used: perceptual; goal statement; behavioral; and demographic. These formats may sound familiar because some of them were discussed in the section on common data sources for environmental assessment in Chapter 2. An example of each of these four response formats is given below.

Perceptual format example: Use of a Likert scale, which includes discrete points for respondents to use in indicating their judgment. For instance:

Very Satisfied	Satisfied	Neutral	Unsatisfied	Very Unsatisfied
(1)	(2)	(3)	(4)	(5)

The degree of your involvement in campus activities: 1 2 3 4 5

Goal statement format example: Use of a discrepancy between "actual" and "ideal" ratings of goal statements to measure perceptions. For instance:

Goal of Student Activities Office

Of no Importance	Moderately Important	Very Important
1	2	3

To provide special activities for off-campus students.

Actually ☐ ☐ ☐
Ideally ☐ ☐ ☐

Behavioral format example: Statement of items about behavior and the environment in action terms. Respondents are asked to indicate how frequently or how seldom they engage in these activities. For instance:

	Once	2 - 5 Times	Never
I study in the main library each week.	1	2	3

Demographic format example: Categories that are of interest are established (such as age, sex, grade point average, and so on). Category levels are set with a computer code number attached to each level. For instance:

Where do you live off campus?
1 - Apartment (and not with family)
2 - Co-op
3 - With family
4 - Trailer court

Demographic data are useful for describing the respondents for cross-tabulating categories of respondents with perceptual, behavioral, or goal statement data (for example, comparing patterns of library usage between off-campus students who live in trailers and those students who live in cooperatives). Perceptual, goal statement, and behavioral formats can be used, also, with environmental referents, which will be considered later in this chapter.

In Step 4, writing items, following selection of a response format, the team members can turn to item construction. The comments of Moos reported earlier in this chapter regarding conceptual, methodological, and practical criteria are very pertinent to item writing. The focus here, however, is on precision in stating items. Some of many issues to consider about writing good items follow.

Each item needs to be written clearly, concisely, and in a way that is understandable to the respondents, so that they can easily reply. Professional jargon should be avoided in favor of language that communicates more effectively (for example, change "alienated" to "feeling different from others"). Instructions for completing item response formats must be stated clearly so that respondents will know what they are being asked to rate, and investigators, in turn, will be able to know to what respondents have replied (for example, change "Students flunk out because they don't study" and/or "Students flunk out due to the lack of study spaces"). For other suggestions, refer to Aulepp and Delworth (1978).

Developing an Environmental Referent Form. Use of environmental referents (ERs) characterizes phase two of the ecosystem environmental assessment approach. ERs are considered fundamental to later design because of the specific, concrete information they yield. ERs allow respondents to describe the ratings they provided in phase one by writing qualitative statements that explain why they responded the way they did, what environmental aspects contributed to or caused their reactions, and what could be done to improve the existing situation.

Although it is impossible to go into detail here in delineating various alternatives for developing ER forms and for collating the information they generate, several variations have been developed as prototypes. One such ER format is shown in Figure 3.1.

FIGURE 3.1: ER Example and Form

	What things in the environment exist or have happened to make you feel this way?	How have you responded to this situation or feeling?	What could be done to change the environment (physical, organizational, functional, etc.) to improve the situation?	RATING
Example: I am dissatisfied with my apartment	There is no decent place to study; no privacy, too much noise.	I stay out of my apartment as much as possible—study at library.	Develop some adequate (cheaper, more frequent) transportation to campus libraries.	1

Source: Adapted from Corazzini, Heubner, and Wilson in Lou Ann Aulepp and Ursala Delworth, *Training Manual for an Ecosystem Model*, © 1976, Western Interstate Commission for Higher Education, Figure 5, p. 47.

Note that the ER format example contains instructions for completion, that it provides a means for tying respondents' rating of an item to their ER comments (in the last column), and that it asks why respondents respond the way they do, how they have coped so far, and what change recommendations they would suggest for future improvements. As pointed out earlier, this qualitative information can greatly facilitate subsequent design because if contains diagnoses, coping strategies, and change directions. As a trade-off, however, one must weigh the costs involved in collating, interpreting, and summarizing the wealth of data that this method yields when summed across several respondents; it can be a very time-consuming business. Aulepp and Delworth's (1978) suggestion of using students trained to implement this task (in exchange for academic credit) seems a most sensible one. In fact, experience has shown that people from the setting involved in these projects generally have been willing volunteer participants in such activities. Of course, if students or other setting "implementers" are used in the data collation stage, their training becomes an important issue that must be addressed effectively.

Despite the complexities implicit in the ecosystem environmental assessment approach, it has much to commend it. The contribution that ERs make in furthering understanding of the person-environment interaction and in propelling a project toward design is a particularly useful consequence of the specific change-oriented information that is generated. Moreover, it has been found that use of this format seems to exert an unexpected attraction-enhancement force in many respondents toward the environmental assessment project. Perhaps having an opportunity to share the reactions they have to their environment is in itself reinforcing, thus facilitating continued, motivated participation in design.

Open-System

Chapter 2 briefly presented the open-system (Katz and Kahn 1966) model of environmental classification, noting that it is particularly relevant to organizations. As may be recalled, this model is based on an input-throughput (transformation)-output cyclical framework in which the organization is viewed as being constantly influenced by, and in turn is constantly influencing, its external environment. The open-system schema provides a basic but elegant framework for classification and it can serve a heuristic purpose in generating other models and approaches.

Three such environmental assessment approaches will be examined here. The first is the so-called "six-box" approach to organizational diagnosis (Weisbord 1976, 1978); the second is the systems approach of Kast and Rosenzweig (1970). Both of them are based on sociotechnical perspective to organizational assessment that is derived directly from the open-system model. The third approach is termed "Model A," (Egan and Cowan 1979), and it presents a basic logic, underlying system design. Model A can be seen as an indirect outgrowth of the open-system model.

62 / ENVIRONMENTAL ASSESSMENT AND DESIGN

Six-Box Approach. Although the open-system model is a very helpful theoretical tool for classification purposes, it fails to provide necessary operational specification. For instance, students are usually quite bewildered about its practical merits. In the six-box approach, one can find some concrete directions for application of the open-system model to organizational environmental assessment.

The six boxes represent organizational processes that are assessed in order to understand an organization more fully. Assessment data resulting from this process can then be used in environmental design of the organization. These organizational processes (the boxes) are comprised of formal and informal purposes, structure, rewards, helpful mechanisms, relationships, and leadership; additionally, the organization-environment interface is considered as a critical element. Figure 3.2 portrays the six-box approach.

FIGURE 3.2: Six-Box Approach to Environmental Assessment in Organizations

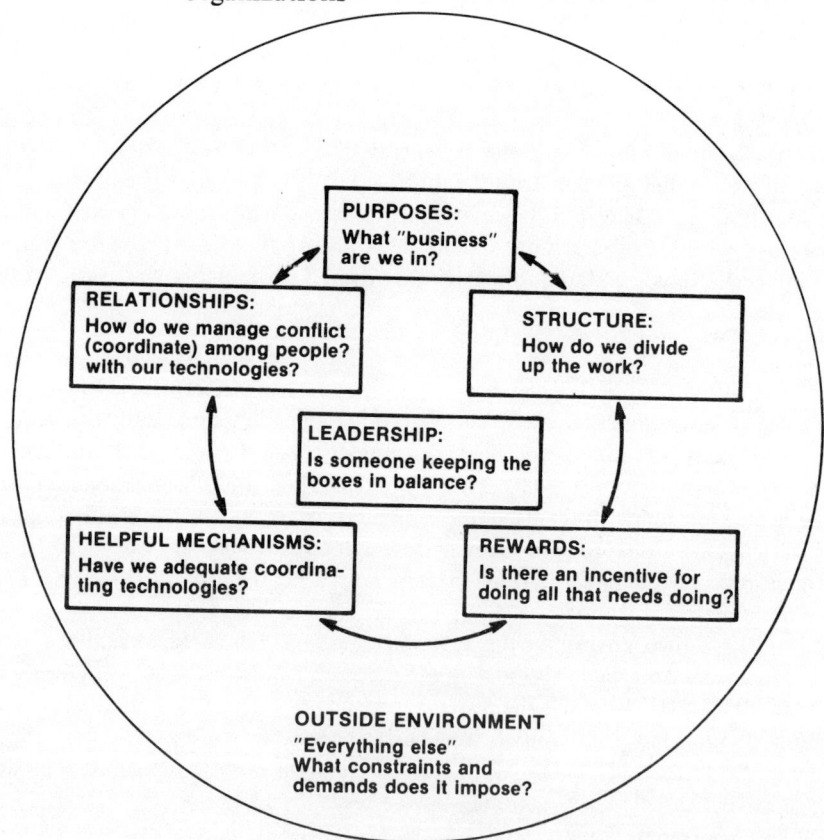

PURPOSES: What "business" are we in?

RELATIONSHIPS: How do we manage conflict (coordinate) among people? with our technologies?

STRUCTURE: How do we divide up the work?

LEADERSHIP: Is someone keeping the boxes in balance?

HELPFUL MECHANISMS: Have we adequate coordinating technologies?

REWARDS: Is there an incentive for doing all that needs doing?

OUTSIDE ENVIRONMENT "Everything else" What constraints and demands does it impose?

Source: Weisbord, *Organizational Diagnosis,* © 1978, Addison-Wesley Publishing Company, Inc., Fig. 1, page 9. Reprinted with permission.

Weisbord suggests that the boxes can be used as a radar screen. Organizational problems show up as "blips" in the boxes involved, thus indicating that work on important tasks is being blocked. Although, as he points out, a blip in any one box cannot be managed apart from its relationship with other boxes, this radar-screen approach provides six points for conducting environmental assessment in organizations.

These six boxes can be located within the transformations process of the open-system framework. This relationship is shown in Figure 3.3.

FIGURE 3.3:   The Six-Box Approach within the Open-System Model

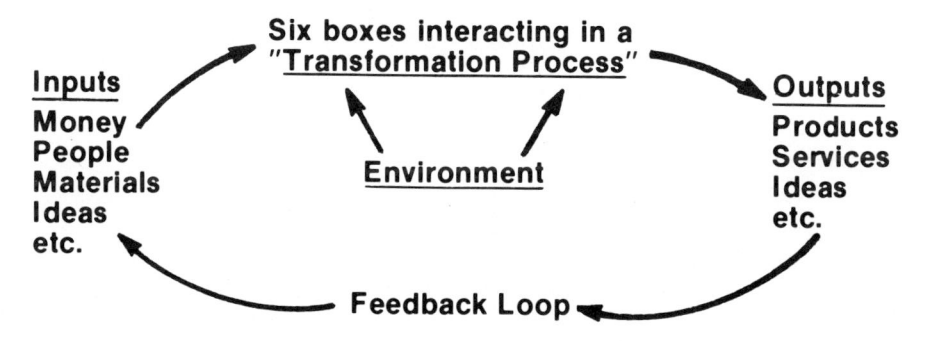

```
                    Six boxes interacting in a
                    "Transformation Process"
    Inputs                                           Outputs
    Money                                            Products
    People                                           Services
    Materials           Environment                  Ideas
    Ideas                                            etc.
    etc.
                    ← Feedback Loop ←
```

Source: Marvin Weisbord, *Organizational Diagnosis,* © 1978, Addison-Wesley Publishing Company, Inc., Fig. 2, page 12. Reprinted with permission.

"Transformation process" is a term that refers to the involvement of people, external environment influences, and technical systems within the organization to convert inputs into outputs. The environmental assessment of an organization in this approach involves investigating the sociotechnical processes occurring within and among the transformation process boxes. What works is a function of the existing "fit" between an organization and its external environment (Lawrence and Lorsch 1969) and between people (employees) and the organizational environment itself (for example, French, Rogers, and Cobb 1974).

How is this approach actually used in assessment? Components of the six-box approach will be parsimoniously addressed to show its application.

In each box, both formal and informal systems must be considered, because frequently great differences exist. The formal system refers to what is written down as, for example, in the organizational chart or the stated mission of the organization. The informal system refers to what actually happens. For example, functions of a designated organizational administrator in reality may be carried out by others and the actual mission may be more related to organizational survival than to idealized conceptions contained in the written statement.

The external environment and its ongoing relationship with the organization must be considered in environmental assessment. This boundary sets the "domain" of the organization's activities and, in an open system, these environment-organization-environment boundaries are critical contact points. Relevant external domains of a human service organization, for instance, might include (adapted from Vaill 1976, cited in Weisbord 1978):

Clientele (distributors and/or users)
Suppliers (of materials, capital, equipment, space)
Competitors (for clientele and resources)
Regulatory groups (government, certifying groups)
Parent organizations (executive board, university, central headquarters, and the like)

As mentioned earlier, Weisbord uses the analogy of "scanning the radar," that is, of applying each of the boxes to an organization in order to identify its sociotechnical strengths and weaknesses. Problems are indicated wherever blips occur on the radar screen. The processes to be scanned are addressed below, beginning with purposes.

Organizational purposes (variations of mission, goals, and objectives) emerge from a negotiation of what is required for the organization to do and what organizational members want to do. Three areas of assessment are important: goal fit, the relationship between a goal and demands arising in the external environment (for example, is there funder support, are clients interested?); goal clarity, the degree of shared understanding that organizational members possess; and goal agreement, the degree to which organizational members' behavior is in agreement with the stated goals.

Organizations establish structures to coordinate their tasks, roles, and functions. This structuring usually takes one of three general forms: according to function, where specialists work together (for example, in business sales or production, or in school administration or teaching); according to product, program, or project, where people perform multiple tasks and use divergent skills that are necessary for producing an output (for example, in interdisciplinary teams, intake service); according to matrix (mixed), which combines aspects of function and product forms (for example, a teacher may also be a researcher or a member of an interdisciplinary team investigating school truancy). In an assessment of structure, its relationship to organizational purposes and its facilitation of division of labor are important considerations.

Organizational relationships can be assessed at three levels: those between people in the organization, those between units that perform different tasks, and those between people and the technologies they use on the job. Thus, human relations processes, such as communication, intergroup cooperation and competition, conflict, power and authority, decision making, participation, involvement, trust, feelings, and values (for example, Katz and Kahn 1966; Schein 1969) are very important to consider, as are employees' competency and comfort in using needed technical systems, equipment, and methods.

How an organization rewards its members also can be assessed. Weisbord shows, in the work of Maslow (1954) on hierarchy of needs and of Herzberg (Herzberg, Mausner, and Snyderman 1959) in work motivation, that a formal reward system (for example, of pay increases) may not be as continuously motivating as incorporating informal means (for example, based on personal growth or recognition) for rewarding meritorious effort. The critical matter is to assess whether reward theory has been translated into the fabric of organizational life and how members regard the effects.

Organizational leadership is a process that has been much studied, and several systems exist for categorizing it (for example, Fiedler's situational model, 1967; Lewin, Lippitt, and White's abdicrat, democrat, autocrat schema, 1939). Stogdill (1974) has comprehensively summarized much of the research literature on leadership covering over 30 years. Yet, as Weisbord points out, "No one knows for sure what makes for good leadership in every situation" (1978, p. 40). His view is that leaders should systematically monitor organizational functioning and initiate corrective action whenever potential problems are threatening. In addition to behavioral and interpersonal skills, organizational leadership requires an ability to assess the environment-organization-environment interface and to design mechanisms to keep formal and informal systems in balance. An assessment of the leadership function would take these functions into account.

The last of Weisbord's boxes is termed "helpful mechanisms." By this term he means those activities that assist in the coordination, integration, and monitoring of work. They are developed to help interrelate the processes contained in the other five boxes and are meant to facilitate intraorganization understanding and cohesion. Possibilities of helpful mechanisms include memos, bulletin boards, coffee rooms, newsletters, informal socializing, staff development, reports at staff meetings, and more formal management systems that include planning, budgeting, and measurement. The critical assessment question is not how many of these mechanisms exist but whether those that are present promote work that is consistent with organizational purposes, whether the work is allocated reasonably (structure), whether work relationships are basically healthy, and whether the rewards are adequate.

Kast and Rosenzweig's Systems Approach. Prior to the work of Weisbord, Kast and Rosenzweig (1970) related the open-system concept of Katz and Kahn (1966) to the structured sociotechnical system posited by Trist et al. (1963). The sociotechnical term has been used earlier with reference to Weisbord's work. The Trist et al. concept of sociotechnical system results from an understanding that organizational output requires a technological organization (for example, equipment, structure) interacting with workers who are organized in a social system. Thus, an organization cannot be seen simply as a technical or as a social system, but as the product of the two factors; "it is the structuring and integrating of human activities around various technologies" (Kast and Rosenzweig 1970, cited in Weisbord 1978, p. 79).

Kast and Rosenzweig described five sociotechnical subsystems that, as in the six-box approach, comprise the transformation process in an open-system model. These subsystems are goals and values, technology, structure, psychosocial, and managerial.

There is a similarity between this approach and that of Weisbord. Both concretize the transformation process of the open-system model into sociotechnical dimensions to be assessed. Both approaches examine goals and structure. In the present approach, the technical subsystem (task requirements, equipment used, facilities layout) is assessed in relation to the psychosocial subsystem (its "climate," comprised of the relationships, values, rewards, sentiments, expectations, and so on, of organizational members). The managerial subsystem includes organizing and effectively maintaining interrelationships among all the subsystems within the organization and between the organization and its external environment.

"Model A": Logic for System Design. Egan and Cowan (1979) have proposed an environmental assessment approach that is based implicitly on the open-system model, but which varies noticeably from the previous two approaches just considered. They indicate that this approach can help in understanding "the structure and function of any given system; it can be used to help design a new system or to diagnose a system that is already in existence" (p. 121).

Briefly, "Model A" can be used to assess a formal or informal organizational environment (for example, a family) according to the following criteria:

> The degree to which basic principles of behavior and behavioral changes (for example, reinforcement) are effectively used
> The association between organizational products and the assessed needs and wants of recipients
> The association among organizational mission statements, goals, philosophy values, and recipient needs and wants
> The clarity of goals and the nature of members' commitment to them
> The association between programs and the goals they are meant to meet
> The association between program demand and the working knowledge and skills required of program personnel for satisfactory execution
> The availability of resources (other than working knowledges and skills)
> The association between structure and goal achievement; the division of labor makes program implementation more efficient; roles are clear
> The relationship between roles and structure, where individual roles and interrelationships between work teams are unambiguous and system members respect each other

The quality and directness of the communication processes and information flow that are necessary to execute programs and to carry out system-related tasks

The degree to which the internal environment or climate of the system is enhanced, facilitating both good human relations and productivity

The degree to which the system is open to and effectively initiates and responds to its external environment

Figure 3.4 illustrates the main ingredients of Model A.

Egan and Cowan indicate (much as did Weisbord with his six-box approach) that Model A provides the framework for a system checkup that can be used to locate system problems or danger points. They also maintain that Model A suggests specific technologies for handling these problematic areas. For example, if blips occur in the radar screen regarding concrete goals, then goal clarification techniques may be appropriate; or if it appears that programs developed by the organization to meet stated goals are ineffective, then it may be that program-centered consultation is in order.

The Funcions of Physical Settings

As was pointed out in Chapter 2, the functions-of-physical-settings model is a sociophysical model. It focuses on the effects of physical environment (the built environment, as compared with the natural environment) on social functioning.

One example may serve to bring the model quickly back to mind. Courses that have an experiential component are often taught—courses in which for instance, students may be placed in role-playing situations or may engage in small-group discussion. Such experiential activities depend on a classroom physical setting with movable chairs. This requirement conflicts with bolted-down permanent chairs that predominate in the majority of classrooms. Therefore, unless a classroom with movable chairs is located, it becomes necessary to consider modifying the course activities, and thus the kind of educational and social experience for students in that course. This example well illustrates the relationship existing between the physical and social environments settings.

How can these sociophysical effects be assessed? Steele (1971, cited in French, Bell and Zawacki 1978) describes one casual way:

> I found rich data by just walking around an organization, trying to become aware of what the physical setting can tell about life there. Nothing can tell more quickly about the impersonality of an organization than seeing an area where there is very little individual influence on the space (decorations, maskings, personal items, or whatever) by the people who actually work there. This can give a real "gut" sense of how little influence they may feel they have over the social system. (p. 310)

FIGURE 3.4: "Model A:" Logic System Design

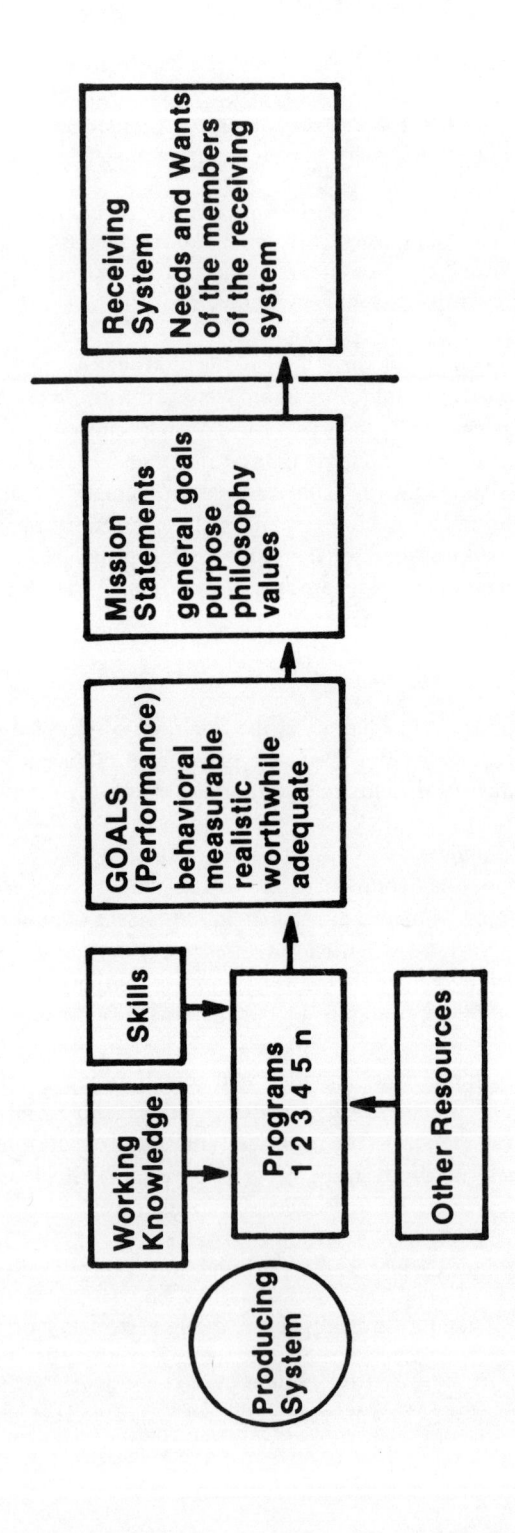

Source: From *People in Systems: A Model for Development in the Human-Service Professions and Education* by G. Egan and M. A. Cowan, p. 138. Copyright © 1979 by Wadsworth, Inc. Reprinted by permission of the publisher, Brooks/Cole Publishing Company, Monterey, California.

This unsystematic yet useful approach to the environmental assessment of physical settings is based on the sensitivity of observational skills. Good observation skills, in fact, are at the root of the more systematic approach that Steele has developed (1973). Supplemental assessment sources in his approach include interviews conducted with users of the settings to identify their subjective responses, the so-called "touring interview" (which combines observations and interviews by asking users to "free associate" about a space as they walk through it), and an analysis of users' reactions to recent change events that have occurred in the setting (for example, how they feel about new office locations). Whatever the data source, a change agent assesses how each of the six functions of physical settings (security and shelter, social contact, symbolic identification, task instrumentality, pleasure, and growth) affect users.

In practice, these functions are not usually independent. They often can be found to interrelate. For instance, a setting that is pleasurable may be positively associated with social contact, because it draws and holds people more substantially than would a nonpleasurable setting. In other cases, a setting might be assessed positively along certain functions but negatively for others. This situation can be seen when a library study room is so highly security- and pleasure-oriented (for example, deeply cushioned easy chairs, availability of cassette tapes and stereo headphone equipment, lots of plants, and a delightful view of the ocean) that it fails to stimulate growth (for example, problem solving and learning) and task instrumentality (such as reading, studying, and writing). Occasionally a setting may not appear to be providing certain of the six functions. For example, a beach with no lifeguard may be a setting that provides no security and shelter functions; in such a case, it would be assigned a neutral rating for that one function. The assessment process itself involves translating data obtained from the various sources mentioned above into ratings and short descriptions of the functions.

Steele (1973) organizes the assessment process into three parts. First, the assessor must rate a place that is of importance to a client system. Somehow this place must relate to ongoing issues in the setting, and there should be an expectation on the part of the client system that environmental assessment information about the place will potentially aid in resolving the issues. Second, the assessor selects specific elements within the chosen place that are likely to affect social functioning. Elements can come in three forms: a particular thing, such as a desk, a wall, a couch, the color of a chair, and so on; the pattern of a set of elements, such as the arrangement of seats in an airport lounge, the location of offices on a floor, the spatial arrangement of a reception room; and a sociological factor, such as a set of norms that govern use of the television in a dormitory lounge. The third part of the rating process involves the actual application of the function of physical settings classification model to the element(s) resulting in numerical ratings and descriptive comments. Each element is given a rough numerical rating on the six functions using a simple three-point scale of positive (+), neutral (0), and negative (-). (Steele also reports using at times a more discriminating scale ranging from -3 to +3, followed by short comments that illustrate the ratings.)

To guide the assessment of elements, questions can be asked within each function, as follows (adapted from Steele 1973, pp. 97-98):

Function	Examples of Rating Questions
Security and Shelter.	Does the element provide protection from physical and psychological stresses? Can users withdraw when they need to? Does this element aid, block, or not affect that process?
Social Contact.	Does the element facilitate, detract from, or not affect human interactions? Does it structure relative locations, control mobility, signal who should be interacting with whom?
Symbolic Identification.	What are the messages the element sends about the owners or users and the image they desire to convey? What symbolic information is communicated about the system, people in it, and individuals? (Note this function is rated from high information content to low or zero, rather than positively or negatively.)
Task Instrumentality.	How does the element help or hinder the kinds of tasks being done (for example, physical, interactional, and internal tasks)?
Pleasure.	To what degree does the element provide pleasure for users? What visual, auditory, olfactory, and tactile senses are stimulated by the element? Does the element trigger memories of past experiences for users?
Growth.	To what degree does the element promote growth for users? How much does the element stimulate growth-producing contacts? What is the degree of problem-solving demand, surprise, diversity, and visible feedback about certain results?

What does a rating form look like? Figure 3.5 provides an example given by Steele (1973, p. 102), in which the environment of an airport waiting lounge (place) is assessed through rating seven elements by the functions of physical settings.

A lot of information is compressed into this figure. Note several points. The seven elements run vertically down the form while the six functions run horizontally across it. The functions are abbreviated, explained under Symbols at the bottom of the form. The ratings are simple and of two kinds: signs (+, 0, -), which can be easily convertible to numeric ratings later, if that is desired; and descriptions, including brief observational comments of the observer (indicated by "m" for "me") or of other users in the setting (indicated by "u" for "users"). Last, a concise summary of all the data is provided by the assessor.

As can be seen, much information is gathered through such an approach. In this case, one gets a pretty good sense of this airport waiting lounge's perceived effect on the assessor and others involved for that one assessment period. These ratings and descriptions are basically structured impressions of a physical environment and its social effect on users. The data obviously do not result from a procedure based on test construction techniques that would meet psychometric criteria. Yet the data can be of much potential use for describing a setting and for generating ideas and hypotheses about potential action steps.

As Steele emphasizes, the value of the ratings obtained must be determined by the client system. It is not inherent in the ratings themselves. For instance, while plastic chairs in the airport waiting lounge were rated negatively for pleasure (see Figure 3.5), this fact does not mean automatically that their use is good or bad. Rather, it is a perceived state to be evaluated by the relevant consumers. Issues related to data usage and change approaches associated with the sociophysical approach will be examined in the next chapter.

Mapping Approach

Mapping is a means for assessing an environment either through cognitive or through geographic processes. Although both means are spatial representations, they arrive at end-points differently and the end-points themselves have different realities. That is, the cognitive map is always an abstraction of an environment as people believe it to be at one point in time, while a geographic map attempts to illustrate graphically an existing physical reality. Nonetheless, the two mapping approaches to understanding environments share many similarities, so that psychologists and geographers are combining their efforts to develop theory, research, and practice in this area (for example, Gould 1973; Stea and Blaut 1973).

Cognitive Mapping. As Downs and Stea (1973) indicate, pragmatics for improving the quality and process of using cognitive maps in environmental design are lacking. There is a growing body of research, however, that shows potential for such movement. This research involving cognitive mapping has revealed that individual and intergroup differences exist in cognizing settings. For instance, Lucas (1963) found that the perceived spatial extent of a wilderness recreation area in the northeastern United States was defined differently by various user subgroups and by administrators. Ladd (1970) showed that two brothers produced surprisingly discrepant cognitive maps of their neighborhood. McKay (cited in Gould 1973) constructed a cognitive map showing Canada

FIGURE 3.5: A Functions of Space Coding Sheet

Place: Airport Waiting Lounge   Date: Nov. 7, 1970

Element or Pattern	S/S	So	Sy	T	P	G
Linoleum floor (grey)	(m,u) : (−) cold, drafty, glare	(m) : (−) with fixed chairs, reduces contact, can't sit on floor	cold, efficient, clean, unfriendly, says it's a business place	0	(m,u) : (−) ugly, glare, color is wearing	0
Plastic chairs around periphery of space; none in the center, bolted down.	Slightly (−) - hard after long use.	(u) : (−) people can't talk. One group said they were split up by it.	impermanence mass movement (like cattle)	(m) : (−) for business chats, only 3 at the most can be near each other	(m,u) : (−) we all thought they were ugly and not comfortable.	(m) : (−) no movement or experimenting possible
Windows on one side looking out on airfield	(u) : (−) for those sitting under them, drafty; (0 for others)	(u) : (slightly−) as people stared out windows (for those facing windows)	shows what the place is about—air travel	0	(u) : (+) for those facing. 0 for those not.	0 (or slight + for those facing)
Location of lounge—at far end of corridor, away from all counters	(u) : (slight −) away from bathrooms	(m) : (−) No contact with other travelers;(+) increase contact with some flight	says that this flight is slightly "out of it"—not regular schedule	(m) : (−) for agents and staff; don't get down here to help passengers	0	(m) : (slight +) pass through many airport areas to get here.

72

One narrow entrance to working area, past check-in counter	0 (except (−) if fire started)	(m) : (−) people seeing others off slightly intimidated	clear message about where to go – no ambiguity	(m,u) : (+) for agent: can control crowd from one spot	0	0
Flourescent lights fairly intense	(m,u) : (+) no eye strain	(m) : (slight −) no intimacy possible in that light	cold, harsh, says there is nobody's personality here.	(m,u) : (+) good for reading	(m) : (−) I don't like the look of it. Feel the glare (with floor)	0
Temperature about 60° in the lounge	(m,u) :(−) several people complained, felt stiff.	0	Don't know; may be that this is a transition zone— neither inside nor out	(m) : (+) for agents: public don't fall asleep. Keep moving (−) for reading	(m,u) : (−) doesn't feel good or homey(!)	(m) : (−) people keep coats on, see little of one another, learn nothing new.

Summary: Not bad for its purpose. Good design for the agents, not so good for travelers. Hard to talk, or sit for long; good for reading till you get cold. Probably easy to clean, but unpleasant because of it. A transition area, not a place of its own, really.

(m) = my own observations; (u) = data from other users.
* Symbols: S/S = shelter and security; So = social contact; Sy = symbolic identification; T = task instrumentality; P = pleasure; G = growth.

Source: Steele, *Physical Settings and Organization Development*, © 1973, Addison-Wesley Publishing Company, Inc., Fig. 10.1, page 102. Reprinted with permission.

through French Canadian eyes that was uniquely unlike its actual parameters. Orleans (1973) showed many instances in which various groups of urban residents held differential cognitions of their city, concluding that knowledge of the spatial environment (and one way in which it is visualized and symbolized) results from experience in and with it. In a more humorous view, there is the *New Yorker*'s "View of the United States," which pictures New York City as figure and all else west of the Hudson River as ground! Of course, those New Yorkers who are from upstate would hold a much different conceptual map.

Techniques are needed for using cognitive maps in environmental assessment. Asking people to draw their own detailed maps of a setting is one approach. As an example of this method, Orleans (1973) and Panati (1976) report how the Los Angeles Planning Commission asked various ethnic and economic groups to draw as detailed maps as they could of Los Angeles. Results obtained showed that Westwood upper-class residents had a vast and differential knowledge of the city, including museums, beaches, airports, and universities. Black residents of Avalon (near Watts), however, conceived Los Angeles as much more truncated— an inner city with but few main streets. Hispanics from Boyle Heights produced maps that contained their own neighborhood and, in addition, only City Hall, Union Station, and the bus terminal. Although poor blacks and Hispanics were aware that the city really was larger than their own neighborhoods (City Hall, and so on), these other areas were depicted only with empty circles. Orleans, the architect who studied the Los Angeles project, indicates that the way people perceive their city determines to a large extent how they will use it.

These results are startlingly clear. Methodologically, however, obtaining mapped impressions using blank sheets of paper and no cues needs refining and it may be more of a liability than an asset (Orleans 1973). Many confounding variables exist. For instance, it is possible that the capacity of a respondent to draw a detailed map may be more closely associated with socioeconomic level and related correlates of familiarity with maps and how to draw them than with actual experiential knowledge of a particular environment.

Orleans (1973) suggests some alternative approaches to cognitive mapping:

> It might well be that a series of partially completed base maps—maps showing, for example, major streets, civil divisions, geologic features, important landmarks, and the like—would elicit a more detailed, coherent, and consistent imagery. Such maps should be administered to the respondent in a series, increasing in detail, as with a focused interview. For some purposes, it might be sufficient to ask the respondent to locate certain items on an outline map, or to piece together a cut-apart map. The procedure employed would depend upon the purposes of the research. (cited in Downs and Stea 1973, p. 129)

Geographic Mapping. Contrasted with cognitive mapping, assessment methodologies are well defined for geographic mapping. Environmental assessors using these techniques are able to relate personal demographic characteristics (such as age, sex, ethnicity, academic performance) and measured affective states (for example, perceived safety, depression) to geographic spatial locations of respondents. These literally are mapping techniques. Three of these techniques have been described and illustrated by Smith (1979): geocode analysis (drawn from geography), trend surface analysis (from geology), and social area analysis/ecological analysis (from epidemiology). The following description of two of these approaches, geocode and social area analysis, two divergent perspectives to geographic mapping, will rely heavily on Smith's account.

The technique of geocode analysis relates geographic distribution to certain personal characteristics. It uses the individual as the analysis unit and aggregates individual data over definable geographic areas. Geocoding (geographic coding) in this process uses symbolic codes to indicate geographic location; thus, street addresses and census tract numbers are examples of geocodes. Individual personal characteristics data of interest are then integrated with the geocode being used to produce a contour map of individual characteristics by geographic location. The advent of computers, with computer printing and plotting capabilities, has made it possible to reference geographically large collections of individual data and to summarize and analyze such data graphically.

Figure 3.6 contains a geocode analysis plot from Smith (1979) that shows the math achievement scores of sixth graders by geographic location.

As can be seen, students living near schools F and H are performing at or above sixth-grade level in math, while those students living near schools D and G and near the river are doing much more poorly in this area. In addition to the

FIGURE 3.6: **Social Area Analysis—School Cluster Based on Student Demographic Data**

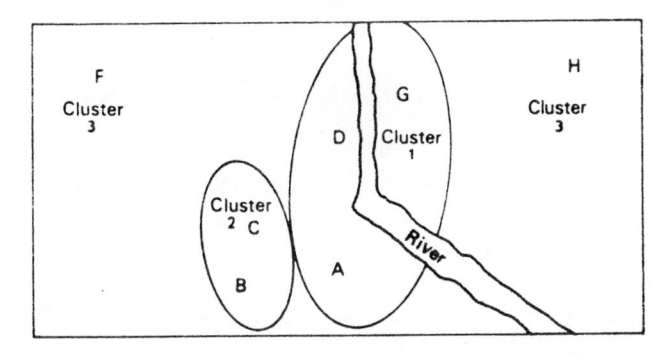

Source: From Nick L. Smith, "Techniques for the Analysis of Geographic Data in Evaluation," *Evaluation and Program Planning* 2 (2), 1979, Fig. 1a, page 121. Reprinted with permission.

math plots, others could be constructed for these same individuals in different achievement areas (for example, English, social studies) and in other areas such as educational level of parents, perceived locus of control of the students, ethnic distribution, and feelings about school. Multiple overlays of these plots could then be produced (much as in an anatomy text) to provide pictures of the geographic relationships existing among these variables that would enable the informed study of subpopulations within the school district to occur.

The second technique, that of social area analysis/ecological analysis, is not a discrete procedure, but a point of view and a collection of techniques. It is used to study group characteristics within defined geographic areas, such as census tracts, counties, or service regions called catchment areas. Thus, the level of analysis in this approach is groups that are taken as organized wholes. Social area analysis is used to determine characteristics that differentiate among subpopulations and that predict other characteristics or behaviors of interest. For instance, Smith points out that social area analysis has been used to study relationships between census tract characteristics and health problems (Kay 1978) and between social area characteristics and health service use (Brandon 1975). It is an appropriate approach to use when association between groups and geographic areas are of specific interest, especially in regard to education, health, and welfare service delivery.

Smith (1979) indicates the steps that would be involved in a complete social area analysis:

1. Define the geographic region of catchment areas of interest and the collection of relevant demographic data.
2. Develop theoretically meaningful and psychometrically stable indexes of catchment area characteristics through factor or cluster analysis.
3. Identify similar catchment areas through profile analysis.
4. Collect data on conditions, behaviors, or characteristics of interest, studying relationships between these variables and catchment area indexes through multiple regression.
5. Verify apparent relationships found through direct inquiries of group members, experimentally controlled studies of treatment interventions, or time series designs.

Returning to the sixth-grade achievement score example discussed earlier under geocode analysis, Smith suggests that social area analysis could be applied to produce the clusters contained in Figure 3.7.

In this case, a cluster analysis based on such variables as household income, ethnicity, and level of parental education could be used to identify types of student backgrounds. Each school could then be classified according to the cluster most representative of it (clusters 1, 2, and 3 in Figure 3.7). The relationship between school cluster and levels of academic achievement in the various subject areas could then be studied by using multiple regression.

FIGURE 3.7: Geocode Analysis of Math Scores by Student Address

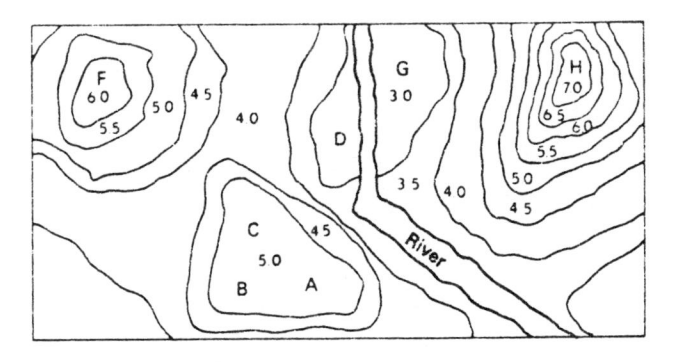

Source: From Nick L. Smith, "Techniques for the Analysis of Geographic Data in Evaluation," *Evaluation and Program Planning* 2 (2), 1979, Fig. 1c, page 121. Reprinted with permission.

Social area analysis/ecological analysis, geocode analysis, and trend surface analysis (which was not described) all approach the geographic display of human characteristics in different ways. All three procedures are labor-intensive, require sophisticated computer facilities, and are relatively expensive. But, as Smith indicates, "they offer new options for the analysis and presentation of geographic data in evaluation and will significantly strengthen the methodological repertoire of evaluators who make the effort to learn and apply them" (p. 125).

SUMMARY

Chapter 3 is devoted to the identification and description of environmental assessment methodologies and procedures and their role in environmental design. Environmental assessment was defined as a new form of appraisal that is used to measure person-environment fit. Several environmental assessment instruments used in higher education and in business were described. Most of this chapter contained environmental assessment procedures that are associated with each of the five classification models discussed in Chapter 2: social ecological, ecosystem, open-system, functions of physical settings, and cognitive and geographic mapping. Specific illustrative material was presented for each model in order to give a concrete indication of how each one is used to conduct environmental assessment.

4

ENVIRONMENTAL DESIGN: ALTERING THE HUMAN ENVIRONMENT

The first three chapters have shown that the environment is a significant influencer of human behavior and that it can be a force for planned change (Chapter 1), that human environments can be understood through classification (Chapter 2), and that their effects on people can be measured (Chapter 3). This chapter will now consider methods that are appropriate for the evaluated, intentional, collaborative change of human environments, a process referred to as environmental design. This process extends and integrates the applied research functions of environmental classification and assessment by adding to them an environmental change phase that itself includes applied research. This change phase is used by a change agent(s) (Lippit, Watson, and Westley 1958) to help a client system (individual, group, organization, or community) improve its human environment by converting environmental assessment data to environmental change. The discussion of environmental design begins by looking at applied research, followed later in this chapter by an in-depth exploration of a variety of environmental change approaches that can be used in altering human environments for the better. Following these discussions, an integrated and more extensive definition of environmental design will be provided.

APPLIED RESEARCH IN ENVIRONMENTAL DESIGN

Environmental design is the "evaluated, planned, collaborative change of human environments." This definition contains strong emphases on the intentionality, researchability, and participative nature of the change process. The first two of these dimensions will be addressed here, leaving participation until the end of the chapter.

What are the distinguishable forms of applied research and how do they relate to the characteristics of intentionality and researchability that adhere in environmental design? Rossi, Wright, and Wright (1978) have provided a typology of applied research that is useful in addressing this question. Their review and analysis of the vast range of applied research activities shows that five general types exist; parameter estimation, monitoring, modeling of relevant phenomena, ongoing evaluation, and social experimentation. The first four of these types will be briefly defined and then they will be related to the environmental design characteristics of intentionality and researchability.

Parameter estimation is used to identify, describe, or document demographic or distributional characteristics of some relevant phenomenon existing in a particular environment. This is an evaluation of the context of the phenomenon of interest. How much unemployment exists in a city for young black males? How do users of the county clerk's office regard the services provided? Are students satisfied with the quality of their educational experience at the university? These and other similar questions illustrate instances in which this applied research form can be used. Environmental assessment is primarily a parameter estimation technique.

Monitoring extends parameter estimation by following trends in parameters over time. The Institute for Social Research's (at the University of Michigan) 10-year longitudinal national study of 5,000 families is a project that illustrates monitoring—in this case, of family conditions occurring over an extended time frame. The campus environmental assessment project of Illinois State University offers another example, where certain parameters such as campus social climate were monitored monthly for their effects on students over a four-year period. Environmental assessment can be used as a monitoring technique.

Modeling of relevant phenomena is used to proceed beyond estimating and monitoring to understanding those phenomena. The models used in this effort may be relatively sophisticated, empirically based, and causal or they may be more ad hoc, intuitive, and simplistic. They are used, however, in an attempt to depict as fully as possible the causal processes of parameters (which causes what?) and to provide direction for planned environmental change. Moos's social ecological model, illustrating how person, environment, and mediating variables interact in relation to outcomes, provides an example of environmental classification that fits this type of applied research.

Ongoing evaluation of an environmental change effort follows estimating, monitoring, and modeling. This continuous evaluation research process (formative and summative) is critical to environmental design (Conyne et al. 1977, 1979). It is used to discover whether the change program is being implemented as planned and whether it is accomplishing what it was intended to do. For instance, slippage frequently occurs between an intended change and its delivered form. Whether, in fact, a new admissions policy to enable 10 percent of a student body to be comprised of black students in five years actually reaches that goal is really an empirical question and should not be accepted simply because it is "on the books." The discrepancy between the detailed bus transportation plan and its actual implementation at the Lake Placid 1980 Winter Olympic games provides another example of slippage. Applying ongoing evaluation procedures to planned environmental change represents a type of applied research that addresses process and product effectiveness.

These four applied research types can be related to intentionality and researchability characteristics in environmental design, as follows:

Environmental Design Characteristics	*Applied Research Type*
Intentionality	Parameter estimation
	Monitoring
	Modeling
Researchability	Ongoing evaluation

Intentionality in environmental design is achieved through effective use of the applied research types of parameter estimation, monitoring, and modeling. Environmental assessment and environmental classification can be used to conceptualize, develop, and maintain a change program.

Researchability in environmental design is accomplished through systematic, periodic evaluative research of environmental changes that have been implemented. Descriptive, formative, quasi-experimental, and (less frequently done due to real-world limitations) experimental summative research designs are used to shape the environmental change program in effect. Figure 4.1 shows the applied research/environmental change/applied research cycle, in which environmental change is "sandwiched" between applied research functions. This relationship is analogous to the open-system model where throughput is sandwiched between input and output. That is, the intentional applied research function provides necessary input (for example, environmental assessment data) that is used to intentionally construct an environmental change program (throughput) whose output, in turn, is tested for effectiveness through evaluation research. This relationship is pictured in Figure 4.2.

The preceding section on applied research and environmental design should give a working knowledge of environmental design as "evaluated intentional environmental change." The role of applied research in environmental design has been briefly examined, indicating that it contributes to intentionality (through input and planning) and researchability (through evaluation of output). It goes without emphasis that an environmental designer must possess well-developed competencies in applied research.

Next to be examined is environmental change, the throughput section of the environmental design cycle. After defining environmental change, several generic change approaches, strategies, and models that can be useful in promoting it will be described. The five environmental classification (Chapter 2) and assessment (Chapter 3) models previously discussed—social ecological, ecosystem, open-system, functioning of physical settings, and mapping—will again be used to describe the environmental change processes that are associated with each of

FIGURE 4.1: Environmental Design Cycle

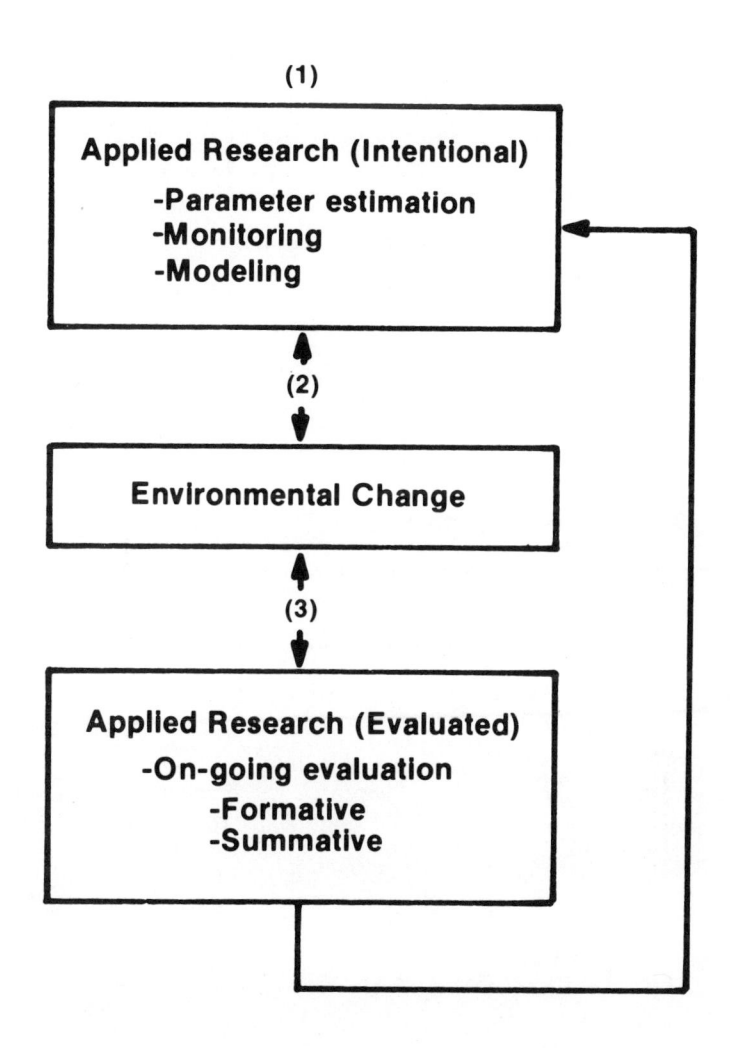

(1)
Applied Research (Intentional)
- **Parameter estimation**
- **Monitoring**
- **Modeling**

(2)

Environmental Change

(3)

Applied Research (Evaluated)
- **On-going evaluation**
  - **Formative**
  - **Summative**

Source: Constructed by the authors.

FIGURE 4.2: Environmental Design Cycle in Open-System Format

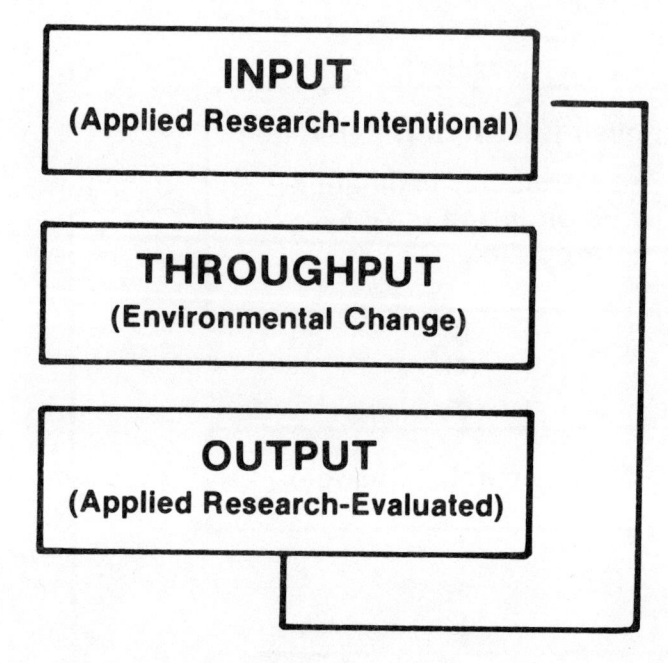

INPUT
(Applied Research-Intentional)

THROUGHPUT
(Environmental Change)

OUTPUT
(Applied Research-Evaluated)

Source: Constructed by the authors.

them. Finally, one environmental change approach will be identified that cuts across these models and seems to have special potential for the general process of environmental design. This approach will then become the focus of Chapter 5.

ENVIRONMENTAL CHANGE: THE THROUGHPUT OF ENVIRONMENTAL DESIGN

What is Environmental Change?

Environmental change is an indirect method used to seek client system improvement. It is indirect because the change target is not people themselves but, rather, the environmental contexts of relevance for them (Huebner, in press). By relevant environmental contexts the authors refer to the definition of an environment presented in Chapters 1 and 2 which includes physical features (for example, an office corridor), institutional dimensions (for example, reward structures), social characteristics (such as race balance in a work group), ecological climate (for instance, reaction to a town where one lives), and how these components are processed and responded to by environmental members Environmental change involves the use of change approaches to assist client systems to alter those aspects of their environments that are assessed to be excessively misaligned with human needs.

The role for the change facilitator in environmental change efforts has been labeled variously: "ecological problem solver" (Conyne and Rogers 1977), "action-oriented consultant-researcher" (Steele 1971), "environmental consultant" (Conyne et al. 1976), "environmental change agent" (Holahan 1979), and "ecological action researcher" (Holahan 1980; Holahan and Wilcox 1977). Steele (1973) indicates that the activity of changing physical environments has been termed alternately, "sociophysical organizational development," "ecological consultation," "environmental organizational change," "settings and organizations change," and so on. As can be seen, environmental change is associated with considerable flexibility, given its relative youth as a client system improvement approach. The variety of descriptors for change facilitators roles and for the activity itself, however, appears to share considerable commonality. In sum, it can be said that environmental change is used to advance client system improvement by applying change approaches and models within a person-by-environment ecological model.

Generic Views of How Change Occurs

What are the general strategies, approaches, and models that have been developed to promote change and what is the nature of their contribution to environmental change? This question can be considered by overviewing three broad views of change: summaries of change approaches (Greiner, cited in Huse 1975) and of change strategies (Olmosk 1972); meta-strategies (Chin and Benne 1976) and meta-perspectives in change (Crowfoot and Chesler 1976); and change models. The latter includes a discussion of five models that are representatives of change induction: Lewin's change model (1947); research, development, and diffusion (Clark and Guba 1965); linkage (Havelock 1969); planned change (Lippitt, Watson, and Westley 1958); and action research (Lewin 1946, 1947).

An understanding of these basic views of how change occurs is necessary as a precursor to conceptualizing how environmental change can be stimulated. For a more expanded discussion of change models see Havelock and Havelock (1973); and Sashkin, Morriss and Horst (1973).

Summaries of Change Approaches and Strategies

Greiner (cited in Huse 1980, p. 20) has summarized what he considers to be the seven most commonly used approaches to organizational change. They are presented below, ranked in terms of power from unilateral power (decree), to collaborative power (group decision), to shared influence (T-group).

The Decree Approach. This comes from the top and is passed down through the organization with "one-way" communications.

The Replacement Approach. In order to bring about change, one or more individuals, usually in high-level positions, are replaced by others. The basic assumption is that personnel changes bring about organizational changes.

The Structural Approach. In this approach, change is brought about by modifying the structure of the organization and the required relationships of subordinates in the situation. By changing the nature and structure of organizational design and relationships, organizational behavior is also affected.

The Group Decision Approach. This involves group members' participating in the selection and implementation of alternatives specified by others. Others identify the problem; the group agrees on a course of action from available alternatives.

The Data Discussion Approach. Information is obtained about the client system and feedback is given to the client system by an internal or external change agent. Organization members then develop their own analysis of the data to identify and solve problems.

The Group Problem-Solving Approach. In this model, problem identification and problem-solving occur as the group generates its own data with the help of a change agent external to the group.

The T-group Approach. Here, the group is trained to understand the processes of individual and group behavior. Changes in work relationships and patterns of work are assumed to follow from the changes in interpersonal relationships. This approach focuses first on the interpersonal relationships and then works toward improvements in work practice.

Reflecting for but a moment on one's own experience in organizations (work, religious, volunteer, and so on) should provide enough data to immediately concretize these change approaches. How many times, for example, has one seen major shake-ups in leadership (a replacement approach) reported for large corporations, baseball teams, and governments? Most people have at some time participated in a setting where decisions were always made by the leader (decree); or in a setting where decisions usually resulted from group consensus (group problem solving). Each of these general methods of change represents a relatively unique approach that has implications for environmental management and change.

Kurt Olmosk (1972) has taken a broad approach to how change is fostered in individuals and groups. He describes seven "pure" strategies and one combination strategy for change. He indicates that, in practice, one strategy may predominate along with modifications derived from one or two other strategies, and that seldom are the pure strategies used alone. In his analysis, the change strategies are as follows:

Fellowship, where change is realized through the development of good, warm, interpersonal relations and a premium is placed on treating everyone and all opinions equally. Arguments are infrequent and conflict is generally avoided.

The emphasis on making everyone happy means that priority setting and determining direction suffer, and over time the group finds it difficult to maintain member commitment. Olmosk sees this strategy used most often by groups that have few financial or physical resources to use in rewarding or punishing member behavior (for example, voluntary groups).

Political, where change is accomplished by getting influential people to agree to take certain action. The main motivators for groups using this strategy are control and attention. Much effort is expended to obtain decisions that are favorable to these groups and to communicate their influence in the decision-making to others. The mobilization of power and implementation of decisions is the hallmark of this change strategy, which is achieved at the expense of maintaining credibility over time. The political strategy is used most often by those already in power.

Economic, where the change emphasis is on acquiring or influencing all forms of material goods, such as land, money, stocks, and so on. Once relevant marketable resources are controlled or can be manipulated, decisions are rather easily implemented. This asset is countered, however, by difficulties experienced by users of this strategy sustaining change, since material rewards are only temporary satisfiers (Herzberg 1966). Olmosk observes that although this strategy is used most by corporations and the very rich, other groups (the have-nots), such as the poor in Operation Breadbasket, are beginning to use it.

Academic, where change is based on the assumption that people are rational and will make required changes if enough pertinent facts are made available to them. This strategy emphasizes an objective, analytical, dispassionate, empirical approach to solving problems where data and reports provide the stimuli for change. While relevant information, analyses, and recommendations may be produced through the academic strategy, Olmosk points out that its track record is mediocre. Doing research and writing reports is time-consuming and frequently results reach administrators too late for use in decision making. Implementation of findings is difficult also, because usually only the researcher has been involved in the study. Later readers of a report, therefore, often feel uncommitted to the process used in the study, a condition that may result in their unwillingness to read the report enthusiastically and thoroughly. Despite these difficulties, the academic strategy is used habitually by many consultants and by people in staff (as opposed to line) positions.

Engineering, where change in people is attempted through changing their environment or surroundings. This approach places strong emphasis on the environment of a client system, involving physical layout, information flow, structure, policy, interactions, and so on. Modifications of environmental conditions (for example, reorganization) that excessively constrain individuals can be a powerful and efficient change strategy. Some of its deficiencies surround the frequent lack of opportunity given environmental members to participate in the change process (they may feel it was foisted on them), unintended side effects produced by the change (tightening the organizational structure for increased clarity may jeopardize individual freedom), and the relative disinterest paid in general to how people will feel about the changes (compared with the main attention given to rationality and efficiency). Olmosk indicates that this strategy is used most often by top management.

Military, where change is based on the use or threatened use of physical force. Users of this strategy (Olmosk points out these are not only the military but also, in various forms, many police departments, revolutionary student groups, and some teachers) believe that people react to real threats and that with enough physical force they can be made to do anything. This approach endorses "might makes right," and it can be useful for keeping order or initiating radical changes. Its difficulties are that changes imposed on others through physical force usually disappear when the force is removed, and that force begets force, meaning that the threat of counterrebellion is always present.

Confrontation, where nonviolent conflict is used to produce change. Argumentation, anger, and challenge are primary means employed for generating and sustaining conflict. This strategy forces people (opponents) to consider, and often to deal with, issues the confronters are pressing, and its use brings attention and publicity to the resolution of these issues. As Olmosk suggests, "It is very hard to ignore a thousand people marching down Main Street" (p. 169). Some drawbacks to the confrontation strategy are that solutions to problems may not be proposed by the confronters, and the strategy may polarize people, creating a backlash rather than obtaining the desired change. Groups using this strategy are often the disenfranchised or those who feel they have no other effective way of making themselves heard (such as students, the poor, civil rights groups, and so on).

Applied behavioral science, where change is approached from the view that a variety of strategies is usually required to achieve a solution to complex and overdetermined problems. Therefore, a broad-based, inclusive path is taken to explore problems and to act on them. A considerable range of information and perspectives is used and integrated in moving toward decisions. These points represent the strengths of this change strategy. A limitation is that it can be an excessively differentiated approach, so selective and complex that it can be confusing and unwieldly. The applied behavioral science strategy is typically used by human relations consultants.

Meta-Strategies and Meta-Perspectives for Change

Robert Chin and Kenneth Benne (1976) and James Crowfoot and Mark Chesler (1976) both offer molar classifications of change strategies or perspectives, respectively. Whereas, for example, Greiner and Olmosk identified several change approaches and strategies, each of which accounted for a range of "strategy variance," the present typologies are even broader in scope, approaching the level of factors.

The meta-strategies of Chin and Benne are termed empirical-rational, normative-reeducative, and power-coercive. Under these three labels the authors have organized change theorists and change systems ranging from enlightenment and classical liberalism through therapists, trainers, and situation changers, to lobbyists, power brokers, strikers, and pressure groups.

In the empirical-rational meta-strategy, a reliance is placed on rationality. It is believed that people will pursue their rational self-interest once it is effectively revealed to them through information, data, and theory. Examples of change approaches used in this meta-strategy include basic research and the dissemination of knowledge through general education, systems analysis, applied research and the diffusion of research, and educational research.

In the normative-reeducative meta-strategy people are seen as being in a transitional relationship with their environment, actively shaping it and being shaped by it. Change occurs not only through rational, intellectual means, but through personal and sociocultural levels (for example, norms, roles) as well. Normative reeducation is a phrase that conveys the importance given in this meta-strategy to value and cultural redefinition. Other critical elements in promoting change include collaboration between a client system and change agent, the client system accepting responsibility for change, and the future benefits to the client system of change principles and methods. The variety of change approaches falling under the normative-reeducative meta-strategy includes psychotherapy, action research, laboratory method, training, counseling, process consultation, organization development, and others.

The power-coercive meta-strategy emphasizes the use of political, economic, and, to a lesser extent, moral sanctions in the use of power. Chin and Benne observe that, in general, power-coercive strategies of changing "seek to mass political and economic power behind the change goals which the strategists of change have decided are desirable" (p. 40). Thus, court-ordered busing as a means to increase racial integration in the schools, state legislation requiring the licensure of professionals to practice their trade, federal appropriations granting funds to schools for so-called basic education (reading, writing, and computing), and fire fighters who strike to protest the laying-off of fellow employees are all examples of power-coercive change methods.

In a similar vein to the above meta-strategies, Crowfoot and Chesler (1976) have identified and compared three contemporary meta-perspectives to planned social change, termed professional-technical (PT), political (P), and countercultural (CC). They compare these perspectives according to their general image of society and of individuals, their diagnoses of contemporary society, and with regard to their change priorities. As with the previous change technologies covered, this work can be only briefly summarized.

In the professional-technical (PT) change meta-perspective, society and most organizations are believed to be basically sound, although they are judged to be in need of learning better adaptation techniques for coping with constant change. The PT meta-perspective views individuals as rational information processors and problem solvers who are committed to prevailing norms and roles. It calls for change methods in which professionals manage ongoing, incremental planned change that is accomplished with existing social groups and organizations through rational problem-solving approaches. Important PT change agent activities include system diagnosis, small-group skills, process facilitation, force-field analysis, and consultation, among others.

The political (P) change meta-perspective views social organizations and institutions as being comprised of groups that vary by sex, age, race, ideology, and in other ways, and that are in competition for the acquisition and control of scarce resources. What tends to result from this competition is that certain groups (the haves) control most resources while others (have-nots) are denied them. In the P perspective, change can occur through divergent concern for advancing the interests of either the elite or the oppressed groups through political, economic, or moral means. Tactics used by P change agents include negotiation, compromise, coalition building, motivating the oppressed, and fostering collective action, among others.

In the countercultural (CC) change meta-perspective all relevant subunits of contemporary society are judged as being overtechnocratic and overbureaucratic, resulting in an inhibition of individual development and an undesirable increase in conformity. The CC meta-perspective heavily emphasizes individual changes, resulting in a variety of alternative life styles and organizations based on values such as racial and sexual equality, interpersonal cooperation, and concensual decision making. The CC change agents can be found in such alternative institutions as food cooperatives, communes, and free schools. They are heavily committed to living new cultural patterns themselves as a main preparation for their often unpaid work. More specific preparations components include self-development skills (values, spiritual growth) appropriate for achieving new life patterns (such as in establishing cooperative gardens, consciousness-raising groups), and skills in developing and maintaining organizations that support alternative life styles (such as book collectives, free clinics, and marketing cooperatives).

Change Models

Kurt Lewin's Model for Individual and Group Change. Lewin's model is based on the notion that change is precipitated by alterations that occur in the magnitude, direction, or number of factors that support change (driving forces) or resist change (restraining forces), or by a combination of these. Client system stability, or quasi-stationary equilibrium, results when the pattern of these driving and restraining forces is in a dynamic state of balance.

Force-field analysis is a change technique that is used to investigate the relationship in a client system between driving and restraining forces. Figure 4.3 depicts a force-field analysis format.

Force-field analysis can be conceptualized as an environmental assessment device that provides a dynamic picture of the driving and restraining forces at work in a setting. In Figure 4.3 the number, magnitude, and direction of the forces balance to produce a momentary equilibrium. This condition might exist, for instance, in a family where driving and restraining forces balance around issues such as control, finances, geographic location, relationship quality, family policies, and so on. In such a case, the family might be expected to continue as it is until an imbalance occurs that is intense enough to unfreeze existing conditions and to trigger movement of some kind to relieve the mounting tension.

FIGURE 4.3: A Force-Field Analysis Format

Restraining Forces Against Change

Driving Forces for Change

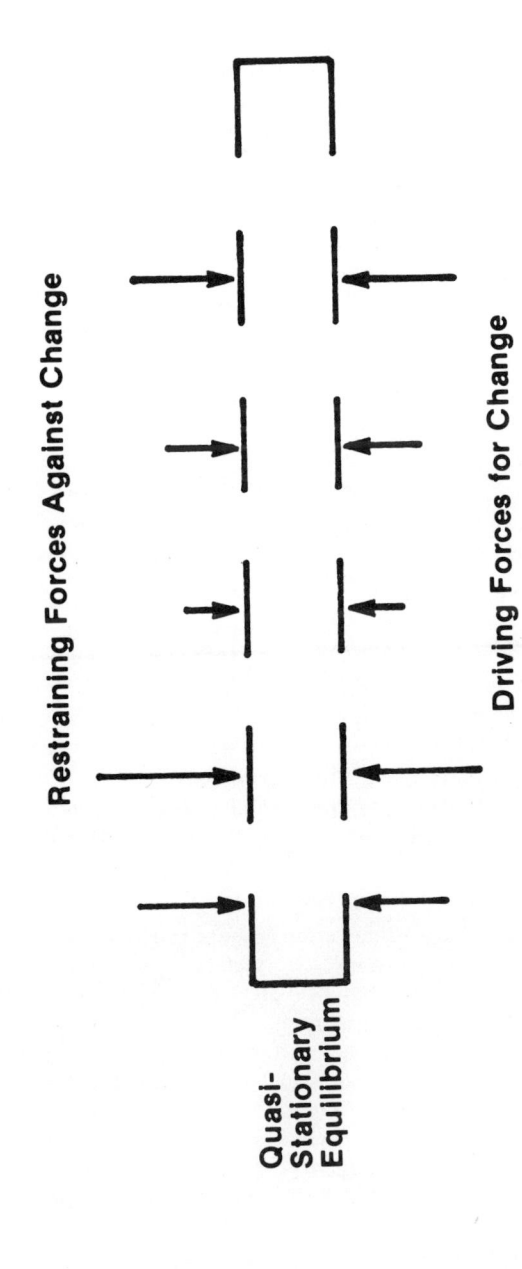

Quasi-Stationary Equilibrium

Source: Constructed by the authors.

Lewin conceptualized the change process as consisting of three phases: unfreezing, where the balance between restraining and driving forces is disturbed; moving, where driving forces are increased and/or restraining forces are decreased; and refreezing, where a temporary, new equilibrium is established from a balancing of driving and restraining forces. He wrote (1947):

> A change toward a higher level of group performance is frequently short lived; after a "shot in the arm," group life soon returns to the previous level. This indicates that it does not suffice to define the objective of planned change in group performance as the reaching of a different level. Permanency of the new level, or permanency for a desired period, should be included in the objective. A successful change includes, therefore, three aspects: *unfreezing* (if necessary) the present level, *moving* to the new level, and *freezing* group life on the new level (p. 34).

In the family example given earlier, member relationships might decay to such an extent that the family would change to seek a new equilibrium level. For example, a member could be expelled from the family, the family could seek outside professional assistance, and so on. Once movement has occurred that serves to satisfy the system need for homeostasis, refreezing occurs and the family functions at a somewhat different level.

Research, Development, and Diffusion. This change model (Brickell 1961; Clark and Guba 1965) systematically organized the processes involved in educational innovation into the phases of research, innovation development, and diffusion or dissemination of the innovation. This general process can be extended beyond educational innovation to considering how any change program (such as environmental change) can be created and promulgated.

Havelock and Havelock (1973) point out that the R-D-D change model is based on at least five assumptions:

Rational sequence. An innovation (change program) is developed through a planned, rational series of steps that includes basic and applied research, followed by development and testing. Effective innovations are mass-produced and packaged prior to wide dissemination.

Planning. Large-scale planning conducted over a long time span is required prior to the initiation of these steps and throughout the life of the project.

Division and coordination of labor. Functions related to diagnosis, information retrieval, research, development, and application need to be assigned differentially as the size and complexity of the project increases. For instance, a small local project would normally require less specialization than a larger national project would require.

Rationality and passivity of consumer. In this assumption, potential users will accept the innovation if it is offered to them in the "right place at the right time and in the right form" (Havelock and Havelock 1973, p. 12). The user is seen as an effective information-processing recipient rather than as an active participant in the change process.

High initial development cost. Substantial time, energy, and money are contributed early in the innovation development stage. Such an investment of resources in development is assumed to insure long-term innovation efficiency and quality and its suitability for mass dissemination to users.

Figure 4.4 pictures the research-development-diffusion change model. As Huse (1975) observes, the basic problem with this systematic model is that it is too rational. For instance, it ignores the long time lag between innovation and adoption, which sometimes takes 20 to 40 years, as well as generally disregarding the affective and situational barriers that accompany change efforts.

Linkage. Havelock (1969) suggests that this change model possesses aspects that might serve to integrate other models (namely diffusion and problem-solving models). The linkage concept begins with viewing users as problem solvers who experience a felt need that leads to a diagnosis and a problem statement. Users then work through phases of search and retrieval to arrive at a solution and finally to the application of that solution. Linkage extends beyond an internal user problem-solving approach, however, to stress that users must be meaningfully related to outside resources through the creation of reciprocal relationships. These relationships allow for mutual and appropriate stimulation and response. When these conditions are met, a useful linkage occurs, where exchange can take place between users (who ask for help) and resource systems (who provide it) that may lead to immediately effective solutions and the possibility of future collaboration.

Havelock (1969) elaborates on this basic linkage between a user system and a resource system to include overlapping linkages among a series of user and resource systems. He refers to such multiple linkage as forming a chain of knowledge utilization (p. 24), and suggests that such linkages contain the essential process in any effort at planned social change.

Planned Change. Lippitt, Watson, and Westley (1958) first advanced the model of planned change. Frohman and Sashkin (1970) and Kolb and Frohman (1970) are among others who have redefined the model, but the Lippitt, Watson, and Westley discussion remains the classic treatise on the subject. By planned change they mean, "change which derives from a purposeful decision to effect improvements in a personality system or social system and which is achieved with the help of professional guidance" (p. vi). In discussing planned change, these authors also defined key terms such as change agent, client system, change forces, resistance forces, phases of change, and methods of change; these terms have come to be significant ones in most discussions of change.

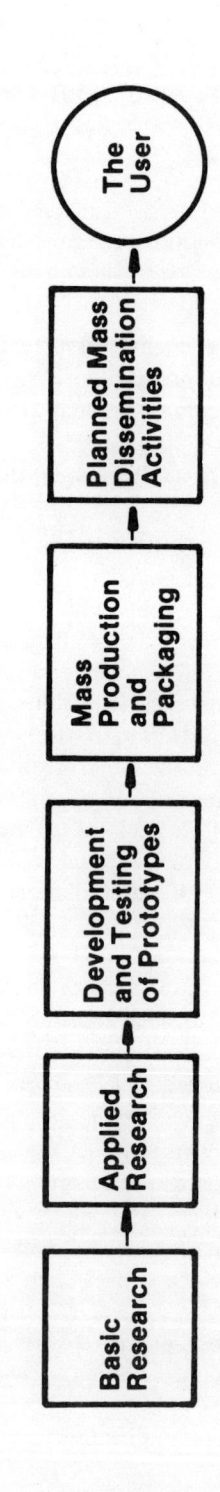

FIGURE 4.4: The Research, Development, and Diffusion Change Model

Basic Research → Applied Research → Development and Testing of Prototypes → Mass Production and Packaging → Planned Mass Dissemination Activities → The User

Source: Adapted from Ronald G. Havelock and Mary C. Havelock, *Training for Change Agents*, © 1973, Institute for Social Research (CRUSK), Ann Arbor, MI, Figure 1.2, page 13. Used with the permission of the publisher.

The planned change model builds from Lewin's three phase typology, discussed earlier, which includes phases of unfreezing, moving, and refreezing. Lippitt, Watson, and Westley extended these three phases into seven:

1. Development of a need for change (Scouting).
2. Establishment of a change relationship (Entry).
3. The clarification of the client system's problems (Diagnosis).
4. The examination of alternative routes and goals; establishing goals and intentions of action (Planning).
5. The transformation of intentions into actual change efforts (Action).
6. The generalization and stabilization of change (Generalizing).
7. Achieving a terminal relationship (Termination).

Figure 4.5 relates the phases of Lewin's model with the phases of the planned change model. As can be seen, phases of the planned change model are sequential, proceeding from scouting through terminating. Recycling back to

FIGURE 4.5: Comparing Lewin's Change Typology and Planned Change

Lewin's Typology   **Lippitt, Watson, and Westley's Typology**

Lewin's Typology	Lippitt, Watson, and Westley's Typology
Unfreezing	Scouting, Entry
Moving	Diagnosis, Planning, Action
Refreezing	Generalizing and stabilizing, Terminating

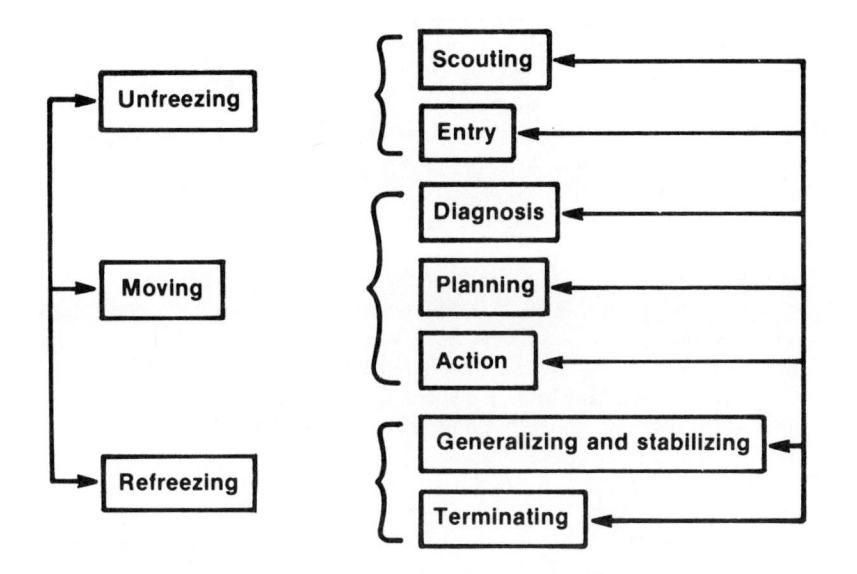

Source: Adapted by permission from *Organization Development and Change*, Second Edition, by E. F. Huse, copyright © 1980, West Publishing Company, Fig. 1, p. 98.

previous phases however, is always possible and often necessary. Thus, for example, a planned change program that is currently in the planning phase may be recycled for more diagnosis before further planning can continue.

What goes on in each of the seven planned change phases? These activities are summarized below.

Phase 1: Scouting. Here, mutual commitment between the client system (individual, group, organization, or community) and the change agent (external or internal professional facilitator) has not yet occurred. The former is in the process of converting problem awareness to a desire for change and the latter is considering potential entry points. Both are exploring the possibility for working together.

Phase 2: Entry. This very critical phase involves "contracting" change agent services with client system needs. Mutual expectations, goals, roles, and methods are discussed in an attempt to define acceptably the nature of the helping relationship and how it will proceed. This contract is developed to provide a guiding structure that is always modifiable, dependent on emergent activities. Entry is a significant planned change phase because "the success or failure of almost any change project depends heavily upon the quality and the workability of the relationship between the change agent and the client system, and many aspects of this relationship are established very early in the helping relationship" (Lippitt, Watson, and Westley 1958, pp. 135-36).

Phase 3: Diagnosis. The client system and change agent collaborate to identify problems in the client system. Interviews, questionnaires, observation, and archival data are used to provide information needed to locate problems. Diagnostic considerations include the problem(s) as perceived by the client, client goals, client resources, and change agent resources (time, skills, knowledge).

Phase 4: Planning. In this phase, the client system translates diagnoses into plans of action by generating alternatives, considering them, choosing a way or ways to proceed, and then by designing a strategy to reach desired goals. This planning is done cooperatively between the client system and change agent (as are all planned change phases) so that feasible directions are selected and that mutual commitment is obtained.

Phase 5: Action. Here, planned strategies are transformed into actual change efforts. Success in this phase is dependent on whether activities involved in the previous four phases have been satisfactorily accomplished. Issues that the client system must face during the action phase include eliciting support from the change agent, maintaining involvement from members of the client system during the change, and obtaining adequate feedback on change consequences.

Phase 6: Generalizing and Stabilizing Change. The interest in this phase is to determine if any implemented changes remain over time and if they are adopted by other subparts of the same system or by neighboring systems. Answering these questions satisfactorily requires that some form of evaluation be conducted. Unfortunately, as Huse (1980) observes, appropriate evaluation is rarely conducted, or when present it is often anecdotal rather than systematic. Further, he states that "in the ideal situation, this stage [evaluation] should be conducted throughout the change process and should be used by both the client system and the change agent in order to determine whether further work is necessary or whether the change agent should terminate the relationship with the client" (Huse 1980, p. 97).

Phase 7: Termination. A variety of terminal adjustments exists among client systems and change agents. For instance, termination may occur at any point in the planned change process after phase 2 (entry), work on one phase may be temporarily terminated to recycle to additional work on a previous phase, termination may be a final stoppage of contact between a change agent and client system, or the agent may continue to be available to the client on a periodic basis. An overriding concern in phase 7 is the degree to which a client system has improved and can apply learnings gained to new and different future problems to be encountered when the change agent is no longer present.

Action Research. In Chapter 1 Kurt Lewin's seminal contributions to psychology were discussed and earlier in this chapter his change model was reviewed. An overview of action research is presented next, a methodology that he pioneered to carry out his change model and to relate it to critical issues that people face. For instance, some major action research projects conducted under Lewin were in areas of gang behavior, law and social change, social integration, group loyalty, integrated housing, community discrimination, bigotry, and sensitivity training. Alfred Marrow, an associate and biographer of Lewin's, has said in *The Practical Theorist: The Life and Work of Kurt Lewin* (1969):

> . . . I described Lewin's aim as discovery of what determined changes in human relations. Such an aim, he had disclosed, is ideal for a scientist who integrates his role as scientist with his responsibities as a citizen of a democratic society that must keep bettering its works and ways. The patterns of action research were developed primarily as ways of realizing this ideal, developed because Lewin was a socially conscious individual who believed that only science provided dependable guides to effective action and wanted his labors to be of maximum social usefulness as well as theoretical significance. (p. 230)

Lewin's oft-quoted dictum, "There is nothing so practical as a good theory," characterizes the action research spirit. How is that orientation actually carried out?

The process of action research is highly similar to that used in planned change, just reviewed. This is not surprising, since the models originate from the same roots (Huse 1980), collaborative problem solving (Havelock and Havelock 1973). Therefore, the individual action research steps will not be elaborated here. Rather, the emphasis will be on where differences occur between the action research and planned change models. Further, the next chapter will be devoted to describing an adaptation of the action research (environmental change technology) that seems especially well suited to the environmental change component of environmental design.

Two differences between the models are most striking. The first is the definite integration of action and of research throughout the change process that typifies action research. In practice, this means that change projects are set in researchable frameworks and that every phase of the action project is researched (not just at the end), with resulting feedback used collaboratively by the client system and the change agent to shape progress. Figure 4.6 illustrates this aspect of action research.

The second significant difference between planned change and action research is the intent in the latter model to produce findings that are not only useful to the client system but that can be generalizable to other settings and problems as well. This larger purpose contributes to the general advancement of scientific and practical knowledge. Thus, action research projects address such real and global social problems as "Which procedures in giving jobs to minority members serve to increase, and which to decrease, group tension?" "How can one avoid the 'shot-in-the-arm' effect, which improves intergroup relations for a while, only to have them fall back again to earlier or even lower levels?" (Marrow 1969, pp. 175-76). Results generated are used by the client system and they are also meant to contribute to the public and scientific storehouse of knowledge.

From Generic Change Views to Environmental Change

As will be recalled, the authors set out to explore a general view of how change occurs (through strategies, approaches, models) in order to find a foothold from which how environmental change occurs can be specified. It was found that change can be conceptualized in several ways. Rational, collaborative, political, action, and linkage are but five of the many change technology variations considered. All of these were examined also because environmental change does not exist independently from general change technologies. Indeed, it will be seen that environmental change is attempted through the application of generic change technologies, such as those reviewed, within an ecological focus.

This ecological focus to change provides the boundaries within which environmental change must be considered. Traditionally, in the human services (for example, counseling, therapy, consulting, case work) the focus of change has been person-centered. Change agents have applied various technologies, such as planned change, to directly assist a client system to improve in some desirable manner. An individual is helped in psychotherapy to become more insightful or assertive, family members are taught better communication skills in family counseling, organization development is conducted to improve team functioning in an industrial division, or community members are instructed through public health education to redefine their personal dietary habits as a preventive measure to lower heart-attack risk, and so on. The common change focus that spans these examples is that of direct person change.

FIGURE 4.6: A Diagrammatic Model for Action Research

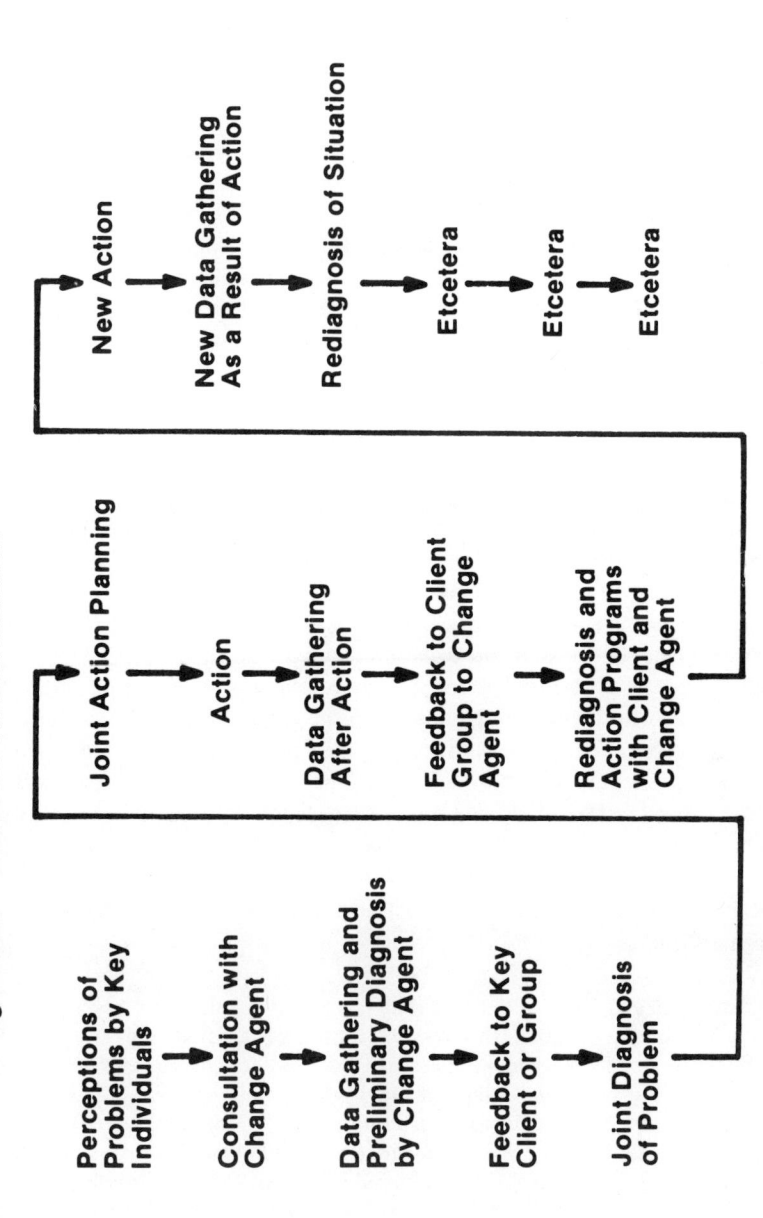

Perceptions of Problems by Key Individuals → Consultation with Change Agent → Data Gathering and Preliminary Diagnosis by Change Agent → Feedback to Key Client or Group → Joint Diagnosis of Problem → Joint Action Planning → Action → Data Gathering After Action → Feedback to Client Group to Change Agent → Rediagnosis and Action Programs with Client and Change Agent → New Action → New Data Gathering As a Result of Action → Rediagnosis of Situation → Etcetera → Etcetera → Etcetera

Source: Adapted from Wendell French, 1969, "Organization Development: Objectives, Assumptions, and Strategies," *California Management Review* III, (No. 2 1969), p. 26. Reprinted by permission of the Regents.

Of course, there is much that is sensible about this change focus. When members of a client system need to gain information, knowledge, or internal personal skills (such as clarifying values, developing a physical skill, or meditating) it may be a change method of choice. When members of a client system need to gain social-interaction skills, however, (for example, in forming relationships with others) or system-involvement skills (for example, in obtaining suitable employment or modifying a detrimental office procedure), an ecological focus provides a more useful change perspective.

As pointed out in Chapter 3, an ecological perspective takes into consideration the transactions of a client system with its environment. While either person change or environmental change can follow from an ecological perspective, neither has fully endorsed it. Person change attempts have tended to exclude environmental considerations by emphasizing thoughts, feelings, and behaviors of client system members. Environmental change efforts have reversed this tendency by emphasizing environmental influences, thus minimizing personal adaptation. In their extreme manifestation, these two change orientations take on what have been referred to as blaming characteristics.

Victim blame (for example, Caplan and Nelson 1973; Gregg, Preston, Geist, and Caplan 1979; Guskin and Chesler 1973; Ryan 1971) exaggerates personal change attempts, where people who experience problems are held culpable for being the cause of the problems they suffer. Thus, poor people are poor because they lack knowledge and skills necessary to acquire and hold jobs, a couple divorces due to inabilities of the partners to communicate effectively, and so on. In victim blame, environmental factors such as inadequate schools or inequitable employment opportunities are ruled out of consideration as contributing factors to people's poverty. The change focus becomes that of changing the victim, without altering environmental factors. All that is needed, in this view, is for victims to acquire better skills and more knowledge in order to cope more effectively.

Ellen Goodman, the syndicated columnist, has decried this orientation to mental health in a recent column, "Help Professions Aren't Shrinking" (Goodman 1980):

> Inflation—like DC-10s, and Three Mile Islands, and Cold Wars—is bad for your mental health. But there is a difference between dealing with these problems as social diseases or as psychological ones. It's the difference between giving the unemployed jobs or giving them leaflets on how to explain to their children why they aren't getting birthday presents. The whole psychiatric, psycho-babble approach to major social problems makes me cringe. It puts the responsibility on the person who often is least powerful. It smacks of blaming the victim. (p. A-16)

System blame (for example, Heller and Monahan 1977; Rappaport 1977) exaggerates environmental change attempts, where the environmental system is held responsible for the problems that people face. The people affected adversely by these systems are viewed as being controlled by dominating external conditions. Thus, in the examples cited earlier, environmental design projects might create jobs for the poor, and couples might be provided with easy access to a variety of helping resources. The change focus in system blame is on the environment—physical, social, institutional factors—exonerating the place of personal responsibility in the process.

There is no intention here to place the environmental change function of environmental design within a system-blame perspective. The authors agree with Heller and Monahan's view (1977) that neither person-blame nor system-blame perspectives are independently adequate:

> Just as a person-blame orientation can reinforce the status quo, so too can a system-blame perspective become an excuse for inaction. If individuals are simply passive "victims" of their environment, personal responsibility and accountability for one's own behavior can be avoided. A further perspective would indicate environmental influence is not a one-way process—environments influence behavior, but persons also have the capacity to shape environments. What is needed is a more complex and sophisticated view of causality. (pp. 9-10)

The ecological frame of analysis would seem to provide such a view for underlying environmental change. Its inclusion of mutually interacting person and environmental variables enables a holistic approach to change to be taken, which minimizes neither side while calling for the examination of their combined influence.

Placing generic change approaches, strategies, and models within an ecological framework means that they are used to attend to broader aspects of a client system's condition and that change is undertaken to improve both personal and environmental dimensions. For environmental change, particularly, generic change technologies that are conducted ecologically means that coping and adaptation activities engaged in by a client system within environmental settings can become a specific focus for change.

With the application of an ecological focus to generic change in mind, let us now turn to an examination of the change elements within each of the five environmental classifications and assessment models that were featured in Chapters 2 and 3, respectively: social ecological, ecosystem, open-system, functions of physical settings, and cognitive and geographic mapping.

Environmental Change Models

Social Ecological Model

Chapter 3 discussed the variety of social climate scales developed by Rudolf Moos and his associates for use in assessing the psychosocial climate of a number of human environments (such as classrooms, correctional institutions, and groups). Focusing on the change technology in this section will emphasize the translation of data collected through use of the scales to components that comprise environmental change.

Moos has written in a number of sources about this matter (for example, Insel and Moos 1974; Moos 1979a, 1979b). It can be said, however, that his emphasis to date has been on the development of sound environmental assessment methodologies and not on the change process. Nevertheless, his conception of how environmental change can occur through a social ecological approach seems to contain the following components:

Data Base. Environmental change is planned. It is based on information that is collected through the use of assessment measures that meet scientific and ecological criteria.

User Participation. Environments are not to be changed by external experts or by a select few from the environment. Rather, "the likelihood of achieving an optimum environment is greatly facilitated when critical decisions about changing the environment are in the hands of the people who function within the environment" (Insel and Moos 1974, p. 187). More correctly, everyone in an environment is given an opportunity to describe how the current environment is functioning and how they would like to have it function ideally. This assessment process yields data (through use of the appropriate social climate scale) upon which change efforts can be based.

Feedback. Results of these assessments are then organized and presented to the respondents or their representatives (for example, see Daher, Corazzini, and McKinnon 1977; DeYoung 1977; Holahan and Wilcox 1977). Emphasis is placed on similarities and differences in two areas: the perceptions of various important groups in the environment (for example, in a classroom, teacher versus students), and between the actual and ideal social climates these groups perceived.

Moos has cautioned that feedback alone is not enough. Rather, it needs to occur within a coherent, planned approach and to conform to certain guidelines. Drawing from McKeachie's work (1976), Moos (1979b) emphasizes that feedback must provide relevant information to recipients, be received by people who are motivated to change, and be associated with a range of alternative solutions. Further, Moos reports that feedback for environmental change purposes must attend to three additional factors: targeting relatively small social settings (for example, a residential floor instead of a whole residence hall, a ward rather than an entire hospital) that are very important for their constituents; selecting aspects of settings that people can do something about rather than elements that are not under their control (for example, teachers can change the degree of support they give to students but cannot readily change the length of the school year); and directly considering people's needs for environmental and personal efficiency.

Planning and Instituting Changes. Changes may occur in any of the three broad divisions of social climate: relationship, personal growth, and/or system maintenance and system change. For instance, in a project that Conyne was involved with on a university residence hall floor, residents reported through a modified form of the URES that the atmosphere of their floor inhibited growth and relationship building. During planning sessions they decided that one way to ameliorate this situation was to change the long, cold-looking corridors by painting them attractively. This action was taken with dramatic improvement found through evaluation.

Price (1976) has presented a data-guided feedback method that gives directions as to how recipients' responses to feedback can be channeled through a set of program development steps to result in environmental change. Daher, Corazzini, and McKinnon (1977) and Schroeder (1979) have outlined similar environmental change strategies for social ecological design projects. In addition to generally following the feedback guidelines mentioned above, these change strategies include substages of selecting environmental values, goal setting, translating goals to specific actions, developing social contracts, and implementing resulting plans. The Daher, Corazzini, and McKinnon and the Schroeder approaches combine a guided-data-feedback change approach with aspects of the ecosystem change model, to be discussed in the next section.

Helping a group convert environmental assessment data into a planned change effort requires what Insel and Moos (1974) have termed a "social systems change facilitator." Krasner (1980) also has used similar terms in describing this role ("social change agent," "learning facilitator," and "environmental designer," pp. xi, xii). Moos (1979b) has recently pushed beyond this view of facilitation to suggest a proactive role of environmental educator. Such a person would be available "to teach people how to create, select, and transcend environments, that is, to enhance environmental competence" (p. 244). As will be seen later, the notion of environmental competence is an important one underlying the work of Steele (1971, 1973) in physical setting design.

Reassessment. Once a change is instituted, the environment is reassessed with results fed back to the participants for their continued evaluation. The goal is that this systematic assessment-change-reassessment cyclical design process will eventually help participants to attain the kind of environment they desire. In the corridor-painting example referred to earlier, residents reported a dramatic increase in relationship and personal growth opportunities following the change project, a result that may have been as much (or more) a reflection of the group painting process inself than it was of the painted corridors that were produced.

Several generic change approaches are combined and expressed through the social ecological model. Notable among them are the empirical-rational (data base, planned approach) and normative-reeducative meta-strategies (feedback, value consideration); collaboration (active role of users); action research (cyclical assessment-change-reassessment process); and applied behavioral science (integrated use of multiple change approaches).

Ecosystem Model.

Huebner (1979) has summarized the ecosystem interventions process as generally containing the following seven steps:

(1) some effort at gaining institutional or area support for the project;
(2) the establishment of a working group ("planning group" or "team") composed of representatives of the major constituencies in the setting;
(3) the design of the project, including instrument construction (most of these assessments design their own survey instruments for use in the project);
(4) data collection, typically done using a sampling technique;
(5) data analysis;
(6) interventions based on the data, often including the dissemination of analyzed data to the original respondents or to subunits responsible for the various areas assessed;
(7) a reassessment of the environment after interventions have been made and some period of time has elapsed since the original assessment. (p. 12)

In the earlier discussion of the ecosystem model in Chapters 2 and 3 the model was overviewed and assessment questions dealt with in some depth: the instrumentation used, designing local measures, and so on. Here the various change forms used within the ecosystem model will be emphasized.

Hurst and Ragle (1979) have summarized three organizational structures that have been used to support ecosystem change efforts (the team approach of Aulepp and Delworth 1978; the campus design center of Fawcett, Huebner, and Banning 1978 that we described in Chapter Three; and the on-site design team, of Huebner and Corazzini 1978). They then discuss their own environmental assessment and intervention team model that is lodged in a Dean of Students office. Other models (Huebner 1979) include those used in housing offices (Daher, Corazzini, and McKinnon 1977; Schroeder 1979; Schuh 1979); and in total campus design (Conyne 1975, 1978). The point here is that the administrative organization and proper location of an ecosystem project in a campus (or other) system are critical issues that have been approached successfully in a range of ways in different situations.

Regardless of how these important contextual issues are resolved, the ecosystem change process, as Huebner observed earlier, usually entails the collaborative collection, interpretation, and use of ecological data. Of fundamental importance seems to be the creation and effective functioning of an interdependent steering group whose members are appropriately respresentative of environmental constitutents. The belief seems to be that if this group is constituted carefully and maintained satisfactorily, then change is more likely to be possible and effective. Change efforts conducted over the years by community and environmental psychologists have shown that setting participants (users) must be actively involved in changes that are to occur in their space. Failure to work with the users, instead choosing to do things (like changing environments) for them, guarantees unsuccessful efforts that are typified by low participation, high attrition, and little if any positive effects.

Although, as Huebner (1979) indicates, "Possible interventions that may arise out of an ecosystem project are almost limitless" (p. 17), precious little has been advanced to demonstrate the change mechanism itself. What appears to be implied, however, is that redesign occurs when planning group members themselves initiate changes in their own environment by using environmental assessment data or when other decision makers are influenced by these data (as presented in reports or through consultation, for instance) to institute changes.

This process seems to be based largely on a research-dissemination-utilization model that is heavily invested in the empirical-rational meta-strategy of change. This emphasis on an intellectual, rational academic change approach may be overly minimizing the importance of affective and political dynamics. Although Aulepp and Delworth (1978) have suggested the use of normative-reeducative change strategies such as consultation and workshops, the literature is scant in reporting such efforts. Most evidence available relies on the use of data dissemination through oral and written reports as the prime change strategy.

One example, however, of how a workshop can be used effectively as a change strategy was reported recently by Conyne (1980). He and his colleagues presented the salient results of a four-year campus environmental assessment project (Conyne 1975, 1978) to the directors of student affairs agencies in a data-based workshop series. This format used social climate data as triggers for small-group discussions, role-plays, and planning sessions related to campus issues and potential change approaches. Such an approach recognizes the importance of values, attitudes, norms, and political dynamics in relation to any change considerations. Emerging from this workshop series was a planning-group-sponsored prevention program to assist new university students who live off campus to accommodate more adaptively to the university and city environment.

Open-System Model

It will be recalled that three environmental assessment approaches were discussed in relation to the open-system model that Katz and Kahn (1966) proposed for understanding organizational functioning: Weisbord's (1978) six-box approach; Kast and Rosenzweig's (1970) systems approach; and Egan and Cowan's (1979) Model A. In this section on environmental change an attempt will be made to identify the change processes that evolve from these approaches.

At issue is what organizational interventions (environmental changes) are appropriate for correcting or improving deficits (Weisbord's blips) revealed through environmental assessment. For instance, how can deficiencies be ameliorated in organizational structure, leadership, goals, relationships, staff knowledge and skills, "climate," external involvements, and so on? Two change orientations that address this question will be described and interrelated. The first, proposed by Egan and Cowan (1979), is based on a general problem-solving approach, and is termed by them Model B. The second, summarized by French and Bell (1973), is organization development.

The Model B change approach contains four stages (diagnosis, goal setting, program development, and implementation/evaluation), with each of these stages having an expanding and a contracting step, as follows:

(1) *Diagnosis.* The system, Using Model A, takes its pulse.
(2) *Focusing.* The system centers on elements in need of renewal.
(3) *New perspectives.* New ways of carrying out the activities of the subsystem in need of renewal are considered.
(4) *Goal Setting.* Behavioral goals are set, based on the new data considered in Step 3.
(5) *Possible programs.* Different means for achieving established goals are considered.
(6) *Choice of programs.* The system commits itself to specific programs in order to achieve goals.
(7) *Implementation.* The programs are carried out.
(8) *Evaluation.* The system determines the effectiveness of programs in light of behavioral goals. (p. 141)

Figure 4.7 illustrates the four stages of system change with the expanding and contracting steps in each stage. The widening, left-hand half of each of the four diamonds represents an expanding step in this system change approach, while the narrowing, right-hand half of each diamond represents a contracting step. Thus, in Model B, environmental change results from a continuous broadening and focusing of interlocking and overlapping change steps that are applied to concern areas in the environment related to structure, leadership, relationships, and other variables.

Step 5 of Model B indicates that a variety of change approaches can be used to obtain organizational change. One major technology is organization development.

Organization development (for example, Beckhard 1969; French and Bell 1973; French, Bell, and Zawacki 1978; Huse 1980) is an effort that is "(1) *plan-*

FIGURE 4.7: An Overview of Model B

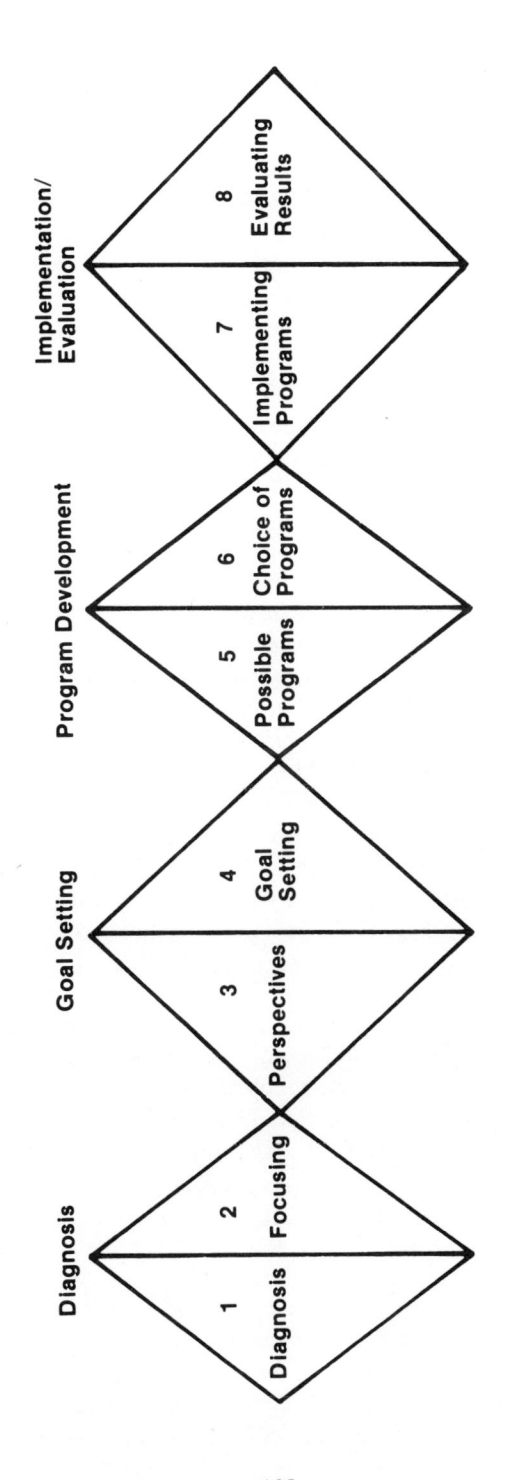

Diagnosis	Goal Setting	Program Development	Implementation/Evaluation
1 Diagnosis / 2 Focusing	3 Perspectives / 4 Goal Setting	5 Possible Programs / 6 Choice of Programs	7 Implementing Programs / 8 Evaluating Results

Source: Adapted from *People in Systems: A Model for Development in the Human-Service Professions and Education*, by G. Egan and M. A. Cowan. Copyright © 1979 by Wadsworth, Inc. Reprinted by permission of the publisher, Brooks/Cole Publishing Company, Monterey, California.

ned, (2) *organization-wide,* and (3) *managed* from the *top,* to (4) increase *organization effectiveness* and *health* through (5) *planned interventions* in the organization's "processes," using behavioral-science knowledge" (Beckhard 1969, p. 9). Organization development (OD) contains a variety of interventions that can be used in attempts to change organizational environments. OD can be seen as a broad-net intervention from which any number of possible change programs can be selected for application in environmental change within organizations.

French and Bell (1973) have organized this broad net of interventions economically into two useful classifications that are based on these questions: Is the OD intervention primarily oriented toward individual or group learning and does it focus mainly on task or on process issues? And is the OD intervention designed to enhance the functioning of individuals, dyads/triads, teams and groups, intergroup relations, or the total organization? In terms of environmental change within organizations, each of the many interventions presented in Figures 4.8 and 4.9 needs to be interpreted ecologically. For example, T-groups used with organizations' members have traditionally placed a premium on personal and interpersonal learning with little if any emphasis placed on environmental matters. Application of an ecological perspective to T-groups, however, would necessitate giving attention to environmental as well as to personal and interpersonal matters. Specifically, personal learning gained during T-group interaction needs to be applied to the organizational work setting. This ecological view (people and environment), then, should be kept foremost in the mind in inspecting the range of OD interventions presented. First to be examined are some representative OD interventions that are organized by individual-group and task-process dimensions.

It can be seen in Figure 4.8 that a variety of interventions exist for different purposes and that some of the same interventions can be used to meet different purposes. Thus, for example, survey feedback can be used with groups to work on both task and process issues.

OD interventions can be organized, also, according to the target group at which they are directed. Figure 4.9 illustrates this relationship.

Once again variety and overlap are observable in these OD interventions. This condition reflects the actual use of various OD interventions. Examination of the contents in Figures 4.8 and 4.9 also shows that certain types of OD interventions are omitted that may have significant import for environmental change. These are action research, which French and Bell (1973) have stated arguably (see Frohman, Sashkin, and Kavanaugh 1978) as being basic and common to all OD efforts, and sociophysical interventions (Steele 1971, 1973) which will be explored in some detail later. It has been seen earlier that cyclical steps of assessment, action, and reassessment have tended to characterize environmental change; therefore, action research needs to be restated here as an important OD option. Sociophysical interventions emphasize environmental contributions to the change process, and for that reason require inclusion.

FIGURE 4.8: Some OD Interventions Organized by Individual-Group and Task-Process

| | Individual vs. Group Dimension ||
	Focus on the Individual	Focus on the Group
Focus on Task Issues	Education: technical skills; decision-making, problem solving, goal setting, planning Career planning Job enrichment	Technostructural changes Survey feedback Team-building
Focus on Process Issues	Process consultation Group dynamics Planned change T - groups	Survey feedback Intergroup activities Team-building

(Task vs. Process Dimension)

Source: Adapted from Wendell L. French/Cecil H. Bell, Jr., *Organizational Development: Behavioral Science Interventions for Organizational Improvement,* © 1973, pp. 106-7. Reprinted by permission of Prentice-Hall, Inc., Englewood Cliffs, N.J. 07632.

Therefore in seeking change, many OD interventions can be used that correspond to the transformation component of the open-system model. Once these interventions are cast within an ecological perspective, environmental change options become readily available for potential use.

Functions of Physical Settings

As has been seen, the built environment (for example, buildings, parking lots, classrooms) affects human behavior. Robert Sommer (1974), for instance, has compared "hard" and "soft" architecture in relation to their differential

FIGURE 4.9: Some OD Interventions Organized by Target Groups

Target Group	Some Types of Interventions
Individuals	T-groups Counseling Education
Dyads/Triads	Process Consultation Third-party peacemaking
Teams & Groups	Team building Process consultation Survey feedback
Intergroup Relations	Organizational Mirroring Technostructural interventions Process consultation
Total Organization	Technostructural activities Survey feedback Strategic planning activities

Source: Adapted from Wendell L. French/Cecil H. Bell, Jr., *Organizational Development: Behavioral Science Interventions for Organization Improvement,* © 1973, pp. 106-7. Reprinted by permission of Prentice-Hall, Inc., Englewood Cliffs, N.J. 07632.

impacts on people. Hard architecture, he says, typifies many institutional and public places. It is designed to be strong (for example, made of steel and concrete, bolted down) and resistant to human imprint. Soft architecture, conversely, is pliable and flexible and it is constructed of plastics, foam, and inflatable materials. He argues that while hard architecture conveys impersonal dehumanizing messages and yields minimal flexibility for use of the space, soft architecture suggests a humanizing, warm, modifiable space that welcomes human interaction. Sommer reports several studies that lend general support to these notions.

This line of study, the research conducted in the area of fixed and pseudo-fixed physical settings done by Sommer (1974) and others, and explorations in related areas (such as the effects of windowless buildings on people, uses of office plazas, and the personalization of anomic buildings) all verify the importance of physical settings in people's lives. The mother of one of the authors, for instance, told him that the brand-new, expensive state office building in which she works, which replaced the (supposedly) run-down building that had been in use for decades, is very unsatisfactory and depressing to her and others: its shiny metal walls project a sanitary, antiseptic sense, the walls cannot be decorated due to state regulation, windows cannot be opened because of similar regulation and, most of all, the place just does not "feel like home anymore."

Steele (1971, 1973) suggests a sociophysical approach to change that is meant to address such conditions as hard architecture and other problematic issues that the built environment raises for users. Clearly, these issues are central to an ecology of human functioning, for they directly target environment-person and environment-organization interactions. He indicates five broad sociophysical change approaches that can be taken to promote what he terms environmental competence, a concept that will be described later. Each of these five sociophysical change approaches is discussed below.

Changing an organization's spaces (relocation) to provide a better setting for the users. The six functions of physical settings described in Chapter 3 (security and shelter, social contact, symbolic identification, task instrumentality, pleasure, and growth) can be applied to collect data about how a spatial location affects users. When unsatisfactory spatial locations are revealed in the data, this change approach can be used to relocate spatial features more satisfactorily. For example, departmental offices that are scattered across three floors in a building may inhibit social and work contact. Rearranging office locations so they are in closer proximity would increase opportunities for interpersonal contact, also leading potentially to enhanced productivity.

Changing physical settings to support a social-system organization development process. Counseling offices whose walls are partial partitions that do not reach the ceiling fail to provide adequate privacy to allow the function of counseling to occur freely. Classrooms with bolted down chairs arranged in parallel rows facing the teacher do not set the physical conditions suitable for discussion and other experiential classroom activities that involve active student participation. Offices that overheat in the summer and underheat in the winter are not pleasurable for most people and the resulting uncomfortable temperatures can diminish productivity. In these cases, extending the walls to the ceiling, replacing bolted chairs with movable ones, and regulating the temperature more adequately would serve to support necessary functions more sufficiently.

Using sociophysical approaches to enhance the problem-solving ability of a client system. Steele believes that using the six functions of physical settings system for diagnosis and change can often generalize to using a problem-solving approach in other areas of personal and organizational functioning. In this sense, the sociophysical change approach can be used to develop in users problem-solving skills that they can put to use in other ways.

Using organization development processes to facilitate physical-setting changes. OD is used most frequently in relation to human processes and their effectiveness—such areas as decision making, communication, leadership, and so on are usually of interest. However, OD can be used also to address the relationship between organizational functioning and physical settings. As has been seen, a brand-new office building does not necessarily mean it will be a better place than the old setting for employees and clientele. As Steele points out, consultation using a sociophysical perspective that is conducted during the creation of new office plans can be very useful in creating functional spaces in the future.

Effective use of these general sociophysical strategies can lead to what Steele (1973) has termed environmental competence in people. By environmental competence he means people becoming aware of their surrounding environment and its impact on them, and being able to use or change settings appropriately. He sees increased environmental competence as emerging from the application of a sociophysical perspective to the general problem-solving process (Steele 1973) by

> (a) asking what we are trying to *do* in the setting; (b) asking what spatial arrangements would be adequate or useful for our purposes; (c) specifying the present spatial arrangement and comparing it with our needs; (d) asking what can be done to change the setting to make it more appropriate and how much energy is required to carry out the changes; (e) choosing an alternate and acting on it and (f) taking note of the consequences of our choices for inclusion in future problem-solving tasks. (p. 116)

Several approaches are available for learning the sociophysical problem-solving process. For example, environmental members (users, consultees, trainees, students, or others) can be taught the six functions, be trained in them through the use of experiential exercises, can collaborate with architects or designers, and/or they can receive process consultation that attends to both human and physical process. Whatever routes are chosen, Steele thinks that the sociophysical problem-solving approach can help to increase environmental competence in individual and organizational change projects.

Cognitive and Geographic Mapping Model

Two challenges are presented when environmental change procedures associated with mapping models are considered. The first corresponds to the assessment results that are produced in mapping. As has been seen, these results are in the form of graphic-spatial maps, as compared with the quantitative and/or verbal—descriptive displays with which people are more familiar. Translating pictorial maps to change interventions demands a different approach in moving from data analysis to change. The second point is that mapping is basically a research tool that is being developed in order to describe and compare environments. Consequently, little work has yet been conducted that focuses on action methodologies. The potential user of cognitive or geographic mapping in environmental design, then, will find its assessment component considerably more developed than its change component.

Due to the absence of any specified environmental change approach in mapping, one is free to invent alternatives. Turning to the generic change approaches discussed earlier in the chapter can be very helpful here, as well as considering the change components that are associated with the other environmental models that have been examined. For instance, data contained in maps could be combined within an action research model, used to formulate policy by decree, framed within an empirical-rational feedback approach, and so on.

Despite the unavailability of change methods developed especially for mapping, the authors believe that environmental assessment data depicted through maps present inherent benefits over nearly any other mode of presentation. "A picture is worth a thousand words," said one sage. Maps depicting spatial distributions of people in relation to important issues they face (such as access to public transportation or perceived safety of various neighborhoods) serve to identify needs and problems concisely and sharply, perhaps with more immediate meaning and impact than do other more popular forms of feedback such as written reports.

The authors believe that the superior form of feedback that maps afford can expedite change. Information can be parsimoniously organized and conveyed through maps in such a way that it is pertinent, easily interpretable, and relevant; in short, it easily becomes cognitively acceptable (Blanton and Alley 1978). Cognitive acceptability needs to be accompanied by affective acceptability. Factors to be considered include decreasing resistance to change, increasing involvement in findings, making implications clear, timing feedback appropriately, and other considerations (Blanton and Alley 1978; Davis and Salasin 1979; Kiresuk and Lund 1979). Enhancement of affective acceptability should be a primary concern in selecting an appropriate environmental change approach to use with mapping.

Conyne and his colleagues have incorporated the geographic mapping technique of geocode analysis in a campus ecosystem design project referred to earlier. This project is being conducted to assist current undergraduate students who are new to the university and who live off campus (client system) to cope effectively with both city and university environments. Among other assessment devices, geocode analysis was used. (A good advantage of having an interdisciplinary planning group is shown by this example. A geography professor, who was very interested in finding real-world cases to which his students could apply new computer mapping equipment purchased by his department for applied geography purposes, headed up this aspect of the ecosystem design project.) Through this approach, it has been possible to produce contour maps that display the physical location of off-campus students according to any number of demographic variables that seem important, including the distribution of off-campus females in relation to physical assaults, low academic achievers, and students who indicated particular concern about being able to become actively involved in the university. Being able to pinpoint where selected target members live who may be at risk for certain problems, such as women at risk for physical assault, greatly facilitates the mounting of environmental change programs that are intended to lower the risk.

Mapping, therefore, provides advantages of economical data presentation that is readily understandable. Its use enables a change agent to contact client system members with a degree of precision not heretofore available through other means. These advantages, coupled with use of appropriate follow-up change approaches, give the use of mapping approaches in environmental design a bright future.

APPLIED RESEARCH REVISITED:
CHANGE EVALUATION AND ITS USAGES.

As will be recalled from the discussion earlier in the chapter of the environmental design cycle, environmental change is conducted within the context of applied research. In fact, analogous to the open-system model of input-throughput-output, the environmental design cycle is conceptualized as consisting of interlocking applied research/environmental change/applied research elements. Where the first applied research element is used primarily to generate the input for change efforts, the second element is employed mainly to evaluate the effects of any intervening change effort and to find ways to utilize the results programatically.

Applied research used to evaluate change programs was briefly examined earlier. Here this phase of the design cycle is extended by focusing on the critical issue of data usage by decision makers. As shown in the discussion of the environmental design cycle (see Figure 4.1, for instance), this issue is an important one not only after a change has been accomplished, but throughout all phases of design.

Michael Quinn Patton (1978) has provided a penetrating analysis of the usability of evaluation results by policy makers. He indicates that there are two fundamental requirements in what he terms utilization-focused evaluation and that the rest is a matter of negotiation, adaptation, selection, and matching between evaluator and decision maker:

> First, relevant decision makers and information users must be identified and organized—real, visible, specific, and caring human beings, not ephemeral, general, and abstract "audiences," organizations, or agencies. Second, evaluators must work actively, reactively, and adaptively with these identified decision makers and information users to make all other decisions about the evaluation—decisions about research focus, design, methods, analysis, interpretation, and dissemination. (p. 284)

The active-reactive-adaptive evaluator role implied above is used to accommodate rather than to manipulate the views of decision makers (Davis and Salasin 1975). Utilization-focused evaluation employs this role to organize evaluators (change agents), decision makers, and information users in such a manner that all participants share responsibility for planning, modifying, and implementing an evaluation that is both useful and of high quality.

Patton claims that this kind of evaluator role is totally compatible with the hope expressed by Davis and Salasin (1975) that evaluators can perform a change consultant role. He points out that the change consultant role begins at the very first step of utilization-focused evaluation when relevant evaluators and decision makers are identified and organized to begin working together to "actively engage in discussions about what a program is doing, where it is going, how it could be improved, and what information is needed to reduce uncertainty about program implementation and effects—these processes are in themselves change producing" (p. 290).

This notion that evaluation can serve a continual, collaborative, change function captures the essence of environmental design. The next step now is to consider an integration of the separate pieces of environmental design (applied research/environmental change/applied research) that have been discussed throughout this chapter.

Leonard Krasner (1980) in his edited book, *Environmental Design and Human Behavior: A Psychology of the Individual in Society,* draws from Colman (1975) to define environmental design as

> ... the planning of a coherent program and set of procedures to effect the total human and non-human environment in ways that increase the probability that certain goals or "needs" will be achieved. The goal of environmental design would relate to social behavior, such as planning an educational or therapeutic system, as much as to aesthetics such as constructing an awe-inspiring church. Input into environmental design problems must then include knowledge related

to modifying human behavior and social systems as well as structural information from engineering and perceptual psychology. The field would expand toward a new view of man, always powerfully effected [sic] by his physical and social environment, now actively developing an environmental design model and methodology that would place the effect of the total environment on his behavior more in his own control, and the responsibility for the design and control of the environment on his behavior, in himself. (cited in Krasner 1980, p. 3)

This definition of environmental design integrates the aspects that have been addressed throughout this chapter: it is an intentional and evaluated change process that is conducted, at least in part, by setting participants. This latter point, which is concerned with who controls the design process, is immensely important. The authors agree with Krasner (1980) who has said that "the designing and planning should and must come from the participants of the setting in which the design is taking place" (p. 4); and with Hutchison (1980), who has discussed issues such as the importance of informed consent, allowing the client to select the goal, and community involvement in planning. This ethic of optimizing user participation is fundamental to carrying out environmental design effectively and openly, devoid of the manipulation of people's lives conjured up by notions of "big brother."

SUMMARY AND PROSPECTUS

Throughout the lengthy discussion of environmental design in this chapter an attempt has been made to describe its components of applied research/ environmental change/applied research and to show how they fit together. The predominant focus of this chapter has been on the environmental change component. In that regard, the reader was presented with a range of generic change approaches that have potential for environmental change. Particular emphasis was placed on the five environmentally oriented change models considered throughout the book and to their potential use in environmental design projects. Table 4.1 contains a summary of predominant ecological assessment and change emphases in the environmental change models.

Next, the question to be addressed is whether there is a basic technology of environmental design that integrates applied research and environmental change dimensions and that meets the necessary criteria of intentionality, researchability, and collaboration. The authors believe such a basic technology is available. Variations of it have been referred to previously by Conyne and Rogers (1977) as ecological problem solving, by Holahan and Wilcox (1977) as ecological action research, by Price and Cherniss (1977) as research for social action, and by Steele (1971) as action-oriented consultation-research. These labels (mentioned previously) may be recognized as deriving from the Lewinian action research

TABLE 4.1: Predominant Assessment and Change Emphases for the Five Environmental Change Models

Environmental Change Models	Ecological Assessment Emphasis	Ecological Change Emphasis
Social ecology	Social climate	Data-based feedback
Ecosystem	Environmental referents	Change team/planning group
Open-system	Organization-environment interface	Organization development (sociotechnical change)
Functions of physical setting	Sociophysical elements: security/shelter, solid contact, symbolic identification, task instrumentality, pleasure, growth.	Organization development (sociophysical change)
Mapping	Cognitive/geographic maps	Unspecified

Source: Compiled by the authors.

model, placed within ecological, social change, or consultation contexts. Regardless of the label used, the generic process that is being addressed has these elements: it includes integrated and cyclical research planning and action phases; it is lodged within an ecological people-by-setting assessment and change perspective; and setting participants are actively and systematically involved throughout all phases. The new nomenclature of Environmental Change Technology will be used to represent the generic technology underlying environmental design and the entire next chapter will be devoted to its elucidation.

5

ENVIRONMENTAL CHANGE TECHNOLOGY: A METHOD FOR ENVIRONMENTAL DESIGN

The previous chapters have discussed the effects of environment on human behavior, the conceptualization, classification, and measurement of environments, and an overview of methodologies and strategies for environmental change. This chapter will describe a model and detail methods for implementing environmental design. And to conclude the chapter the authors will give a description of a case from their own experience in which environmental design was implemented.

DEVELOPMENT OF ENVIRONMENTAL CHANGE TECHNOLOGY

The method, Environmental Change Technology, is an amalgamation and adaptation of the Lewin typology, of Lippitt, Watson, and Westley's (1958) Planned Change Model, and of action research paradigms. The Lewin typology serves as the most general of the models. It delineates planned change into three basic parts: unfreezing, moving, and refreezing. In comparing the Lippitt, Watson, and Westley model of planned change to the Lewin typology in Chapter 4 (Figure 4.6), it was noted that planned change is a more detailed extension of the three-part model, and thereby gives the applied practitioner better guidelines from which to operate when working with a change process. The action research model of Huse (see Figure 4.7), however, is also impressive, due to its emphasis upon the involvement of and continual feedback to the client system throughout the change process. Further, one should note the overall consistency of the action research model with both the Lewin typology and the Lippitt, Watson, and Westley Planned Change Model. All three are useful: Lewin's typology for its generic description of change processes, Lippitt, Watson, and Westley's model for its attention to detailed steps in planned change, and action research for its

118 / ENVIRONMENTAL ASSESSMENT AND DESIGN

emphasis upon client involvement and research as an ongoing part of the change process. The most salient features for environmental change have been drawn from each of the three in the development of a model of Environmental Change Technology. This development is shown in Table 5.1, and the processes of Environmental Change Technology are shown in Figure 5.1.

Environmental Change Technology: Certain Assumptions and Premises.

The evolution of the environmental change technology (ETC) model emerged from certain assumptions and values held by the authors, which include the following:

It is imperative to include representatives of the environment of reference in all phases of the change process. This premise is based upon ethical considerations (addressed in Chapter 6), and pragmatic considerations that indicate change is best fostered by the inclusion of the client in the process, thereby reducing resistance to change (Huse 1980; Coch and French 1948; Beckhard 1969) by creating openness and collaboration (Beer and Huse 1972). Thus the development of a change team occurring early in the Environmental Change Technology will be noted.

It is necessary and desirable to include ongoing research activities in the change process so that a data base exists to support all aspects of assessment, change, and follow-up procedures.

The change model should be encompassed within an ecological perspective of both people and their environment. Environments affect people and people affect their environments. These interactional effects must be considered when planning environmental change.

An environmental change agent having expertise and skill in environmental design is required for the effective and efficient development and implementation of planned environmental change.

Definition of Terms

In describing the nature and activities of environmental change technology it is necessary to use a number of terms that have specific meaning in this particular context. In order to make the description both more understandable and easier to read, these terms are defined and explained here.

The terms environment of reference (E_r), environment, environmental setting, and target environment will be used to refer to an entity comprised of a delineated physical space, governed by a set of rules, laws, and policies (both formal and informal), and containing a prescribed set of people. At certain times, in order to be specific, the environment of reference will be referred to as the organization, the neighborhood, and the manufacturing plant, as examples.

Environmental constituents, inhabitants, or participants are those individuals who reside, work, play, or use the environment of reference. Upon occasion

TABLE 5.1: The Development of the Environmental Change Technology Model

Lewin's Typology	Action Research	Planned Change	Environmental Change Technology
Unfreezing	Perceptions of problems by key individuals	Scouting	Preparation Initiation
	Consultation with change agent	Entry	Contracting Change team development
Moving	Data gathering and preliminary diagnosis by change agent	Diagnosis	Action Environmental assessment
	Feedback to key client or group		
	Joint diagnosis of problem	Planning	Change planning
	Rediagnosis and action programs with client and change agent		Change implementation
	New action	Action	
Refreezing	New data gathering as a result of action	Generalization and stabilization	Follow-up Monitoring (evaluative research)
	Rediagnosis of situation	Termination	Modification
	New action		Stabilization
	Etcetera		Withdrawal

Source: Compiled by the authors.

FIGURE 5.1: Environmental Change Technology Flow Chart

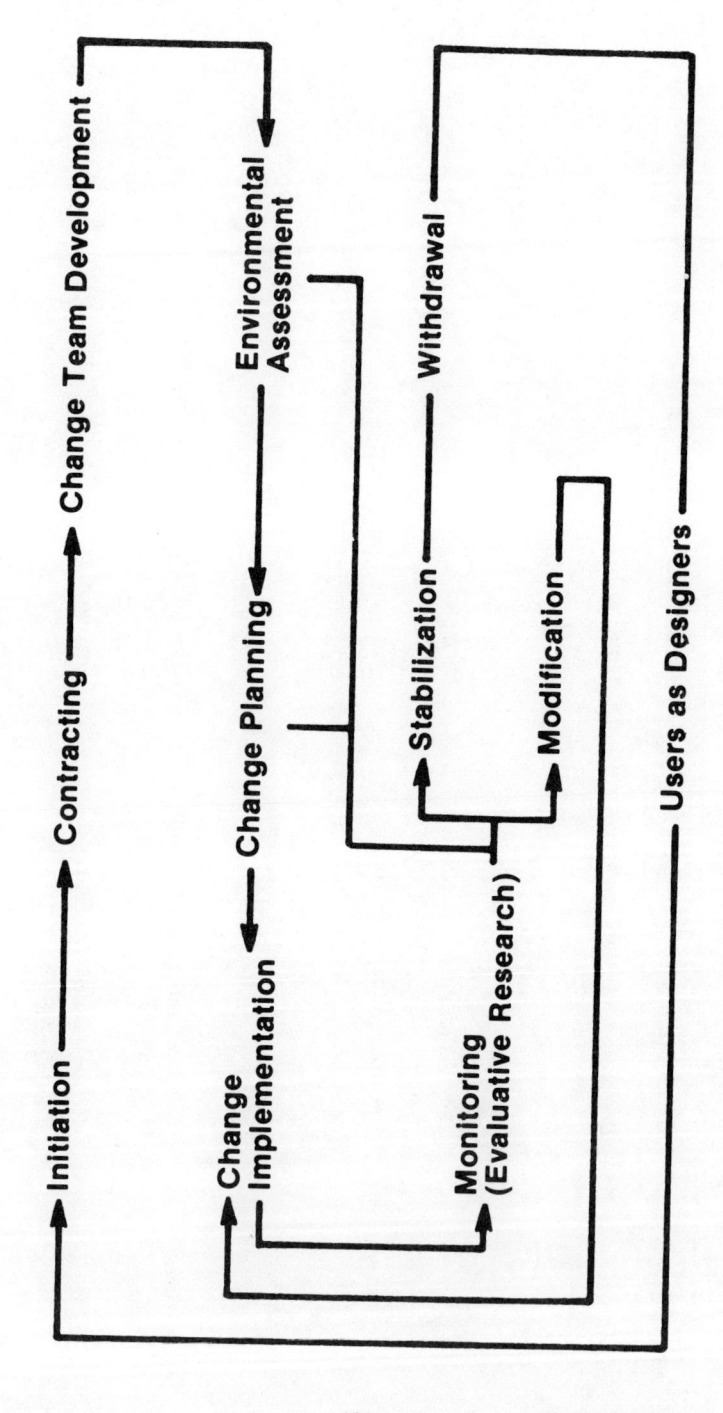

Initiation → Contracting → Change Team Development → Environmental Assessment → Change Planning → Change Implementation → Monitoring (Evaluative Research) → Stabilization → Modification → Withdrawal → Users as Designers

Source: Constructed by the authors.

such terms as residents, users, personnel, and respondents will be used as being interchangeable with environmental constituents.

The term client system is used to describe those who have some form of direct or delegated responsibility for the use of the environment of reference. The term client system is viewed as either singular or plural. The client system employs the environmental change agent and is considered ultimately responsible for decisions that govern the planned environmental change process. At various, times, in order to be descriptive, the client system will be referred to as the administration, administrators, superintendents, or the boss.

The environmental change agent, at various times shortened to change agent or the agent, refers to that individual who has expertise in environmental design including environmental assessment and environmental change technology. This individual serves as both technical expert and process consultant within an environment of reference when a planned environmental change project is in progress.

An environmental change team, the change team, or the team, is a group of environmental constituents who have volunteered, been appointed, or elected as representatives of some portion of the environment of reference. They perform duties in concert with the environmental change agent during an environmental change project.

A GUIDE TO ENVIRONMENTAL CHANGE TECHNOLOGY

Chapter 4 defined environmental design as a cyclical process used for the evaluated, intentional, collaborative change of environments. Environmental design was further designated as encompassing the applied research functions of environmental classification and assessment, an environmental change technology, and an ongoing evaluative research function. The remainder of this chapter will be devoted exclusively to describing the throughput of the environmental design cycle, or environmental change technology. It will be described as a step-by-step process that proceeds through three major phases: preparation, action (changing), and follow-up.

Preparation Phase

The preparation phase of environmental change technology includes three elements: initiation, contracting, and change team development. The overall purpose of the preparation phase is similar to Lewin's unfreezing, that is, to negotiate and develop a contract for environmental change and to prepare environmental constituents for the processes that follow. The outline below gives a map to use in considering the different steps in this phase.

Initiation
    Determining background and impetus toward change
    Clarifying demands and expectations upon client system
    Determining ability of client system and change agent to work together
Contracting
    Detailing goals for change
    Specifying expected outcomes
    Specifying time considerations
    Delineating roles and responsibilities
    Outlining action research and accountability procedures
    Specifying costs and fees
Change Team Development
    Formation of change team
    Team building
    Skills training

Initiation

The initiation of environmental change may occur either reactively or proactively from the perspective of the environmental change agent. Reactive initiation would indicate that three conditions exist: first, that some problem situation, or its potential exists in a particular environment of reference (E_r); second, that some individual or group residing within or responsible for aspects of the E_r is aware of the effects or potential effects of this problem or situation; and third, that a client system contacts an environmental change agent by requesting assistance. In this case, the environmental change agent is in a position of reacting to a potential client or client group regarding an existing problem or situation in the E_r. Reactive initiation is then characterized as being the change agent's response to a request from a setting representative(s), where an already existing problem has been identified.

Proactive initiation is different from reactive in several ways: (1) the environmental change agent initiates the change process by (2) identifying some existing or potential problem or situation within an environment or reference, and (3) brings this situation to the attention of the client system, with (4) a request that planned environmental change be initiated. The critical difference between reactive and proactive initiation of planned environmental change is determined by who takes the steps to start the change process.

Another characteristic of Environmental Change Technology becomes apparent at the time of initiation and relates to the purpose of the proposed intervention. It may be noted from the above descriptions that some existing or potential problem situation has been identified as a part of the initiation, whether by a client system or by the environmental change agent. If an existing problem has been identified at the time of initiation, the subsequent planned change process is designated as being remedial in nature; that is, a major purpose of the intervention is to dispel or alleviate a preexisting problem within the E_r.

It is not necessary, however, for a problem already to exist for planned environmental change to be initiated or to occur. It is possible for change to be initiated for either preventive or developmental purposes. Individuals or change agents associated with a particular E_r (for example, organization, housing project, school, and so on) may be aware that in E_rs similar to their own a particular problem typically arises after a certain amount of time passes, and they wish to head off, or prevent, the occurrence of the problem by preplanning. Also, it is known that individuals, organizations, neighborhoods, and so forth go through specifiable developmental stages in their growth and development. Since this developmental process is generally predictable, environmental design can be implemented to facilitate that development, by supporting health and orderly growth characteristics and/or by modifying negative ones.

A final concern that needs to be mentioned while discussing the initiation of the environmental change technology is whether the change agent is internal or external to the E_r. Certain critical differences exist in the perspective, methods, freedom of action, and ethics involved when comparing the status of internal versus external change agents. Collier (1962), referring to consultants, noted that the way one looks at a business depends on where the observer happens to be. It makes a big difference whether one is on the outside looking in or the inside looking out. The authors believe that an even more critical concern exists when one is inside looking in. For an environmental change agent to be a member of an environment of reference and take a leadership role within it by promoting assessment and change procedures can be very problematic. The change agent, as a member of an E_r, can be affected by personal loyalties, status and security considerations, information obtained outside the context of a proposed environmental change project, personal ambition, and so on—in sum, by any aspect of the planned change project that impinges upon the agent's role as a member of the E_r or his/her personal being. There is the potential for change agents to have their perceptions distorted, to be coopted, to take compromise positions, or be fired while assessing or implementing change as a result of being internal agents. On the other hand, environmental change agents working within their own environments may be able to inject a wealth of knowledge, information, and understanding unavailable to one not familiar to the particular E_r.

An external environmental change agent is one who is brought in from the outside of a particular E_r for the purpose of environmental design. The external agent will not be subject to many of the dilemmas faced by the internal agent, and thereby may be able to be more objective, to view the E_r from a fresh new perspective, and not be influenced by personal loyalties and existing political and status considerations. Therefore an external change agent may not be susceptible to some of the drawbacks faced by the internal agent. Conversely, the external agent may be deficient in terms of some longitudinal and in-depth data about the environment in question.

The authors do not propose the use of either internal or external environmental change agents on the basis of one form being consistently superior to the other in practice. Potential users and potential agents are encouraged, however, to study the differences and to be aware of the assets and deficits inherent in either approach. For a more complete discussion of the issues involved, see Huse (1980) and Lippitt and Lippitt (1978).

Regardless of whether the introduction of an environmental design project is made reactively or proactively, for remedial, preventive, or developmental purposes, or uses internal or external change agentry, it is recommended that three major steps occur after the original contact is made. These three steps are within a preparation phase, and are preliminary to any formal agreement. As a matter of fact, the purpose of the initiation step is to explore the potential of the client system in working with the environmental change agent to develop a mutually defined and designed change project. Broadly speaking, such issues as the current situation within the client system environment, the clients' expectations, the change agents' perspective, expectations, and demands on the client system, and the resulting ability or inability for client and change agent to work together must all be fully ascertained prior to an agreement formally to contract such a project. The environmental change agent is responsible for structuring an interview, meeting sessions, telephone conversations, or correspondence so that the following three steps are taken.

First, the existing situation that is serving as the background for instituting an environmental design process needs to be thoroughly understood by both client and change agent. This calls for mutual clarification of antecedent events, philosophies, recommendations, or whatever led to initiation. Further, a thorough exploration of the perceived need for change should occur, including how the client sees changes as affecting and improving the E_r. If the environmental change agent is in a reactive role, it will be necessary to question and respond to the potential client in such a way as to clarify how the client perceives the situation, the desired changes, and expectations held for the change agent and the process. The change agent, via this process, will need to ascertain both the client's support for and commitment to environmental design.

Second, it now becomes the change agent's turn to express and clarify the expectations and demands that would be placed upon the client system and the E_r if an environmental design process were to be implemented. This exploration requires the change agent to spell out in somewhat specific terms the overall model of change including descriptions of what occurs. The change agent should explicate both potential benefits and dangers that may arise as a result of such a project. In other words, at the end of this explanation, the client should know what to expect.

Third, it is now necessary to discuss the ability of the change agent and the client system to work together. This phase will include discussions of such questions as the following:

Is this proposed project within the domain, scope, and expertise of the environmental change agent?

Do the environmental design concept and the accompanying technology meet the needs expressed by members of the potential client system?
Can the change agent and client system members work together effectively and harmoniously in organizing and implementing the environmental change technology?
Is the change agent an individual who can work effectively with other members of the client system? Will the change agent be accepted by members of the client system?
What are the costs associated with implementing such a change program (for example, money, people's time, printing and duplicating of materials, strain on the system, and so on)?
How much time would it take to implement all phases of the project?

Contracting

If the reactions and responses of client system members and of the change agent are essentially positive throughout the above-described initiation phase, it is then time to pin down the planning of an environmental design project. This is called the contracting step of the Environmental Change Technology. It is preferred that a contract between a client or a representative of a client system and an environmental change agent be a written document. Although putting it in writing is not an absolute necessity to contracting, in many ways the written document offers protection from misunderstandings that are more likely to occur if only verbal agreements are made. It is not necessary, however, that an environmental change contract be a legal document drawn up by legal personnel. To the contrary, it is proposed that the contract be written mutually by the client system and the change agent. It is the task of the change agent to take the lead in the contracting process since it is the agent who has the fuller understanding of how the environmental change technology is implemented.

Contracting has multiple purposes. The overriding function of the contract will be to serve as a guideline for both client and change agent as they work through the environmental design process. The contract should spell out in detail the goals for the environmental design project; the expected outcomes of the project; a time-line indicating when the various activities in the change technology will be introduced and concluded; a specification of roles and responsibilities of all personnel who will be involved in the project, particularly the change team (that is, who does what, how, when, and with whom); evaluation research and accountability procedures; and a specification of the payment of all costs and fees associated with the project.

Change Team Development

Change Team Formation. Once an agreement has been reached between the client system and the change agent, an announcement of the project needs to be made to all personnel who will be affected by the project. Such an announcement includes an overview, goals, preferred outcomes, and a description of and an invitation to active participation in the environmental design project. Depending on the size of the client system and their accessibility, this announcement can be made personally, using an individual, small-group, or large-group format. Or, if personal contact is not feasible, a written announcement to each of the affected personnel is appropriate. The personal contact format is considered preferable, particularly if the change agent is external to the client system. Personal contact gives the change agent an opportunity to explain the environmental change technology thoroughly, to answer questions relating to it, and to allay fears that are often inherent among people faced with the prospect of change. Whether the contact is personal or written, however, it is imperative that all personnel receive valid information stating how their involvement is central to the entire process and that from this point on their opinions and preferences will be used as input in all decisions and plans made and/or implemented.

Once again, depending upon the number of personnel in the target environment it may be possible to include all affected personnel in the change team. If the number of people is large, however, it may become necessary to use some form of representation in the forming of the change team. The formation of a change team can be accomplished by administrative appointment, by election by members of the client system, by members volunteering for membership, by using an existing planning group, or by some combination or permutation of the above methods. In most cases, however, a prime consideration should be that the personnel feel included and involved at this early stage and at all subsequent stages of the change process.

After subsequent team building and training, change team members will become fully involved in the change process. Team members participate actively in all phases of the change technology, using the environmental change agent as an expert resource guide.

Team Building.   Once the change team has been formed it is appropriate for the change agent to engage the group in team-building activities. The amount and scope of team-building activities are dependent upon the size of the project, the number of personnel, and financial support available to the project. Further, the amount of team building is also determined by any previous history of working together the members might have and the attitudes and skills they bring to the team. Team building is particularly important if members of the change team represent divergent segments or departments of the client system. Even if, however, the change team is comprised of a group of individuals who have had a significant amount of experience in working together in the past, time spent in team-building activities is deemed well worth the time and effort expended.

Beer (1975) has suggested that there are four basic approaches to team building, each slightly different from the others, but all containing action research and data feedback as basic elements of the models. Three of these models are seen as appropriate for use with members of an environmental change team within the Environmental Change Technology. These models address goals, interpersonal relations, and member roles, respectively.

The goal-setting model of team building is aimed at the development of group goals that are then used to guide and influence both individual and group behavior. Beer notes that a number of studies have shown that member participation in team goal setting raises the members' commitment to and motivation toward accomplishing stated goals (Beckhard 1969, Wigtil and Kelsey, 1978).

In the particular situation of the environmental change team, major project goals have already been formulated by the change agent in concert with the client. These goals will then need to be explained to and discussed with the members of the change team in order that the goals may be adopted completely or with minimal revision by the members. On the other hand, if a significant number of the members of the change team disapprove of the goals or process of this particular design effort, further exploration is needed of such issues as overall purpose, methods, composition of the change team, role and functioning of the environmental change agent; in sum, the entire process and all personnel involved must be scrutinized. Prior to continuing with the project, issues leading to disagreement and resistance must be resolved. Fortunately, the Environmental Change Technology brings members of the target environment into the change process early on, so that the likelihood of disapproval of goals by change team members is remote.

The second model described by Beer is based on the premise that an interpersonally sound work team is more effective than one that is not. The major focus of interpersonal team building is to effect mutual trust, support, clear communication, and confidence among team members. The development of an atmosphere of trust, support, and confidence, along with effective communication patterns, supports a work team's ability to manage conflict, make decisions, and thereby accomplish tasks.

The third model Beer identifies is that of role models. In this form of team building, team member's roles are clarified in terms of such issues as leadership, power, interpersonal and intergroup relations. This activity leads members to know precisely what is expected of them by the change agent, other team members, and any administrative representative of the client system.

At the conclusion of team-building activities the following description should characterize the members of the change team:

Members will be familiar with all goals for the environmental design project, and with all steps of the environmental change technology used to implement the model. Additionally, members will have agreed to the utility of the project and have endorsed the goals and processes.
Members will have developed a reasonable sense of trust, support, and confidence with regard to other members of the change team, and will be exhibiting

effective communication skills such that the environmental change agent can be confident that the team can work together effectively throughout the course of the project.

Members will know specifically what is expected of them and what they can reasonably expect from other personnel involved in the change project.

Skills Training. With the change team now intact and having developed some sense of cohesiveness and purpose as a result of team-building activities, it is now time to train the members in certain skills they will employ throughout the duration of the project. The initial training will include a basic communication skills module and an overview of assessment methodologies to be used in this specific project. If change team members are functioning as representatives of groups of personnel within the target environment, then attention will be given to training in small-group discussion leadership, including information and collection techniques and feedback mechanisms. The amount of training, like the amount of team-building activity, is to a large extent determined by the size of the project and the amount of personnel and financial support allocated to the project, as well as by the level of relevant skill team members bring to the project.

A sample training curriculum for a newly formed change agent team would include training in basic communication such as the skills delineated by Ivey (1971); attending behavior, open-ended leads, and selective listening skills. In addition Clack's (1975) "negotiation of understanding" skill set, which combines Ivey's paraphrasing and reflection of feeling within a feedback model of communication, is highly appropriate for this type of training. The overriding purpose of this training is to enhance the likelihood that change team members will communicate accurately and understandably with each other, the environmental change agent, any client group constituents, and with any other personnel involved with the project. Once the basic communication skill training has occurred, it is believed that the training can be made to stick. That is, change team members will continue to use the skills if the environmental change agent appropriately model such use, and further, continually promotes the use of the skills in individual and/or group meetings with team members.

If the change project is of large enough scope that members of the change agent team are serving as representatives of some constituent group, wherein they will be required to take a liaison role between the change team and the constituent group, then it is appropriate that members be trained in group discussion leadership skills. If the team members are to perform a liaison role effectively, they will need to be capable of conducting effective group discussions in which information is accurately gathered and disseminated, issues and responses are clarified, maximum participation and involvement is encouraged, and purposes, issues and decisions are clearly understood. Clack and Conyne (1973) developed a module for training beginning group discussion leaders in seven basic skills so that trainees might be proficient in a leadership position. The seven skills are listed below:

Explanation and clarification of the task. The leader is trained to define the task or purpose of the group meeting in specific terms. The leader should encourage questions, comments, and reactions from group members in an effort to assure a common understanding of group task and purpose.

Encouraging participation. The leader is trained to encourage participation in a number of ways. Initially, a statement is given to the effect that all members' opinions are valued and desired. As group interaction develops, individual members who are not active are encouraged by an expression of interest in what they are thinking. No pressure or coercion beyond this invitation to speak is encouraged, however.

Attending and acknowledging. The leader is trained to elicit and sustain group interaction by attending to group members (via eye contact, posture, and verbal following) and by acknowledging participation. Acknowledgment can be accomplished by the leader in many ways: a nod of the head, a thank you, or a verbal response to what a member or members have said.

Clarification and summarization. A leader can be particularly helpful in facilitating group discussion effectiveness if trained to clarify and summarize the content of group interaction. Clarification may be accomplished by the leader restating his/her understanding of what has been said, or by asking a member to restate what he/she has said for purposes of clarification. An occasional summary also helps establish understanding and tends to keep the group on task.

Responding to content and feeling. Verbal messages stated in meetings usually include expressions of both content and feeling. They should be aware of both dimensions and respond appropriately, again in an attempt to assure understanding.

Linking and pairing. The leader can be trained to assist group discussion by noting similarities and differences among the statements made by members. Their skill is used to point out common and differing perspectives held by members of the group.

Closure. The leader is trained to close a group meeting with a summary of what has been done and a prospectus on any future meetings of the group. This procedure prevents the group members from feeling that the session has been incomplete and allows them to prepare for future meetings.

Just as there are interpersonal (communication and group discussion) skills that receive training emphasis, there are also technical skills that must be addressed. At this point in the training of a change team, it is time to turn attention to skills necessary for understanding the environmental assessment methodologies that are to be used in the change project.

The goal of training members of an environmental change team in the technical skills to be used in a partucular project is not to make them experts in assessment methodology, theory, or statistics. The goal of training is pure and simple: for the change team members to understand the procedure so that they know what is being assessed, how it is being assessed, and what the results of the assessment mean. A behavioral objective for members is that they can explain these three aspects to an individual who is unfamiliar with environmental assessment in such a way that the individual will have a basically sound understanding of the process. This part of the training may include a description and explanation of the effects of the environment upon those residing in it (see the model presented in Chapter 2), leading to an explication of what within that total environment is to be specifically assessed. Second, a basic course in measures of central tendency may be included, since means, medians, and modes are the terms most used to summarize and report assessment data. And finally, some instruction and practice is usually useful in learning how to communicate assessment procedures and results in an understandable fashion.

If the change team members are going to be directly involved in data collection—for example, by distributing and/or administering survey instruments, by conducting structured interviews, or by reporting observed data—additional specialized training will be needed. It is believed that the basics of environmental assessment can be learned by most laymen if the training is presented in appropriate language and format with ample opportunity for clarification and practice.

Training in change skills is not presented until after assessment has occurred and environmental change becomes the task at hand. Change team members are then trained to recognize those parts of the environment identified by participants through the assessment process as being the primary targets for change. These targets may be environmental components identified as having significant negative impact that could be targeted for change in order to remove their deleterious effect; components that are described as having neutral effects that could be modified to yield a positive effect; or components already having positive impact that could be increased further through environmental change.

Having formed the change team, used team-building activities to assist the team to function at high levels of cooperation, communication, and commitment, and having trained the group in the basic knowledge and skills of environmental assessment, the team and the change agent are ready to work together. The second major phase of the Environmental Change Technology, action, describes concretely how this work is accomplished.

Action Phase

The action phase of Environmental Change Technology is composed of environmental assessment, change planning, and change implementation. In this phase, the impact of the E_r upon its constituents, the development of ideas and recommendations that become the innovation to be implemented, and the determination of a process for implementing changes are considered. The outline below gives an overview of the steps in this phase.

Environmental Assessment
    Choice of instrumentation
    Administration and data collection procedures
    Reporting of results
    Feedback cycle
    Data review
    Data categorization
Change Planning
    Change ideas
    Change recommendations
    Change plan
Change Implementation
    Notification of constituents
    Implementation

Environmental Assessment

The choices of a particular method and/or instruments to be used in assessing an environment are primarily the responsibility of the environmental change agent, operating in conjunction with the client system members. Although this judgment is made earlier in the process, prior to training change team members in assessment methods, discussion is presented at this point for clarity's sake.

The environmental change agent must take several considerations into account before choosing an assessment methodology and instruments. These considerations include the nature and size of the environment to be assessed, the focus of the design project, the allowable cost for assessment procedures, and the availability of persons and/or places to be assessed. If the environment is small (including the number of people who are participants in it), then assessment procedures using personal contact, such as structured interviews, may be an appropriate assessment method. If, on the other hand, the environment is large and/or contains large numbers of people, some form of survey instrumentation is called for if the interests of time and cost are to be served.

When the number of people associated with a particular environment is small in relation to the number of personnel capable of conducting individual assessment interviews, it may be appropriate for the environmental change agent to select structured individual interviews as a way of collecting data. Jones (1975) describes both the process of and the considerations regarding the use of structured interviews as a data-gathering method in his discussion of "sensing interviews." He notes some of the advantages of this method of data collection: opportunities exist for the interviewer to clarify what the respondent is saying, responses can be amplified, assumptions can be validated, data are "rich" because they come directly from a primary source, data gathered have credibility, its use demonstrates that the interviewee is important, and it helps to get all people affected involved in the project. A modification of the face-to-face sensing interview that has been used with success and satisfaction is a structured, telephone interview format. Although nonverbal reactions and cues available in face-to-face interviews are lost in the telephone method, the other advantages of sensing interviews are available. Besides, telephone interviews are generally much less expensive than face-to-face contacts.

Some of the drawbacks to individual sensing interviews include expense in terms of time, staff, and money; lack of comparability of data gathered from one sensing interview to the next; the data generated not easily summarized; the possibility of threat perceived sometimes by interviewees; and difficulties that can surround gaining access to those people to be interviewed.

Once data have been collected through a series of sensing interviews, it becomes necessary for the change agent to summarize the individual reports into a report that is representative of the expressions of the groups of people. This is a difficult task in that all data have been collected in a narrative form, and even with carefully recorded notes it is difficult to write or state a summary report that reflects all the nuances that characterized the individual statements. On the other hand, the change agent has a wealth of information at a level of depth that paper and pencil surveys have no way of providing. Even though a summary report based on individual interview data may contain inaccuracies as perceived by the respondents, this situation can open the door for further clarification, and thereby provide additional information for the change agent to use. In fact, one of the most profitable data-gathering sessions ever spent by one of the authors (Clack) was when he presented a written summary to seven managers of a small manufacturing plant. The managers, in their attempts to "straighten out the report," shared information and perspectives with each other that theretofore had never been discussed. This occurrence opened the door to new understandings, and later to several positive administrative and personal changes.

When the target environment is too large, or when for other reasons (for example, a need for confidentiality) individual sensing interviews are deemed inappropriate, paper-and-pencil environmental assessment instruments can be used. As mentioned in Chapter 3, there are three major assessment methods available to the environmental change agent when considering a paper-and-pencil survey approach: use of an existing standardized environmental assessment instrument, a modification of an existing standardized instrument, or the development of a new instrument designed specially for the assessment at hand. As noted earlier, it is recommended that existing instruments be used whenever appropriate and possible, due to the difficulty and expense involved in modifying or developing an assessment instrument. Many of the existing environmental assessment instruments and formats available to practitioners were discussed in detail in Chapter 3, as well as guidelines to be used in developing one's own instruments.

Once an environmental assessment instrument is selected, there are several variables to be considered prior to the actual administration. Among these considerations are developing a clear set of instructions for presenting the instrument to respondents and for directing the administration process; the method of administration, whether face-to-face or by mail, individually or in groups; anonymity of respondents or not; and a time-frame within which assessments are to be completed.

Once the administration of the survey instrument has been completed, the data must be tabulated and a summary prepared for presentation to members of the client system. A guideline to use in selecting a format for preparing a summary of environmental assessment data is to put it in simple, uncomplicated terms so that all members of the target environment may readily understand the results of the assessment. Frequencies, percentages, and arithmetic means have been found to be useful ways of summarizing quantitative data, and brief narratives are a preferred method for describing trends in qualitative data. To dazzle the participants with statistical knowledge and professional jargon may be gratifying for the change agent, but counterproductive in terms of fostering the planned change process. It is also recommended that the change agent be conservative in any interpretations or speculations made in regard to the data, particularly any emanating from reactions to narrative responses. In general, it is better to allow the data to stand for themselves in the original summary statement, and then encourage client system members to be active in drawing implications from the data. Of course, the environmental change agent can be as active in this part of the process as is appropriate and wise. The major point here is that the change agent, particularly an external one, is in no position to be all-knowing in regard to the respondents' environment, and certainly does not want to appear in that light. It is particularly important to maintain a climate of cooperation and collaboration during this data-dissemination, sharing, and reaction phase of assessment.

The data may be shared with the members of the target environment in any number of ways: via oral presentations to individuals, small groups, or to a large group comprised of all respondents; through written summary, charts, graphs, maps, and so on; directly from change agent to respondents or through members of the change team who meet with subgroups of respondents. All methods have advantages and disadvantages; there are, however, some guidelines that can assist the change agent in deciding on the most appropriate method in a given situation.

First, it is wise to present the data to the client or client representative(s) prior to releasing it to other members of the E_r. This follows from an often-stated principle of consultation, "Never surprise the boss." One easy way to bring an early and incomplete ending to an environmental design project, for instance, is to invite the boss to the initial presentation of a data summary to the change team, when those data are highly critical of the boss or the system he/she directs. This situation places the client (the boss) in an embarrassing and somewhat indefensible position, from which an extremely negative reaction to both the change agent and the entire project is likely to emerge. It is best for the environmental change agent to hold a preliminary private review of the data with the client, (that is, the boss) to discuss how sharing of the data with change teams and respondents is to occur, to respond to questions and concerns the client may express regarding the data summary, to gather additional inputs and reactions, and to prepare the client for upcoming activity in the design project.

Second, the data should be shared with the change agent team in a group meeting. Careful clarification of the data and summary statement must be made and reactions of team members recorded for future use. If part of the project plan is for change team members to play a liaison role with a wider population, then careful training of the members in accurately reporting the data and in the collection of reactions and input must occur. It is recommended that each member of the change agent team perform a rehearsal (role-play) of reporting the data summary and in leading the reaction and input discussion that follows.

Third, the data summary is presented to all respondents via whatever procedure the change agent has selected. The use of some type of face-to-face format that allows and maximizes the opportunity for the gathering and recording of additional information is encouraged. This information is helpful in the environmental design process, particularly when change recommendations are sought. In the sharing of the data summary with the general respondent population it is important that the information reach all respondents at approximately the same time. This time dimension is critical because respondents often tend to ascribe significance to the order in which different individuals or subgroups receive the data, often arriving at implications and suspicions that have no basis in the change agents' purpose. Such an unintended side effect can become a barrier that must be broken through if the project is to continue with maximum support and commitment from the wider population. Further, experience has shown that data are often interpreted idiosyncratically by respondents, frequently to support some pet position held by individuals or subgroups. Data reaching respondents at widely varying times can exacerbate opportunities for misinterpretation, rumor spreading, and distortion of the data as they proceed through the client system grapevine. Widespread distortion of the data, in this case, then becomes another barrier that must be hurdled before the project can be moved forward.

Following discussion of the data summary by client system members and the collection of their subsequent reactions, inputs, and change recommendations, the change agent must decide whether this process yielded significant new information. If so, an additional feedback procedure may be initiated to make this new information available to client system members. Once again, the change agent should decide on the most appropriate format to accomplish this activity. Generally, this summary of reactions and inputs to the original data summary need not be lengthy. In fact, a brief written summary distributed to members of the target environment is often satisfactory. Still more data may be elicited easily at this point by inviting members to share any additional responses they may wish, either in writing or by interview. Theoretically, it is possible for this assessment—summary feedback—input cycle to continue indefinitely, as in the case of the individual who can never make a decision because all the information relevant to the decision can never be obtained. In reality, however, the number of cyclical repetitions is few, limited in part by the quality and scope of the original assessment.

Data Review. Following assessment of the E_r, the environmental change team is convened for the purpose of reviewing the assessment results. Such a review gives direction for gathering any additional information that will help to clarify, explain, or support the assessment data and for categorizing the data into workable units preparatory to change implementation.

The first task of the change agent in working with the change team members in this step is to help them carefully review the results of the entire assessment process. This procedure can be enhanced when the group looks for clear, consistent statements that emerge from the data gathered from the entire respondent population, and from particular subgroups. The second task is to look for trends suggested by the data, but not clearly recognized or supported across the total respondent population. And third, the change agent helps the team members to identify areas of inconsistency in the data arising from contradictory responses in the assessment.

Next, the change agent and team should make efforts to gather other necessary information that will help clarify and explain any unclear assessment data. It is again important for the change agent to meet with the client system (or representative) in order to share any newly found information as well as to gather additional information that may help the change agent and team better understand the assessment data. Further, the agent and/or team members may wish to contact other members of the environment or ask outside help in seeking to acquire a complete understanding of the data. Through these clarification procedures the change team should feel that they have exhausted all reasonable resources in conceptualizing the data and their meaning.

Data Categorization. The agent and team now turn to the task of placing the data into categories so that they may be worked with more readily. The decision of categories to be used is arbitrary and is governed by consideration of how the data can best be grouped to promote future change procedures. Four general approaches can be used in this task: examine quantitative data (for example, ratings of physical, institutional, social, and ecological climate of environmental components); examine qualitative data (such as narrative descriptions of environmental components); examine data corresponding to the four environmental components taken separately; and examine data drawn from the entire setting, across all environmental components. Obviously, several combinations of the above four methods are available to the change team.

A useful procedure for ascribing value to the data that result from categorization is to sort them roughly into positive, neutral, and negative effect

136 / ENVIRONMENTAL ASSESSMENT AND DESIGN

groupings. Such a sorting yields the matrix contained in Figure 5.2, which serves to organize complex data for interpretation, thus lending direction to the change effort.

FIGURE 5.2: Categorization of Assessment Data

Environmental Ratings:

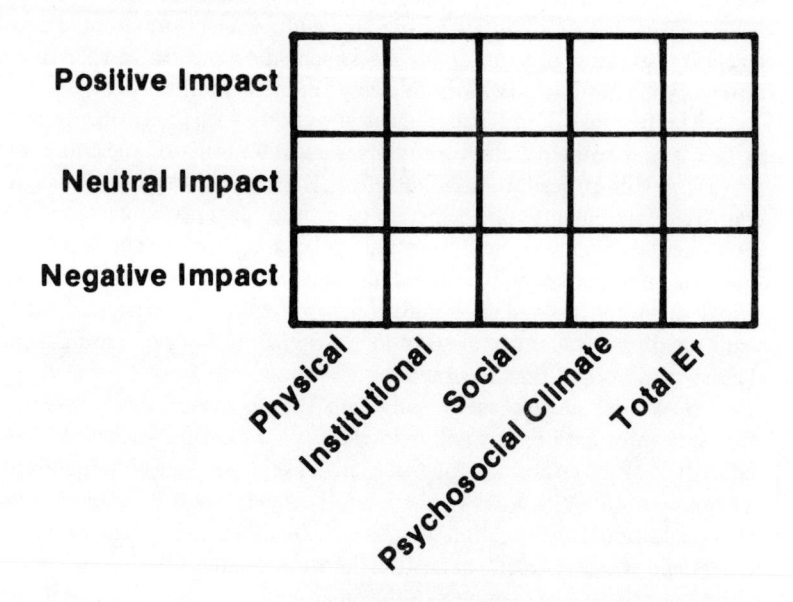

Positive Impact

Neutral Impact

Negative Impact

Physical Institutional Social Psychosocial Climate Total Er

Environmental Components

Once the data have been placed in this form and studied and discussed for meaning and implications, the change team turns to the task of identifying ways in which positive aspects of the E_r can be optimized, neutral elements converted to positive contributions, and negative impact elements eliminated or changed for the better.

Change Planning

Following data organization the environmental change agent and the change team turn their efforts to change planning, the process used in moving an idea for change to implementation, leading, perhaps, to its becoming a stable element in the environment. This section presents a brief overview of change planning, to be followed by a specific step-by-step description later.

In this process, change ideas are originated and generated from a variety of sources. Characteristically, change ideas are statements based on environmental assessment data that suggest innovations or inventions that, if implemented, would improve designated aspects of an environment. As an initial proposal of change, a change idea is characterized as being nonspecific, untried, unproved, and unevaluated, thus having the quality of a brainstorm. In order to raise the potential for individuals and/or groups to be creative in generating change ideas, approval for bringing forth ideas with these characteristics must be present. If ideas are held up to restrictive scrutiny prior to stating them, many excellent ideas may be ruled out because they may not meet some criteria that are thought to exist, but actually may not exist. Therefore, during the generation of change ideas, individuals are encouraged simply to bring forth their ideas without preevaluation.

Once change ideas have been offered, they can be evaluated by the change team members in terms of their reaction to the needs and wants identified in the assessment data, and for their specificity and feasibility. If a change idea passes the evaluation of the change team and is considered appropriate to carry forward, it is converted into a change recommendation. Hence a change recommendation is an idea that has been approved by the change team for inclusion in the change plan. Members of the client system or administrators who have the responsibility and authority for approving new ideas for implementation will receive change recommendations from the change team. Those recommendations that are approved will take their place in the change plan, while those rejected will be returned to the change team, hopefully with reasons given as to why they were rejected. It may be necessary for the change team to place priorities on change recommendations when they forward them for approval, and then for administrators give further priorities as they approve recommendations for the change plan.

Once a preliminary change plan (comprised of approved and prioritized change recommendations) is developed, details for implementing the plan must be completed. These details are usually developed by the change agent who works as adviser to administrators and plays a liaison role between administration and the change team. The details that must be added to complete the change plan include such specifications as who will be responsible, when implementation will occur, where in the E_r the change will appear, how evaluation will be accomplished, and methods for reinforcing the acceptance of change.

Implemented change is the product of a change plan that has been activated. These implemented changes must then be evaluated and tested over a specified period of time. If implemented changes meet evaluation standards over the specified period of time, they become examples of stabilized change. The term stabilized change is used, rather than permanent change. For the authors the concept of permanent change is wrong, because any aspect of an environment is viewed as being continually subject to change. Therefore, an element within an environment can be viewed as stable and not subject to imminent change, but not as being permanent.

From this overview of change planning in the environmental change technology, the discussion turns now to a concrete description of the processes involved in this phase.

Change Idea Sources. Six sources of change ideas will be identified; for particular situations and environments there are undoubtedly others.

Respondents are the primary source for developing change recommendations, particularly if they have been given adequate opportunity and encouragement. No individual or group is more intimately aware of the E_r and its effects than those people who live, play, and work in it daily. The authors have continually been amazed by the innovative and practical ideas for change that come from people involved in changing their own environments.

The change team is another major source for developing innovations. Change team members are closely involved with all phases of the environmental design project, and they hold a relatively unique view of the assessed setting.

The environmental change agent is a major contributor to the design process. As a result of training, management of the planned change procedures, and experience in working with environments and the change process, the agent represents a valuable resource of technical expertise.

The client system representative is a valuable asset in offering change ideas. Also, from this source can come early indication of what is and what is not feasible in terms of change.

External consultants, contracted because of having particular expertise in some aspect of change being considered, frequently themselves generate ideas or can stimulate their development in others. Examples of this type of specialized consultant include architects, telephone system consultants, computer specialists, lawyers, certified public accountants, human relations specialists, and labor relations mediators. Note that these consultant specialty areas all correspond to one of the three environmental components: the first three with the physical, the middle two with the institutional, and the latter two with the social.

The experiences of other people, other organizations, or other environments may be tapped as sources of information. It is common practice to study successful individuals, groups, teams, organizations, companies, institutions, and so on, in order to ascertain characteristics that seem to have contributed to their success.

Using these six sources as a starting point for generating change ideas, the change agent and change team can develop additional change ideas resulting from existing combinations.

Change Recommendations. As the change agent and team develop change ideas and move toward agreement that such ideas should be converted to change recommendations, it is helpful for them to apply certain guidelines. Recommendations should be stated in specific terms. Rather than saying, "The reception room needs to be made a cheerier place," state, "The reception room needs a new coat of paint in a lighter color, some pictures, wall hangings, flowers, and increased lighting." Granted, in this example the members of the change team may have no particular interior decorating expertise, but by being specific in their change recommendations they give clearer information to those who ultimately decide whether, to what extent, and when specific change recommendations will be implemented.

Change recommendations should be attainable in the sense that they are within reason. For a change team to make capricious recommendations that have little or no basis in reality is to place all recommendations it makes in jeopardy. Decision makers may reject a multitude of high-quality change recommendations if they note but a few they view as preposterous. A caution regarding this guideline from an opposing viewpoint is not to lean too far toward conservatism, and not to recommend changes simply because "it hasn't been done that way before," "we've tried that before," or "it won't work." The environmental change agent can assist in establishing the limits of this guideline through clear communication with decision makers.

Members of a setting, when given the opportunity and a sanction to devise and plan changes, can be creative and prolific in their generation of change ideas. Seldom is there a problem in acquiring ideas for innovation; the difficulty comes with the necessity to choose among them, and to apply priorities to the plethora of ideas available. In placing change recommendations in some order of priority, the change team once again uses assessment data in giving them direction. A general rule to apply is to work first with those environmental referents that have been assessed as having potent negative impact, because changes will be highly visible and will tend to generate support for and commitment to other less dramatic aspects of the total change project. Although initial priority may be given to removing or improving elements of negative impact, a second guideline is to not overlook opportunities to improve referents of neutral impact, and to maximize positive aspects of the E_r.

Another general guideline is to give priority to change recommendations that will have impact on the largest number of E_r constituents that is practical; the broader the positive impact, the wider the potential satisfaction with and support for change. Two commonsense principles must be applied, however, in relation to broad impact. The first is "make sure that everybody gets something." This piece of practical advice arises from a knowledge that those who are left out or are given little attention may not only refrain from supporting environmental change, but may even attempt to sabotage change efforts out of spite. The second principle is "do not bite off a piece larger than you can chew." Moos (1979b) has observed that it is critical that the change effort be manageable and doable. When broad impact is mediated by these two constraints the chances for project success are enhanced.

Each change recommendation the team chooses to forward to administrators should include a goal statement and one or more objectives correlated to the goal. The purpose of the goal statement is to state the general purpose of the proposed change, and what negative environmental impact it will lessen or eradicate, or what neutral or positive condition it will improve. Statements of objectives relate to outcomes predicted, with greater or lesser degrees of confidence, as a result of change. Goal and objective statements both help to define clearly the purpose and nature of recommended change and to serve as evaluative criteria for measuring the effectiveness of changes once they have been implemented.

The environmental change team has completed its planning efforts when it is ready to forward a listing of change recommendations, including priority goals and objective(s), to those decision makers who will either approve or reject them for implementation.

The Change Plan. It is the task of the change agent to forward the change recommendations to relevant decision makers for action: discussion, evaluation, approval, rejection, or modification. Decision makers may or may not meet with the change team at this time. In either case, with or without the change team present, the role of the change agent in this process is to provide information regarding change team recommendations. Additional information may be requested, such as the basis upon which the change team made recommendations and selected priorities, the potential impact of implementation, and cost estimates of implementing the various change recommendations. Further, the change agent can now assist the administrator or administrative group in their decision-making process via consultation. In this role, the change agent can help to clarify issues, assist in the exploration of advantages and disadvantages, and provide support while the desirability of the various recommended changes is being evaluated. Because it is often impossible to predict the exact outcome of environmental changes, the change agent can facilitate and give opinions in a discussion of probabilities of desired outcome for the different change recommendations.

After deliberation, decision makers can be expected to approve all or none of the change recommendations, to reject all or none, or they may make revisions in some of them prior to approval. During this time, decision makers may request to consult or meet with the environmental change team. The change agent should encourage this type of meeting since it tends to promote cooperation in the impending implementation of change phase.

Change Implementation

Once decisions about change recommendations have been made and a change plan specified, the change agent and change team have much work to do to prepare the residents or users of the environment for the inception of change.

The first task of the change agent is to be sure that all members of the change team have a clear understanding of the change plan. This understanding must include specifications of the exact nature of each change, of those having responsibilities for it, and of the time schedule for implementation. The next step, then, is to report the change plan and implementation procedure to all personnel in the E_r. The same method that was used earlier in the design project to prepare respondents for assessment and to present the data summary is appropriate for use at this point, also. It is extremely important that all personnel involved be well informed at this crucial point. A few examples of specific changes will illustrate the need for cooperation and support from the personnel of the E_r.

Suppose that a situation exists in which employees at a manufacturing plant (the E_r in this instance) follow company policy by reporting to work at 8 a.m. and getting off at 5 p.m. The plant is located in an urban area and the only parking available for employees is in a company-owned lot adjacent to the plant. Due to a tight production schedule the plant has been operating seven days a week, and thus there has been no opportunity to keep the lot in good repair. It has become riddled with chuckholes and turns into a quagmire of mud when it rains. Since the only entrance and exit to the lot is on a busy major thoroughfare, it is difficult to get into the lot in the morning and employees often wait 30 minutes or more to exit from the lot in the afternoon. Tempers have flared on many afternoons when employees cut in front of others in their attempts to reach the exit more quickly. This condition has led to many crumpled fenders, arguments, and fights in the parking lot. Management attempted to partially resolve this problem by having two security patrolmen direct traffic in the lot, and by ruling that any employee involved in a physical altercation would be terminated. Recently, the company's ace tool-and-die designer punched and kicked one of the patrol personnel for stopping his line of traffic so fast that he was involved in a rear-end collision. The tool-and-die designer was viewed as indispensable by the company management and was given only a warning by the superintendent of personnel, who has since become the object of derogatory remarks from many employees.

In a hypothetical environmental assessment completed by employees of the above manufacturing plant, both the parking-lot condition and its limited access received extremely negative evaluations. The company policy regarding fights and the managerial style of the superintendent of personnel were heavily criticized, as well. The first two assessment ratings appear in the physical, the third in the institutional, and the last in the social category of the environmental assessment. All of these conditions represented by the high negative ratings were given first-priority status when received by the change team.

During planning activity, the change team developed the following change recommendations: (1) repave the parking lot; (2) seek city assistance in installing a traffic light for use during "crunch times" for entering and exiting from the parking lot; (3) revoke the company policy regarding fights in the parking lot if it is not to be enforced; and (4) establish a traffic plan for exiting from the lot.

These recommendations were forwarded to the plant management and, after deliberation and investigation, numbers one and three were approved and placed in the change plan. Recommendation two could not be approved since the city's traffic department would not allow the installation of a traffic light. Therefore, the management arrived at a change recommendation of its own. It stated that while repaving the parking lot the company would open two new entrance-exits onto side streets, which should result in great improvement in both entering and exiting from the lot. Further, the management decided to implement a staggered starting and quitting time for employees, with approximately one-fourth of the work force reporting each 15 minutes from 7:00 until 8:00 a.m., and leaving on the same basis from 4:00 until 5:00 p.m. Management rejected recommendation (4) because the new access to the parking lot combined with staggered work shifts was expected to leave no need for a prescribed traffic plan.

The change plan to be implemented was then returned to the change team who reported it to all employees and sought their support in implementing the plan. Because it was necessary to close the parking lot for two weeks while repair and construction were in progress, employees needed temporarily to locate other parking, to use public transportation, or to ride shuttle buses from a nearly high-school parking lot not otherwise being used during the summer. Further, adjustments among supervisory personnel and employees were needed to compensate for the new operating hours. It is easy to see, in this hypothetical case, why cooperation of all involved personnel would be necessary to implement the described changes smoothly and to make them work effectively.

The change principles involved during the implementation phase, then, include keeping personnel at all levels informed and involved in the process; identifying the connection between implemented changes and the input personnel made via their participation in assessment; reinforcing the positive aspects of change by bringing attention to them; and modifying or removing those aspects of the change plan that are ineffective or deleterious.

Follow-up

The third phase of the Environmental Change Technology, follow-up, consists of four subprocesses: monitoring (evaluation research), modification, stabilization, and withdrawal. This phase serves three major purposes: first, to evaluate the effects of implemented change so that revisions can be made, if necessary; second, to secure those changes that are having positive impact, attaining goals, and meeting objectives; and third, for the change agent to exit from the client system, but leave the inhabitants with a capability of, and interest in, maintaining environmental design as an ongoing activity in the E_r. The four steps are mapped out in the outline below.

Monitoring (Evaluative Research)
    Instrumentation based on goals and objectives
    Administration of evaluative research
    Reporting of results
    Feedback cycle
Modification
    Modification of the change plan in light of evaluative research
    Implementation of revised change plan
Stabilization of Change
    Continuation of evaluative research
    Acknowledgment of acceptance by constituents
Withdrawal
    View environmental design process with constituents; follow-up training aimed at environmental competence
    Termination of formal contract

Monitoring (Evaluaion Research)

    Once environmental changes have been implemented and are in place, the change agent initiates evaluative research for the purpose of monitoring the effects of the changes. The major function of this type of evaluative research is to ascertain if the changes implemented result in the outcomes that were stated as their goals and objectives. In addition, monotoring helps to identify unforeseen, unanticipated outcomes and their effects. Monitoring then becomes the basis for maintaining, revising, or withdrawing actions taken in the change plan. The change agent and the E_r have available to them all those methods of evaluative research explicated in Chapter 4, to meet the purposes and functions of monitoring change. In a general sense, those changes that meet stated environmental change goals and objectives, thereby bringing about more positive environmental impact, are retained and stabilized. Those changes that show marginal, low, or no effectiveness in terms of reaching environmental change goals and objectives are either modified and reimplemented or are withdrawn as being ineffective or inefficient.

    Stabilization of a change involves continuing the support necessary for a change to become established within an environment. After evaluation those changes that show a lack of effectiveness and hold little or no promise for future effectiveness even if modified, are withdrawn from the change plan.

Modification

    As stated above, when implemented changes fail or only marginally meet stated objectives they may be modified and, perhaps, reimplemented. Depending on the relative importance and priority of the change effort attempted, the scope of the modification required, and resources available, much or little of the entire change model may be revised. Redoing an entire change process, however, from assessment to change implementation, is most rare. A more likely occurrence is that decision makers, in conjunction with the change team, will make smaller revisions, notify all personnel, and implement the modification. This modification then becomes subject to another round of monitoring and to the same consequences as any innovations that appear in the original plan.

Stabilization of Change

Stabilization of change is the process of continuing and supporting those changes that, after implementation, meet stated goals and objectives or otherwise contribute to positive environmental impact. Such stabilization occurs over time, resulting from the informal acceptance of the change by environmental inhabitants coupled with formal announcement of the permanence of the change by administrators. Stabilization has occurred when the change is no longer viewed as new, and receives no special attention or evaluation not accorded other elements of the E_r. The change is now taken as a matter of fact.

Withdrawal

The premise in this discussion is that while an environmental change agent is implementing the change process within an E_r, the agent serves not only as an expert resource in environmental design and in the process of planned change, but also as an educational resource. An educational goal of the change agent is to teach members of the E_r the methods of planned environmental change as they experience them during participation in the project. The change agent has a goal of leaving leaders, such as decision makers, members of the change team, and other members of the E_r environmentally competent (Steele 1973), a term discussed in Chapter 4, which generally refers to the capacity of people to use or to change settings appropriately. To carry this strategem further, the change agent strives to leave members of an E_r capable of conducting their own future environmental design projects. In this view, environmental design should become an ongoing process in any setting, and environmental design competencies should be gained by as many setting members as possible.

The notion of leaving members of an E_r environmentally competent is why the term withdrawal is used, rather than termination (Lippitt, Watson, and Westley 1958), as signifying the end point of a particular environmental design project. A major purpose of the withdrawal phase is for the change agent to review the entire process with the significant leaders of the E_r and to educate and train them in keeping environmental design and planned change alive in their environment. If this goal is accomplished well, environmental design can continue after the change agent is gone.

ILLUSTRATIVE CASE

In order to bring Environmental Change Technology to life for the reader, a case one of the authors has been involved in as an environmental change agent will be described in some detail. The environmental change technology applied here can be used in a variety of settings, in a variety of ways, from a very elementary small-scale project, through a complex, multiple E_r approach. This case represents but one such use.

One of the authors (Clack) was approached by a manager of the Word Processing Department of a medium-sized insurance company. The manager was seeking assistance with such problems as high employee turnover and absenteeism rates, constant arguing and bickering among the employees, multiple cases of insubordination, an inordinate amount of equipment breakdown, and vandalism. The Word Processing Department was broken down into sections representing major subdivisions of the company's business: life, fire, auto, theft, and so on. Within these sections, the work load was divided into two major functions: customer billing and customer correspondence. The Word Processing Department dealt only with company correspondence of a mass-mailing nature such as premium notices, advertising letters, and annual reports. The approximately 50 employees operated current word-processing equipment such as electronic typewriters and other devices used to individualize volume correspondence.

The Word Processing Department was located in one large room about the size of two college basketball floors situated side by side. The room was centrally heated and air-conditioned, lighted by recessed fluorescent bulbs in the ceiling, and was painted an off-white color. It was divided into many small cubicles by seven-foot-high partitions. There was a noticeable absence of windows and a steady drone made by the word processing equipment.

The manager assured the change agent that the working conditions were similar to other local operations, that the operators were well paid, had a comprehensive and liberal fringe-benefit package, and that they had a maximum of job security because trained operators were in short supply. On the other hand, she stated that "the girls dragged into work like they dreaded being there," and that she was "beginning to feel the same way herself." Accordingly, she received permission from the director of Personnel and Training to use an outside consultant, and the author was contacted.

During the initiation phase of contact, the manager was asked her opinion of the causes of employee turnover, absenteeism, vandalism, and apparent dread of coming to work. She stated that the only clue she had was that "they might be bored."

After further exploration of existing conditions with the manager, the change agent recommended an environmental design project. A proposal was submitted to the manager and the director of Personnel and Training regarding such a project, who approved a plan having all the essential elements stipulated in the Environmental Change Technology.

The change agent met with the manager and four section leaders who, for expediency, became the change team. The change team met for eight hours on a nonwork day, during which the change agent explained the assessment project and facilitated approximately six hours of basic communication and group-discussion-skills training. The change agent also prepared the section leaders informally to introduce the change project in general and assessment procedures in particular to all operators in their sections. Later, the change agent spent a half-day touring the Word Processing Department, being introduced to the operators, and chatting with them about the impending assessment.

The change agent chose to develop a modification of the Environmental Assessment Inventory (Conyne and Harding 1976) as the assessment instrument to be used in this situation. The instrument was designed to measure aspects of the physical, institutional, and social components of the Word Processing Department, the E_r in this case. Operators were to rate environmental referents used in the instrument on a 1 (negative) to 7 (positive) impact scale, to furnish specific examples that supported their numerical ratings, and to provide suggestions for change. They were also encouraged to add items to the inventory if they felt important issues were not included. The change team assisted the change agent in developing many specific items that were added to general assessment items written by the change agent.

Operators were allotted two hours of regular work time in order to receive specific instructions and to complete the *Work Environment Assessment Inventory* (Clack 1976). Once the assessments were completed, the change agent prepared a written assessment summary that was first returned and discussed with the manager, then with the section leaders. The section leaders distributed summaries to the operators in their sections and discussed the data and collected reactions at one-hour meetings. The assessment summary included mean scores for all items rated, and narrative summaries of clear trends found in both the specific items and the change suggestions completed by the operators.

Although there was a wealth of data available to work with in this project, space prohibits a description of all aspects that were given attention. A description of three significant changes however, will be described, drawn from the physical, institutional, and social components of that E_r.

Although many statements critical of the physical environment appeared as a result of the assessment—for example, lack of windows, glaring lights, excessive noise, and sterile decor—the partitions that were used to "place the operators in their own little cubby-holes" engendered the most violent negative response. The operators complained of feeling isolated from each other and found this condition "very boring and depressing." The change recommendation made by the change team and approved by a company vice-president was to remove the individual partitions and retain ones that would divide the large room into the four major sections. This change was announced to the operators, implemented by a maintenance team over a weekend, and was extremely positively evaluated both initially and at a three-month follow-up. The change stabilized and to the author's knowledge this work configuration remains in use.

An excellent example of the effects of the institutional component appeared when over 60 percent of the assessment inventories completed included mention of the "snow-day policy," even though it was not included as a specific inventory item. Due to severe midwest winter snowstorms, there were days when most roads were impassable. On those days it was the policy of the insurance company to announce over local radio that employees who would face danger or hardship were not to report to work. At the same time, however, offices were to remain open for those employees who could make it to work without excessive hazard. Difficulties arose when some employees reported to work while others did not, and no pay policy existed to cover this situation. Originally, all employees were paid as if they were at work on snow days, whether they were or not. Employees who did report to work began to complain that they should receive an additional day's pay, since they were being paid the same as those who did not report for work. Company management noted that they had no budgetary provision to allow extra pay for these employees, but "in the spirit of fairness," decided that employees who did not report to work on snow days would not get paid. Thus the lines were drawn at the time of the assessment of the word processors.

On the *Work Assessment Inventory,* those who wrote in the snow-day policy as an item consistently rated it as having extreme negative impact, but for different reasons (undoubtedly based upon whether they reported for work or not on previous snow days). Change suggestions also showed this same inconsistency, with approximately half of them recommending extra pay for those reporting and nearly all favoring no reduction in pay for those not reporting for work on snow days. Try as they might, the change team could not arrive at a generally acceptable change recommendation. Also, the issue was far beyond the decision-making authority of the change team or the manager. Nevertheless, the issue and the thoughts expressed about it, including suggestions for change, were forwarded to the director of Training and Personnel. No immediate change was implemented. The author was informed some two years later that the company's board of directors approved a policy whereby employees reporting for work on snow days were paid one and one-half times their regular pay rate. Although this policy change is certainly not directly attributable to the project being discussed, it is almost certain that the assessment data had some influence in the final decision.

The assessment data in the social component was mixed when viewed across all operators in the department. It seemed that two of the sections rated the impact of interpersonal relations, cooperation among employees, and shared concern for each others' welfare higher (more positive) than the other two. These two higher sections also rated their section leaders higher in terms of positive impact. All sections, however, reported that interpersonal relations were most negatively affected by the impersonal physical arrangements (the partitioned cubicles). In addition to the change recommendation that removed the cubicle arrangement, the manager and section leaders as members of the change team decided to make systematic efforts to be more attentive to employees' needs for interpersonal contact and to organize more opportunities for social contact. Further, when this assessment information and the change plans of the manager and the section leaders were detailed to the operators, they suggested that they themselves could contribute to a more positive interpersonal climate. The three-month follow-up survey on this component indicated that interpersonal items that had been rated in the neutral-to-slightly-negative range had moved to mid-range positive. The manager also noted that there had been a turnover of only three employees during that quarterly period, whereas the average turnover rate prior to that time had been nearly eight employees per quarter.

At the time the change agent withdrew from formal contact with the Word Processing Department, the manager had stated she intended to administer the *Work Assessment Inventory* on an annual basis and stated that she had strong support from section leaders and operators for this plan. This activity never came to fruition, however, as the manager took a position with another company approximately eight months after the conclusion of the project. Nevertheless, the manager's intentions and the support of the other employees indicated a movement toward environmental competence.

The author (Clack) might have done things differently in his role as environmental change agent, had he had full grasp of the environmental change technology he and Conyne would forward some four years later. First, he would probably have pushed harder for a change team more representative of the operators rather than of departmental management. Second, he would have planned more feedback loops between the change team and the operators. Third, he would have aided the change team and in particular the manager in being more specific when delineating their change plan as it related to interpersonal relations within the department. And finally, he would have put more effort into making environmental design a more ongoing process, rather than dependent upon the good intentions of one person, the manager.

SUMMARY

This chapter has described the Environmental Change Technology, a methodology for implementing environmental design. ECT is a change process that incorporates constituents of an environment of reference into all phases of implementation. It includes ongoing action research activities that provide a data base for change, encompasses a broad, ecological, perspective of both people and environment, and uses the expertise and skills of an environmental change agent. This technology was described as a process that includes three major phases (preparation, action, and follow-up) and step-by-step guidelines for implementing each of the phases. There are many implications surrounding the use of the environmental change technology, and even more when one considers that it is only a part of environmental design. New roles, functions, and competencies are required of change agents, while new opportunities for involvement in change, with accompanying risks, are available to organizations, groups, neighborhoods, and the like. Unique legal, ethical, moral, and value considerations abound as a result of this new methodology. In the final chapter, 6, the many implications will be considered.

6

ENVIRONMENTAL DESIGN IMPLICATIONS AND CONSIDERATIONS

This chapter will examine implications and considerations related to environmental design. It is clear that environmental design is a unique change approach that evolves from assumptions and includes activities that are in many ways dissimilar to those that constitute typical helping practice. It is these differences that are to be explored in this chapter. Before beginning this process, however, a brief review of some key aspects involved in is order.

BRIEF REVIEW OF KEY POINTS IN ENVIRONMENTAL DESIGN

The preceding chapters have shown that environmental design is a process for assessing and changing human environments that is intentional, collaborative, and researchable. Its three main, cyclical components together comprise what was termed the environmental design cycle of applied research (environmental assessment), environmental change, and applied research (research utilization). Each of these components was discussed in detail, especially environmental change, where several approaches (for example, by decree), strategies (for example, normative-reeducative), and models (for example, planned change) were examined. An Environmental Change Technology was distilled from these procedures as being most suitable for use in altering human environments.

Environmental design is based on an ecological, person-by-environment perspective to behavior for which Kurt Lewin laid the general groundwork in the 1940s. This perspective of behavior and change has been extended by subsequent work, such as in the social ecological model of Rudolf Moos and his associates, which lends conceptual and practical legitimacy to helpgiving that is attempted through environmental design.

From this concise review of the main aspects of environmental design, this discussion now turns to an analysis of the implications. Specifically, this study is interested in the implications of environmental design for practitioners, training programs, and clients, and generally in the ethical and value issues that environmental design raises for consideration. Each of these areas will be taken in order, beginning with implications for practitioners.

IMPLICATIONS FOR PRACTITIONERS

Typical helping practice is predicated on the assumption that individuals who experience psychological problems (termed variously psychopathology or problems in living) can learn more adaptive, effective ways of understanding and/or of handling their problems. Thus, counseling or psychotherapy (common forms of professional helpgiving) are conducted at the request of the problem holder in an effort to ameliorate the problems and to produce competence in place of disturbance.

Note the elements involved in this activity: Problems are experienced by an individual who then seeks professional assistance to help resolve them. The core of this activity, in fact, leads to a paradigm (Kuhn 1970) that is based on a set of shared ways for viewing a world of concern, a set of problem-solving rules, and a set of permissable problems (Rappaport 1977). Its parameters can be described as individual, remedial, and direct-service, which, when taken together, have been termed the Counseling Service Paradigm (Conyne 1980).

A story adapted from Rappaport (1977), may serve to illustrate this paradigm:

> One sunny afternoon a person is picnicking alongside a swiftly moving current. In the midst of her revelry, she hears a scream as someone who fell into the water upstream flails frantically by, struggling to save himself from drowning. Our picnicker quickly jumps into the water and hauls the drowning person to safety. But, lo and behold, the rescuer's job isn't done as the situation repeats itself twice more, each time calling for an emergency response by our picnicker. Frustrated by the crises, she decides to go upstream to see what is causing people to fall into the current and if she can prevent these crises from occurring in the first place.

This drowning-man story exaggerates the Counseling Services Paradigm of individual, remedial, direct-service helpgiving. Egan and Cowan (1979) have labeled it a reflection of "downstream" helping. As can be vividly seen, this form of helping is meted out individually from a professional helper to a needful client after the occurrence of a life problem or set of life problems is already present.

As an alternative to this reactive stance, a professional helper can seek to become more proactive in help provision. Egan and Cowan (1979) have termed such an approach "upstream" helping. It is referred to as preventive, as compared to remedial, helpgiving. The picnicker, for instance, might have been able to enjoy her meal and relax if the individuals upstream had learned previously how to swim and/or if guard rails had been placed alongside the river bank. Both of these events would have served preventive purposes, albeit differently. Learning how to swim reflects a skill-development, competency-enhancement technique of prevention that strengthens the individual in an environmental risk situation; providing guard rails alongside the river bank serves to anticipate possible danger and to protect the individual by decreasing the degree of risk present in a setting, through physical environmental design. The combination of approaches illustrates the ecological (person-by-setting) model discussed in earlier chapters.

This preventive, ecological vantage point to help giving differs from that of the Counseling Services Paradigm in discernable ways. At the very least, it is representative of an alternative world view to helping. Environmental design as a helping intervention is aligned with this preventive-ecological world view. Fairly obvious implication for practitioners stem from its adoption. Three of these implications, related to conceptual, intervention, and competency considerations, will be discussed.

Conceptually, the preventive-ecological world view demands that practitioners reconstrue their notions of how people function in the world, of how behavior change can occur, and of what the practitioner role can become. Once remediation as a goal for helping is replaced (or at least supplemented) by prevention, a different practitioner orientation is mandated. Proaction is substituted for reaction, a population view dominates an individual one, competency enhancement overshadows deficit reduction, and environmental change accompanies people change. Once a clinical perspective to change is broadened to include an ecological focus, then an individual-intrapersonal-change focus is minimized and, instead, translated into a systemic, people-in-environment focus.

Environmental design, as has been seen, is an intervention well suited to this different world view. Its adoption by helping practitioners, however, may not come easily, since that is tantamount to a conceptual revolution in which long-standing traditions in the helping field are overthrown. Success in this venture is a function of accomplishments in other related areas that are examined in sections to follow.

Delivery modes must be created that evolve from a preventive-ecological world view and that support environmental design. Paradigmatic helping interventions, such as individual psychotherapy, conflict with this intent, while the Environmental Change Technology, for instance, is facilitative of it. What cannot be logically expected is that traditional, familiar interventions can be used equally well for both preventive-ecological and for remedial-clinical purposes. Therefore, practitioners who engage in environmental design will need to find ways to channel their existing competencies appropriately. It is hoped that the preceding chapters have given some direction to this effort, particularly Chapter 4 (social ecological change model, planned change) and Chapter 5 (devoted to the Environmental Change Technology).

IMPLICATIONS AND CONSIDERATIONS / 153

Successful implementation of these and of other environmental design interventions is dependent on a variety of factors, with practitioners' competency representing a most critical set. What are the sorts of working knowledge and skills that helpers must possess in order to conduct environmental design effectively? Answers to this fundamental question are currently in the formative stage, although Ford (1980) has presented 13 basic types of skills, and the authors have identified five competency categories. First are listed the 13 basic types (adapted from Ford 1980, pp. 275-76):

Observation Skills: The ability to gather information concerning all relevant aspects of a socio-physical context where an environmental design intervention is to be implemented.
Elicitation Skills: The ability to structure interpersonal interactions (for example, interviews) or sociophysical environments (for example, role-play simulations, furniture arrangements) to elicit data that would not otherwise be observable.
Conceptualization Skills: The ability to develop and use cognitive information processing strategies to screen, assimilate, organize, analyze, and plan data gathered through elicitation and observation.
Problem-Solving Skills: The ability to translate the conceptual scheme and assessment data into concrete interventions.
Facilitation Skills: The ability to redesign sociophysical environments that reflect the change objectives set.
Consecution Skills: The ability to structure the sociophysical environment so that changes are maintained.
Communication Skills: The ability to interact empathically, warmly, and genuinely; to send congruent verbal and nonverbal messages; and to convey messages that enhance change.
Self-Control Skills: The ability to regulate one's own actions effectively.
Process Evaluation Skills: The ability to monitor the effects and efficiency of ongoing change interventions.
Outcome Evaluations Skills: The ability to evaluate the multiple outcomes of a change intervention.
Resource Allocation Skills: The ability to allocate a limited supply of resources to maximize all aspects of an ongoing change intervention.
Coordination Skills: The ability to integrate multiple concurrent intervention programs or subprograms.
Synthesis Skills: The ability to create new paradigms and methodologies and to adapt existing ones to unique setting demands.

As Ford (1980) points out, the specific environmental design skills included in each of these 13 broad types are limitless in number, bounded solely by the resourcefulness of the practitioner. Further, he indicates that the 13 groupings correspond roughly to six basic phases he has identified as comprising an environmental design intervention program: assessment, goal formulation, intervention design, intervention, evaluation, systems maintenance, and generalization.

The authors have envisioned a more general set of five competency classifications that practitioners who are engaged in environmental design might possess. This set corresponds closely with Ford's, but at a more global level.

Communication Competencies. Practitioners must be effective presenters, listeners, summarizers, challengers, and supporters. They should be able to communicate well at both cognitive and affective levels. They must be able to interact satisfactorily with individuals and with large groups, and with groups that are highly compatible or very diverse.

Applied Research Competencies. Assessment skills must be well developed, allowing practitioners to design and implement methods for gathering relevant data from client systems and for converting them to meaningful information. Practitioners should be able to conduct formative and summative evaluations of ongoing projects and to use resulting data for project improvement.

Group Facilitation Competencies. Much of the environmental design practitioners' work is conducted in group settings. Knowledge of group dynamics (such as decision making, leadership, and communication patterns) and skill in effectively organizing and using these dynamics are crucial to successful projects.

Consultation Competencies. Ability to collaborate with client systems is vital to the environmental design role. Consultation, especially of a resource, process, or behavioral nature, provides a systematic model that practitioners can follow in helping client systems mobilize themselves for sustained action. (See Lippitt and Lippitt 1976; Lippitt, Watson, and Westley 1958; or Schein 1969 for extended discussion.)

Action Research Competencies. This model, as illustrated previously, provides the single most fundamental framework for environmental design work. Its sequential, cyclical steps, when set within an ecological change perspective, enable practitioners to integrate research and action in a manner that can be highly facilitative of environmental change. This last set of competencies incorporates and extends those contained in the previous four competency sets just discussed.

Giving consideration to practitioner competencies must inevitably lead to an examination of training programs, a discussion of which follows.

IMPLICATIONS FOR TRAINING PROGRAMS

Although current practitioners in the field can be expected to develop some degree of competence in environmental design through professional activities (for example, reading, workshop participation, sabbaticals, receipt of consultation, and so on), the main source for advancing competence in the delivery of environmental design activities must come from training programs. It is incumbent, therefore, on training programs to offer suitable course work and other educational experiences in environmental design. A significant implication of a role change from, for instance, a sole reliance on a psychologist as a psychotherapist to a psychologist as an environmental designer is that different demands are placed on the orientation and content of training programs. At issue is a training-program response to the unique world view (preventive-ecological), delivery modes, and competencies required in environmental design.

Consider first the preventive-ecological world view of environmental design and its training implications. As Krasner (1980) points out, the designer needs to be an interdisciplinarian. Concepts, research, and methodologies drawn from psychology, sociology, psychiatry, architecture, urban planning, economics, and education, among other fields, can be powerfully pertinent. Presented within a training program based on a coherent preventive-ecological theme, this material can provide the breadth of focus necessary for providing a wide-foundation perspective of human behavior in environments. Such a framework (or world view) mitigates against narrow, discipline-bound approaches to situations, while promoting the generation of hybrid methods resulting from cross-disciplinary sources. Thus, a broadly cast environmental-design world view needs to be transmitted in training programs, a characteristic that is dependent on the program's capacity to establish and maintain an interdisciplinary structure, or at least orientation; this condition illustrates yet another implication that will be simply noted without further elaboration.

This world view must be concretized into training goals, objectives, and into the actual curriculum itself. Curricular matters will be addressed in a general way below. Such a discussion will help to articulate the nature of a training program most clearly and economically.

Ford (1980) has offered useful guidelines for curricular content areas that would provide preparation in necessary environmental design competencies; this discussion will draw from and expand on them. He suggests four ways to consider organizing training around content areas: by the environmental systems in which a practitioner might work; by the kinds of variables that a practitioner might intend to influence; by the type of skills that are relevant; and by a combination of skills and variables within settings. After a brief discussion of these four ways for organizing, a fifth possibility, by intervention, will be added and examined.

Environmental System

Many prototypic environmental systems are potential targets for environmental design. The following systems are examples (Ford 1980, p. 279):

> These include schools, homes, hospitals, prisons, community governments, social service agencies, geriatric institutions, day-care centers, mental health agencies, clinics, welfare agencies, legal aid services, self-help groups, community planning boards, businesses, police departments, park and recreation services, planned parenthood centers, senior centers, youth centers, psychiatric hospitals, special education schools and classrooms, labor unions, and many more.

These settings present unique sets of issues, problems, and characteristics that require practitioners to ply their trade adaptively. Due to these varying challenges, Ford (1980) suggests that specialized training is needed to allow practitioners to deal competently with each setting.

Variables to Influence

Ford and Hutchison (1974) have identified 11 main forms of variables that are pertinent to environmental design and around which training programs can be built. They suggest that a practitioner ideally should be trained to deal effectively with variables of several, if not all, forms. These 11 forms of variables are cited in Ford (1980):

(1) Geophysical (e.g., climate, terrain);
(2) Architectural (e.g., room sizes and accessibility);
(3) Spatial (e.g., territorial boundaries, personal space);
(4) Interpersonal (e.g., person-to-person nonverbal communication);
(5) Cognitive-Interpersonal (e.g., beliefs and personal constructs);
(6) Physiological-Intrapersonal (e.g., hormone levels, muscle tensions);
(7) Intrasocial-Sociopolitical (e.g., decision-making policies and ritualized interaction patterns *within* social groups);
(8) Intersocial-Sociopolitical (e.g., decision-making policies and norms impinging on social groups from *outside* their boundaries);
(9) Intrasocial-Economic (e.g., patterns of resource distribution *within* social groups);
(10) Intersocial-Economic (e.g., patterns of resource distribution that affect social groups but which originate *outside* them); and
(11) Education-Socialization (e.g., childraising patterns). (pp. 279-80).

In examining these 11 forms of variables, the reader may recall the earlier discussion in Chapter 2 of ways to classify an environment. Insel and Moos (1974) presented a similar list of variables that could become a nexus for training content: ecological, organization structure, personal characteristics of inhabitants, behavior settings, functional or reinforcement properties, and psychosocial climate. Likewise, Steele's (1973) sociophysical functions, described in Chapter 3, could provide such a structure: shelter and security, social contact, symbolic identification, task instrumentality, pleasure, and growth.

Types of Skills: The 13 skill types that we described earlier in this Chapter (observation, elicitation . . . synthesis) could provide the framework around which content areas might be developed. As Ford observes, seminars and courses could be created to teach the specific competencies involved in these classes of environmental design skills.

Classes of Skills by Classes of Variables for a Target Setting

Ford has proposed a comprehensive approach to training that includes the interaction of all levels of these two dimensions within specific settings. Such an approach yields as many as 143 potential content areas for environmental design training (13 skill types by 11 variable forms). Training components stemming from this interactive model would allow for consideration of the specific behaviors involved in environmental design skills, for the way each skill type could be related to selected variables of interest, and for analysis of how each skill type might be applied within differing environmental settings.

Intervention

A fifth approach to training, based on teaching selected environmental design intervention, is envisioned. If desired, this approach could be interfaced with the skill-types dimension of Ford. Interventions to be taught would be a function of which ones are thought to be critical, answers to which are not yet at all clear. As starters, however, the interventions of consultation (resource, process, and behavioral), action research, evaluation research, group facilitation, and environmental assessment are suggested.

IMPLICATIONS FOR CLIENTS

The definition of environmental design (Chapter 4) stated that it is "alteration of the human environment through evaluated, intentional, collaborative change." The collaborative nature of environmental design will be discussed in this first part of the discussion of client implications.

The label, environmental design, seems often to stir people's apprehensions about being manipulated, if not overtly controlled, by "Big Brother." In this view, an explicit implication of environmental design projects is that settings are changed by designers without the involvement of setting inhabitants (clients). Thus, company policy may one day be radically different from the past, the mall in a boulevard may be arbitrarily replaced by a widened street, or a new director may create a very different organizational structure—all without the input and participation of the setting constituents who will be affected by these changes. Such occurrences are the result of an expert-client relationship that is defined in "Top Dog/Under Dog, I know/You don't know" terms. Professional control and power are maximized in this format while client freedom and influence are minimized.

By contrast, however, a collaborative approach to environmental design stimulates an entirely opposite set of client implications. Collaboration in environmental design means that the design practitioners and the setting inhabitants find ways to work together to define and execute all phases of the project. As Leland Kaiser (1975) has stressed in regard to campus ecosystem design, "It is immoral to design for people. It is moral to design with people. Students affected by a campus space have a moral right to participate in its design or redesign" (p. 29). And as Krasner and Ullman (1973) have said, "We need to foster greater communication and awareness between influencers (all of us) and influencees (all of us)" (p. 502).

The point here is not only an ethical or moral one (more will be said of ethics later in this chapter) but a highly pragmatic one as well. As Insel and Moos (1974) have indicated, "the likelihood of achieving an optimum environment is greatly facilitated when critical decisions about changing the environment are in the hands of the people who function within the environment" (p. 187).

Two interrelated concepts are important for implementing this collaborative approach to environmental design. The first concept describes the role of the practitioner and the second describes that of the setting inhabitant. When environmental design practitioners articulate their role as participant-observers (Krasner 1980), their behavior concretely encourages, if not requires, the concomitant active involvement of members of the client system. This intervenor role, first expressed by Harry Stack Sullivan for psychotherapy, puts the practitioner in active communication with clients, thus naturally facilitating collaboration. In turn, when clients are viewed as user participants (for example, Cashdan et al. 1978) in the design process, rather than as passive recipients, the conditions for successful designer-user collaboration are further enhanced. As user participants, clients (setting inhabitants) become partners (setting participants) with the practitioners, this relationship shift demands that the noblesse oblige stance that is frequently adopted by professionals be discarded in favor of a working relationship defined by mutual influence and egalitarian expectations and behaviors. Such a partner-participant arrangement between practitioner and client is thought to have both ethical and practical benefits—see the newsletter of the Working Group on Participation, "On Participation" (Cashdan et al. 1978) for the considerably active amount of work that is transpiring around this area.

A second important environmental design implication for clients evolves from the locus chosen for the change effort itself. Earlier, in Chapter 4, the authors argued against adoption of either a victim- or a system-blame perspective on environmental change, and in support of a balanced, ecological conception.

As this preferred conception gets applied in practice, the obvious implication is that clients (setting participants) are freed from being viewed nearly automatically as the problem source. Alternative interpretations become acceptable. Setting participants, for example, may be viewed as members of noxious environments that themselves cause human problems (such as the sweatshops of nineteenth-century America and, some would insist, the nuclear power plants of today). Or, perhaps more frequently, setting participants and settings may be conceptualized in dynamic transaction, both influencing the other (such as the ways a place of residence is used, or the patterns of behavior that occur in a park during different seasons of the year).

The critical implication of environmental design for clients is that generally they cannot be independently praised or blamed for what happens to them; environmental variables must be considered as well. This conceptual shift in attributing causation for human problems seems very much in line with the larger human liberation themes that have been witnessed in relation to civil rights, women's liberation, gay rights, and male liberation movements. Converting this conception to practice, the leverage point of environmental change can lead to more humane, effective, supportive settings for people, thus enabling them to advance their lives in increasingly more satisfying ways.

As setting participants work collaboratively with practitioners in an environmental design project to produce more amenable settings and/or to gain greater environmental competency themselves, a specific implication of the effort becomes possible: that the setting participants become their own future environmental designers (Ford 1980; Krasner 1980). In attempting to promote this possibility for clients, environmental design can be seen as an educational process, totally consistent with goals in other educational processes such as teaching, counseling, and consulting, where people learn to help themselves.

Who, then, can become an environmental designer? Ford (1980) has said:

> virtually anyone—but training, to provide the person with certain key skills, is essential. Parents, classmates in elementary schools, inpatients in psychiatric hospitals, clinical psychologists, teachers, paraprofessional mental health staff-persons, psychiatrists, retarded persons, counselors, nurses, lawyers, economists, politicians, and many more, all have been trained—or could potentially be trained—to serve as environmental designers. (p. 272)

Ford (1980) labels this level of environmental design training as "self-regulation." A self-regulator is an individual who actively participates in a collaborative teaching-learning process in order "to directly improve his/her own functioning or life situation or milieu.... The types of skills that are most relevant for the self-regulator include observation, problem solving (e.g., D'Zurilla and Goldfried 1971), assertiveness (e.g., Rich and Schroeder 1976), and self-monitoring and self-reinforcement (e.g., Thoresen and Mahoney 1974)" (p. 272). Self-regulators learn how to learn and how to be their own teachers (cf. Dewey 1897; Benne, Bradford, and Lippitt 1964) in becoming "autonomous environmental designers" (Ford 1980, p. 272).

A last major set of implications that arise from environmental design is related to ethical and value considerations. Although this area has been briefly touched on in this chapter, this critical topic requires more extensive and intensive coverage. This last section of the book is devoted to several of the fundamental ethical and value considerations surrounding environmental design.

VALUE AND ETHICAL CONSIDERATIONS

Individuals learn values. Important value sources are parents, educators, theologians, colleagues, friends, the media, and so on. In terms of an E_r, all constituents have their own value systems. They also share to a greater or lesser extent, however, a collective set of values representative of the preponderance of the environment's inhabitants. The fact that most E_r constituents hold certain values is certainly no guarantee that the nature of that environment will reflect the majority's preferences. We need only look at totalitarian governments, or many university administrations in the 1960s, to know that power, coercion, and manipulation often set the nature of an environment, rather than the prevailing value system.

A rudimentary way of expressing the role and goals of environmental design and, indeed, those of the environmental change agent, is to say that attempts are being made to improve the quality of human life—to do good. But who is to say what is good, and what characterizes quality in human life? Social scientists are as susceptible to self-deception and selective perception as any other individuals. Their targets, goals, methods, and assessment of outcomes are based on their own value sets, which may or may not be in line with those of a target population.

As Warwick and Kelman (1973) note, the issue surrounding planned environmental change is not only whose interests the outcomes of change serve, but even prior to that, whose conceptual framework determines what the problems are, sets the goals, and decides the methods for implementing change. These issues exist even when representatives of a setting are actively involved in the total change process, because these representatives (an environmental change team for example) may adopt the conceptual framework of the change agent as a function of the training they receive. If this occurs, then E_r constituents can lose their influence in decision making.

This basic concern was also emphasized by Conyne et al. (1979) who observed that social scientists who claim value neutrality in social intervention frequently unwittingly use their own personal values as guidelines in environmental interventions. The danger of value imposition is ever present in any type of social intervention, including environmental design.

The value dilemma does not end with just the concern over the potential of a change agent imposing personal values upon residents of an environment. It extends to issues involved in the change agent faulting his/her own values and ethics for the sake of pleasing an employee or administrator, or to collect a much-needed fee, and to cases where value conflicts become apparent during the course of an environmental design project. For instance, whose values are to prevail and whose are to be subservient in situations where both sets of conflicting values are "good"?—those who support a badly needed sewage system are opposed by those who recognize that the new system would destroy the neighborhood's only park. Both sewage systems and parks are "good" in that they meet basic human desires. But in this case, which one takes precedence?

The Population Task Force of the Institute of Society, Ethics, and the Life Sciences (1971), through an analysis of cultural and legal traditions in the United States, identified four values as being central to the American way of life: freedom—the capacity and opportunity to make one's own choices; justice—fairness in distribution of rewards and punishments; welfare—societal support for health and well-being; and security/survival—freedom from fear of physical or psychological harm.

Goulet (1971) found three common values of all societies that are quite similar to Maslow's (1954) needs hierarchy of physical, security, recognition, esteem, and self-actualization. Goulet's three are life sustenance, to satisfy basic requirements for food, water, shelter, healing and survival; esteem, to give individuals a sense of worth, dignity, recognition, and respect; and freedom, a range of individual choice in the pursuit of perceived good. Although the value issues faced in environmental design projects may never be expressed in as lofty terms as those, the issues and the ethical questions do seem to derive from conflicts over similar high-minded principles.

To summarize this section, environmental design is based on a conceptual framework that holds such activity as being "good," that it will improve the quality of the environment in which people live, and thereby be of benefit to the users. Environmental design, however, (what is changed and how) and implementation of change (the process used) are all subject to and influenced by the change agent.

Obviously, the basic issues of values and ethics have been outlined, but no clear solutions have been given. As in many ethical considerations, there are unfortunately no clear-cut answers that apply under all conditions. There are many well-considered codes of ethics and guidelines, including those of the American Psychological Association (1959, 1973), the American Personnel and Guidance Association (1961), Lippitt and Lippitt (1978), Pfeiffer and Jones (1977). A review of these will give the reader the general essence and intent of ethics as they apply to a range of social scientists and helpers. Their application to environmental change agents may be less direct.

On the other hand, some ethical guidelines that apply directly to environmental design can be mentioned. The authors are the first to admit that these guidelines are a product of their own value systems and experience. Therefore, they are subject to question on the part of the readers who may regard them from a different perspective.

For the environmental change agent, ethical considerations arise in some cases even prior to initiation of a design project. If change agents publicized their services and competencies, these descriptions should be accurate. In particular, no promises of success in terms of either outcomes or process should be made in any way that cannot be backed by fact. To guarantee potential clients that environmental design is the answer to all their problems, that all participants will be happy with the process, and that positive outcomes are assured would be outright deception and fraud. Such a degree of certainty does not exist at this time, and probably never will, in the use of interventions where individual and/or small-group decisions will affect the welfare of a larger population. Accurate descriptions of the agent's professional background, training, and experience, the change model employed, and previous change contracts the agent has held should suffice for advertising purposes. In short, do not promise what cannot assuredly be delivered.

As initiaion occurs and the potential client and change agent address the issue of whether or not they can work together, the change agent should expose his or her values and code of ethics as they relate to environmental design. The change agent will want to inform the potential client of how his/her position can and will affect all aspects of any environmental change project. The agent should seek the potential client's reactions to these statements so that the client will not be disappointed or surprised. In so doing, neither change agent nor client will be placed in a compromising position later in the process. Further, the expressions of the values inherent in the Environmental Change Technology model should be clearly accomplished during the formalization of a contract. For example, if the change agent is given indication that he/she will be expected to conduct activities that would violate ethical standards, withdrawal from the project at that point is the recommended course.

The change agent should take the stance that environmental change teams should be as representative of the total population as is feasible. If through circumstance the change team is not representative, the change agent must keep this fact in mind and compensate for it by paying close attention to the expressions used and positions taken by all respondents throughout the remainder of the design project. Further, in team development and the training of change team members a primary concern of the change agent is to assist members in maintaining their independence and integrity on issues that arise. The team can work together effectively without unanimously agreeing on all issues, particularly with the change agent. The change agent can also help guard against instances where group pressure and norms may be used to coerce a team member into agreement with the team.

As assessment procedures begin, the change agent should encourage active participation from all respondents. The change agent, personally or working through the change team, must negotiate with respondents as to how their opinions and preferences will influence project processes and outcomes, and how they will be kept informed. The change agent is then ethically bound to respect these agreements. Further, the change agent should inform respondents that the assessment methods to be used may not allow them to make complete statements of their opinions and preferences. In such cases respondents should be encouraged to take advantage of open-ended formats in order to state their positions more fully.

As assessment proceeds, all respondents in a setting must be kept informed of results and encouraged to forward further input. This principle must apply throughout the preparation, action, and follow-up phases of the Environmental Change Technology.

Respondents must be clearly informed of the confidentiality, or lack thereof, that will govern the use of any data or statements, written or oral, they make during the project. The respondents must be informed of who will see or hear their responses, and how their responses will be used. If anonymity and/or confidentiality is afforded to respondents, the change agent must guard these promises zealously.

During the change planning step of the model all change ideas must be considered seriously. Although this may be time-consuming, it is a major safeguard against the potential effects of the group think, gravitation toward the mean, or dismissing out of hand those ideas that do not agree with those of the change agent, change team, or majority opinion. Indeed, expressions based upon values that are different from the majority often serve as guidelines to the quantity and quality of change that the client system might potentially accept.

During the implementation of change, the change agent needs to be particularly perceptive of and responsive to feedback coming from setting constituents. The involvement of participants certainly does not end with the change plan, but rather continues in order that subsequent change activities may successfully occur.

Finally, the change agent should strive to help constituents to become environmentally competent, better able to manage future issues with greater facility than they could prior to the project. This ethical guideline aptly demonstrates the important emphasis of environmental design on people as well as on their environments.

These guidelines do not lessen change agents' responsibility for being aware of their own values and their relationship to environmental change. Rather, they should serve to heighten that awareness and to keep the change agent ever vigilant in addressing the ethical issues that unavoidably accompany environmental design.

SUMMARY

This final chapter has discussed several considerations and implications that surround the use of environmental design and its cyclical components of assessment, change, and evaluative research. Environmental design is a unique approach to help giving that requires a conceptual break from the traditional bases of individual psychotherapy. It is grounded in prevention rather than remediation, its client systems are populations rather than individuals, and environmental design attempts to foster competency rather than adaptation.

Operating from this conceptual perspective, environmental change agents find it necessary to implement new methods for fostering change, and to call upon a fresh collection of competencies (action research, consultation, group facilitation, applied research, and communication skills) in their work. Change agents' needs for new concepts, new skills, and new methods beckon training programs to develop responsive curricula.

Environmental design invites clients to participate with change agents as partners in the change process. This collaborative stance nullifies the dependent, passive client role by replacing it with the strategy and ethic of user participation.

The second part of this chapter addressed the knotty area of ethics in environmental design. Some of the explicit values that underlie cultural tradition (for example, freedom, justice, privacy, and esteem) were identified and it was noted how these values, and particularly conflicts that occur among them, serve both to support and to restrict environmental design efforts.

Although no innovative ethical principles were offered in addition to those already published by professional organizations, a unique set of ethical guidelines was identified that seems to be particularly pertinent for use in environmental design.

BIBLIOGRAPHY

Adler, Alfred. 1935. "The Fundamental Views of Individual Psychology." *International Journal of Individual Psychology* 1 (April): 5-8.
_____. 1939. *Social Interest.* New York: Putnam.
Agel, Jerome, ed. 1971. *The Radical Therapist: The Radical Therapist Collective.* New York: Ballantine.
Altman, Irwin, Dallas Taylor, and Ladd Wheeler. 1971. "Ecological Aspects of Group Behavior." *Journal of Applied Social Psychology* 1 (Jan.): 76-100.
American Personnel and Guidance Association. 1961. "Ethical Standards." *Personnel and Guidance Journal* 40: 206-9.
American Psychological Association. 1959. "Ethical Standards of Psychologists." *American Psychologist* 18, 56-60.
American Psychological Association. 1973. "Guidelines for Psychologists Conducting Growth Groups." *American Psychologist* 28 (Oct.): 933.
Astin, Alexander. 1968. "Undergraduate Achievement and Institutional 'Excellence'." *Science* 161 (3842): 661-68.
Astin, Alexander, and John Holland. 1961. "The Environmental Assessment Technique: A Way to Measure College Environments." *Journal of Educational Psychology* 52 (6): 308-16.
Aubrey, Roger, and Francis McKenzie. 1978. "The School Counselor as Environmental Researcher." In *Research Methods for Counselors: Practical Approaches in Field Settings,* edited by Leo Goldman, pp. 237-65. New York: Wiley.
Aulepp, Lou Ann, and Ursula Delworth. 1978. "A Team Approach to Environmental Assessment." In *Campus Ecology: A Perspective for Student Affairs,* edited by James Banning, pp. 51-71. Cincinnati: National Association for Student Personnel Administration.
Bandura, Albert. 1974. "Behavior Theory and the Models of Man." *American Psychologist* 29 (Dec.): 859-69.
_____. 1969. *Principles of Behavior Modification.* New York: Holt, Rinehart and Winston.
Banning, James, ed. 1978. *Campus Ecology: A Perspective for Student Affairs.* Cincinnati: National Association for Student Personnel Administrators.
Banning, James, and Leland Kaiser. 1974. "An Ecological Perspective and Model for Campus Design." *Personnel and Guidance Journal* 52 (Feb.): 370-75.
Barker, Roger. 1968. *Ecological Psychology: Concepts and Methods for Studying the Environment of Human Behavior.* Stanford, CA: Stanford University Press.
_____. 1960. "Ecology and Motivation." *Nebraska Symposium on Motivation.* Lincoln, NE: University of Nebraska Press.
Barker, Roger, and Associates. 1978. *Habitats, Environments, and Human*

Behavior: Studies in Ecological Psychology and Eco-Behavioral Science from the Midwest Psychological Field Stations, 1947-1972. San Francisco: Jossey-Bass.

Barker, Roger and Paul Gump. 1964. *Big School, Small School*. Stanford, CA: Stanford University Press.

Bartz, Wayne R. 1971. "While Psychologists Doze On." In *Toward Social Change: A Handbook For Those Who Will*, edited by Robert Buckhout, pp. 382-84. New York: Harper and Row.

Beckhard, Richard. 1969. *Organization Development: Strategies and Models*. Reading, MA: Addison-Wesley.

Beer, Michael. 1975. "The Technology of Organizational Development." In *Organization Development and Change*, by Edgar Huse, pp. 232-33. St. Paul, MN: West.

Beer, Michael and Edgar Huse. 1972. "A Systems Approach to Organizational Development." *Journal of Applied Behavioral Science* 8, 79-101.

Bell, Roger, George Warheit, and John Schwab. 1977. "Needs Assessment: A Strategy for Structuring Change." In *Program Evaluation for Mental Health: Methods, Strategies, Participants*, edited by Robert Coursey, pp. 68-76. New York: Gruen and Stratton.

Bem, Daryl J. and Andrea Allen. 1974. "On Predicting Some of the People Some of the Time." *Psychological Review* 81 (Nov.): 506-20.

Benne, Kenneth, Leland Bradford, and Ronald Lippitt. 1964. "The Laboratory Method." In *T-Group Theory and Laboratory Method: Innovation in Re-education*, edited by Leland Bradford, Jack Gibb, and Kenneth Benne, pp. 15-44. New York: Wiley.

Blake, Robert and Jane Mouton. 1976. *Consultation*. Reading, MA: Addison-Wesley.

Blanton, Judith and Sam Alley. 1978. "How Evaluation Findings Can Be Integrated into Program Decision Making." *Community Mental Health Journal* 14, 239-47.

Brandon, Richard. 1975. "Differential Use of Mental Health Services: Social Pathology or Class Victimization?" In *Handbook of Evaluation Research* vol. 2, edited by Ernest Struening and Marcia Guttentag, pp. 341-430. Beverly Hills, CA: Sage Publications.

Brickell, Henry. 1961. *Organizing New York State for Educational Change*. Albany: Commissioner of Education, State Education Department.

Brunswik, Egon. 1955. "The Conceptual Framework of Psychology." In *International Encyclopedia of Unified Science*. Chicago: University of Chicago Press, 1, pp. 650-750.

Caplan, Gerald. 1964. *Principles of Preventive Psychiatry*. New York: Basic Books.

Caplan, Nathan and Stephen Nelson. 1973. "On Being Useful: The Nature and Consequences of Psychological Research on Social Problems." *American Psychologist* 28 (Mar.) 199-211.

Carson, Rachel. 1962. *Silent Spring*. Boston: Houghton-Mifflin.

_____. 1951. *The Sea Around Us*. New York: Oxford University Press.

Cashdan, Lisa, Bernd Fahle, Mark Francis, Steven Schwartz, and Peter Stein.

1978. "A Critical Framework for Participatory Approaches to Environmental Change." Center for Human Environments, Graduate Center of the City University of New York for Working Group on Participation.

Centra, John. 1968. "Studies of Institutional Environments: Categories of Instrumentation and Some Issues." In *Institutional Research of Academic Outcomes: Proceedings of the Eighth Annual Forum of the Association for Institutional Research,* edited by C. Fincher.

Chin, Robert and Kenneth Benne. 1976. "General Strategies for Effecting Change in Human Systems." In *The Planning of Change,* 3rd ed., edited by Warren Bennis, Kenneth Benne, Robert Chin, and Kenneth Corey, pp. 22-45. New York: Holt, Rinehart and Winston.

Chrisman, Robert. 1971. "Ecology is a Racist Shuck." In *Toward Social Change: A Handbook For Those Who Will,* edited by Robert Buckhout, pp. 424-28. New York: Harper and Row.

Chu, Franklin D. and Sharland Trotter. 1972. "The Mental Health Complex, Part I: Community Mental Health Centers." In *Nader Report on Community Mental Health Centers,* edited by Ralph Nader.

Clack, R. James. 1975. "Negotiation of Understanding." Unpublished paper. Ausin, Texas.

_____. 1976. *Work Environment Assessment Inventory.* Unpublished. Austin, Texas.

Clack, R. James and Robert K. Conyne. 1973. "Basic Skills of Small Group Discussion Leadership." A mimeographed paper. Normal, Il: Illinois State University.

Clark, David and Egon Guba. *Innovation in School Curricula.* Washington, D.C.: The Center for the Study of Instruction, National Education Association.

Coch, Lester and John French, Jr. 1948. "Overcoming Resistance to Change." *Human Relations* 1, 512-32.

Collier, Abram T. 1962. *Management, Man, and Values.* New York: Harper and Row.

Colman, Arthur. 1975. "Environmental Design: Realities and Delusions." In *Applications of Behavior Modification,* edited by T. Thompson and W. Doches, pp. 409-23. New York: Academic Press.

Conyne, Robert. 1980. *Preventive Counseling: A Primary Prevention-Based Model for Counselors.* Book in preparation.

_____. 1978. "An Analysis of Student-Environment Mismatches." *Journal of College Student Personnel* 19 (Sep.): 461-65.

_____. 1975. "Environmental Assessment: Mapping for Counselor Action." *Personnel and Guidance Journal* 54 (Nov.) 150-55.

Conyne, Robert and R. James Clack. 1975. "The Consultation Intervention Model: Directions for Action." *Journal of College Student Personnel* 16 (Sep.): 413-17.

Conyne, Robert, Douglas Lamb, R. James Clack, Donald Cochran, and Francis LaFave. 1976. "The Use of Faculty Workshops in Campus Environmental Consultation." *Professional Psychology* 7 (Nov.); 565-72.

Conyne, Robert, James Banning, R. James Clack, John Corazzini, Lois Huebner, Lou Ann Keating, and Robert Wrenn. 1979. "The Campus Environment as Client: A New Direction for College Counselors." *Journal of College Student Personnel* 20 (Sept.): 437-42.

_____. 1977. "The Campus Environment as Client: Considerations and Implications for Counseling Psychology." Paper presented at the Annual Meeting of the American Psychological Association, San Francisco. Sept.

Conyne, Robert and Richard Rogers. 1977. "Psychotherapy as Ecological Problem Solving." *Psychotherapy: Theory, Research and Practice* 14 298-305.

Conyne, Robert and Elizabeth Harding. 1976. Environmental Assessment Inventory-Group. *Together* 1, 26-31.

Craik, Kenneth. 1970. "Environmental Psychology." In *New Directions in Psychology.* Vol. 4. New York: Holt, Rinehart and Winston.

Crowfoot, James and Mark Chesler. 1976. "Contemporary Perspectives on Planned Social Change: A Comparison." In *The Planning of Change,* 3rd ed., edited by Warren Bennis, Kenneth Benne, Robert Chin, and Kenneth Corey, pp. 188-204. New York: Holt, Rinehart and Winston.

Daher, Douglas, John D. Corazzini, and Richard D. McKinnon. 1977. "An Environmental Redesign Program for Residence Halls," *Journal of College Student Personnel* 18 (Jan.): 11-15.

Davis, Howard and Susan Salasin. 1979. "Evaluation and Change." In *Improving Evaluations,* edited by Lois-Ellin Datta and Robert Perloff, pp. 257-71. Beverly Hills: Sage.

_____. 1975. "The Utilization of Evaluation." In *Handbook of Evaluation Research: Volume I,* edited by Elmer Struening and Marcia Guttentag, pp. 621-66. Beverly Hills: Sage.

DeBell, Garrett. 1970. *The Environmental Handbook.* New York: Ballantine.

Dewey, John. 1897. *My Pedagogic Creed.* New York: E. L. Kellogg.

DeYoung, Alan. 1977. "Classroom Climate and Class Success: A Case Study at the University Level." *Journal of Educational Research,* 70, pp. 252-257.

Downs, Roger and David Stea, eds. 1973. *Image and Environment: Cognitive Mapping and Spatial Behavior.* Chicago: Aldine.

Drum, David and Howard Figler. 1973. *Outreach in Counseling: Applying the Growth and Prevention Model in Schools and Colleges.* New York: Intext.

Duhl, Leonard, ed. 1963. *The Urban Condition: People and Policy in the Metropolis.* New York: Basic Books.

Dunham, Randall and Frank Smith. 1979. *Organizational Surveys: An Internal Assessment of Organizational Health.* Glenview, IL: Scott, Foresman.

D'Zurilla, Thomas and Marvin Goldfried. 1971. "Problem Solving and Behavior Modification." *Journal of Abnormal Psychology* 78 (Aug.): 107-26.

Egan, Gerard, and Michael Cowan. 1979. *People in Systems: A Model for Development in the Human Service Professions and Education.* Monterey, CA: Brooks-Cole.

Erlich, Paul. 1968. *The Population Bomb.* New York: Ballantine.

Eysenck, Hans. 1952. "The Effects of Psychotherapy: An Evaluation." *Journal of Consultative Psychology* 16: 319-24.

Farson, Richard. 1969. "How Could Anything That Feels So Bad Be So Good?" *Saturday Review* 48 (Sept. 6): 20-21.

Fawcett, Greg, Lois Huebner, and James Banning. 1978. "Campus Ecology: Implementing the Design Process." In *Campus Ecology: A Perspective for Student Affairs,* edited by James Banning, pp. 32-50. Cincinnati: National Association for Student Personnel Administrators.

Fiedler, Fred. 1967. *A Theory of Leadership Effectiveness.* New York: McGraw-Hill.

Ford, Julian. 1980. "Training and Environmental Design." In *Environmental Design and Human Behavior,* edited by Leonard Krasner, pp. 270-301. New York: Pergamon.

Ford, Julian, and William Hutchison. 1974. "Elements of an Effective and Responsive Training Program for Community-Based Psychologists." Paper presented at the City University of New York Action Conference, New York.

Freedman, Jonathan. 1975. *Crowding and Behavior.* New York: Viking.

Freedman, Jonathan, Simon Klevansky, and Paul Ehrlich. 1971. "The Effect of Crowding on Human Task Performance." *Journal of Applied Social Psychology* 1 (Jan.): 7-25.

French, John, Willard Rogers, and Sidney Cobb. 1974. "Adjustment as Person-Environment Fit." In *Coping and Adaptation,* edited by George Coelho, David Hamburg, and J. Adams, pp. 316-33. New York: Basic Books.

French, Wendell and Cecil Bell. 1973. *Organization Development.* Englewood Cliffs, N.J.: Prentice-Hall.

French, Wendell, Cecil Bell, and Robert Zawacki, eds. 1978. *Organization Development: Theory, Practice and Research.* Dallas: Business Publications.

Freud, Sigmund. 1957. *A General Selection From the Works of Sigmund Freud.* Rickman, John (Ed.) New York: Doubleday Anchor Books.

Frohman, Mark and Marshall Sashkin. 1970. "The Practice of Organization Development: A Selective Review." Ann Arbor, MI: Institute for Social Research.

Frohman, Mark, Marshall Sashkin, and Michael Kavanaugh. 1978. "Action-Research as Applied to Organization Development." In *Organization Development: Theory, Research, and Practice,* edited by Wendell French, Cecil Bell, and Robert Zawacki, pp. 137-47. Dallas: Business Publications.

Fromm, Erich. 1941. *Escape From Freedom.* New York: Rinehart.

Gapp, Paul. 1975. *Chicago Tribune,* October 26, pp. 13,18.

Gazda, George. 1971. *Group Counseling: A Developmental Approach.* Boston: Allyn and Bacon.

Gibb, Jack. 1971. "The Effects of Human Relations Training." In *Handbook of Psychotherapy and Behavior Change: An Empirical Analysis,* edited by Allen Bergin and Sol Garfield, pp. 839-62. New York: Wiley.

Goodman, Ellen. 1980. "Help Professions Aren't Shrinking." *Ann Arbor News,* March 30, p. A-16.

Goodstein, Leonard. 1978. *Consulting with Human Service Systems.* Reading, MA: Addison-Wesley.

Gould, Peter. 1973. "On Mental Maps." In *Image and Environment: Cognitive Mapping and Spatial Behavior,* edited by Roger Downs and David Stea, pp. 182-220. Chicago: Aldine.

Goulet, Denis. 1971. *The Cruel Choice: A New Concept in the Theory of Development.* New York: Atheneum.

Gregg, Gary, Thomas Preston, Alison Geist, and Nathan Caplan. 1979. "The Caravan Rolls On: Forty Years of Social Problem Research." In *Knowledge: Creation, Diffusion, Utilization* 1: 31-61.

Greiner, Lawrence. 1975. "Organizational Change and Development." Cited in Huse, Edgar. 1976. *Organization Development and Change.* St. Paul, MN: West Publishing.

Guskin, Alan and Mark Chesler. 1973. "Partisan Diagnosis of Social Problems." In *Processes and Phenomena of Social Change Problems,* edited by Gerald Zaltman, pp. 353-76. New York: Wiley.

Hall, Calvin and Gardner Lindzey. 1957. *Theories of Personality.* New York: Wiley.

Hall, Edward. 1969. *The Hidden Dimension: An Anthropologist Examines Man's Use of Space in Public and in Private.* Garden City, N.Y.: Anchor Books.

Hamer, John. 1975. "Neighborhood Power Staging Comeback." *Sunday Pantograph,* Bloomington-Normal, Ill.: Editorial Research Reports, November 9.

Hausser, Doris, Patricia Pecorell, and Anne Wissler. 1977. *Survey-Guided Development II: A Manual for Consultants.* La Jolla, CA: University Associates.

Havelock, Ronald. 1969. *Planning for Innovation.* Ann Arbor, MI: Center on Utilization of Scientific Knowledge, Institute for Social Research.

Havelock, Ronald and Mary Havelock. 1973. *Training for Change Agents: A Guide to the Design of Training Programs in Education and Other Fields.* Ann Arbor, MI: Institute for Social Research (CRUSK).

Haworth, Lawrence. 1963. *The Good City.* Bloomington, Ind.: Indiana University Press.

Hays, Donald and Joan Linn. 1977. *Needs Assessment: Who Needs It?* Ann Arbor, MI: ERIC Clearinghouse on Counseling and Personnel Services.

Heller, Kenneth and John Monahan. 1977. *Psychology and Community Change.* Homewood, IL: Dorsey Press.

Herzberg, Frederick. 1966. *Work and the Nature of Man.* Cleveland: World Publishing.

Herzberg, Frederick, Bonard Mausner, and Barbara Snyderman. 1959. *The Motivation to Work.* New York: Wiley.

Hiemstra, Horman and Leslie McFarling. 1978. *Environmental Psychology.* 2d ed. Monterey, CA: Brooks/Cole.

Holahan, Charles. 1980. "Action Research in the Built Environment." In *Evaluation and Action in the Social Environment* by Richard Price and Peter Pollitser, pp. 89-105. New York: Academic Press.

_____. 1979. "Redesigning Physical Environments to Enhance Social Interactions." In *Social and Psychological Research in Community Settings,* edited by Ricardo Muñoz, Lonnie Snowden, James Kelly, and Associates, pp. 243-74. San Francisco: Jossey-Bass.

Holahan, Charles and Brian Wilcox. 1977. "Ecological Strategies in Community

Psychology: A Case Study." *Journal of Community Psychology* 5, 423-33.
Holland, John. 1973. *Vocational Choices: A Theory of Careers.* Englewood Cliffs, N.J.: Prentice-Hall.
_____. 1970. *The Self-Directed Search: A Guide to Educational and Vocational Planning.* Palo Alto, CA: Consulting Psychologists Press.
Horney, Karen. 1937. *The Neurotic Personality of Our Time.* New York: Norton.
Howard, Jane. 1970. *Please Touch: A Guided Tour of the Human Potential Movement.* New York: Dell.
Huebner, Lois. In Press. "Theories of the Environment: The Impact of Context." In *A Handbook for Student Services,* edited by Ursula Delworth and Gary Hanson. San Francisco: Jossey-Bass.
_____, ed. 1979. "Redesigning Campus Environments." In *New Directions for Student Services,* Ursala Delworth and Gary Hanson, editors-in-chief, pp. 1-22. San Francisco: Jossey-Bass.
Huebner, Lois and John Corazzini. 1978. "Ecomapping: A Dynamic Model for Intentional Campus Design." *Journal Supplement Abstract Service* 8, 9.
Hurst, James and John Ragle. 1979. "Application of the Ecosystem Perspective to A Dean of Students Office." In *Redesigning Campus Environments,* edited by Lois Heubner, pp. 69-84. San Francisco: Jossey-Bass.
Hutchison, William. 1980. "Ethical and Value Contexts." In *Environmental Design and Human Behavior: A Psychology of the Individual in Society,* edited by Leonard Krasner. New York: Pergamon.
Huse, Edgar. 1980. *Organization Development and Change.* 2d ed. St. Paul, MN: West Publishing.
Hyne, Sue. 1976. "Environmental Assessment Techniques." In *Training Manual for an Ecosystem Model,* edited by LuAnne Aulepp and Ursula Delworth, pp. 112-19. Boulder, CO: Western Interstate Commission for Higher Education.
Insel, Paul and Rudolf Moos. 1974. "Psychological Environments: Expanding the Scope of Human Ecology." *American Psychologist* 29 (Mar.): 179-88.
Ittelson, William, Harold Proshansky, Leanne Rivlin, and Gary Winkel. 1974. *An Introduction to Environmental Psychology.* New York: Holt, Rinehart and Winston.
Ivey, Allen. 1971. *Microcounseling: Innovations in Interviewing Training.* Springfield, IL: Charles C. Thomas.
Jones, Maxwell. 1953. *The Therapeutic Community: A New Treatment Method in Psychiatry.* New York: Basic Books.
Kaiser, Leland. 1975. "Designing Campus Environments." *NASPA Journal,* 13, Jan., 33-39.
Kast, Fremont and James Rosenzweig. 1970. *Organization and Management: A Systems Approach.* New York: McGraw-Hill.
Katsarelas, Nick. 1980. "Think You're Gonna Graduate?" *Michigan Daily,* January 19, 1980, p. 4.
Katz, Daniel and Robert Kahn. 1966. *The Social Psychology of Organizations.* New York: Wiley.

Keating, Lou Ann. 1976. "Assessment Instruments and Techniques." In Training Manual for an Ecosystem Model, edited by Lou Ann Aulepp and Ursula Delworth, pp. 99-111 (Technical Appendix B). Boulder, CO: Western Interstate Commission for Higher Education (WICHE).

Kay, F. Dewitt 1978. "Applications of Social Area Analysis to Program Planning and Evaluation." *Evaluation and Program Planning* 1, pp. 65-78.

Kiresuk, Thomas and Sander Lund. 1979. "Program Evaluation and Utilization Analysis." In *Evaluator Interventions: Pros and Cons,* edited by Robert Perloff, pp. 71-102. Beverly Hills: Sage.

Klein, Donald. 1968. *Community Dynamics and Mental Health.* New York: Wiley.

Koffka, Kurt. 1922. "Perception: An Introduction to the Gestalt Theorie." *Psychological Bulletin* 19, 531-85.

Kolb, David and A. Frohman. 1970. "An Organization Development Approach to Consulting." *Sloan Management Review* 12, 51-65.

Krasner, Leonard. 1980. *Environmental Design and Human Behavior.* New York: Pergamon.

———. 1971. "The Operant Approach in Behavior Therapy." In *Handbook of Psychotherapy and Behavior Change,* edited by Allen Bergin and Sol Garfield, pp. 612-52. New York: Wiley.

Krasner, Leonard and Leonard Ullmann. 1973. *Behavioral Influence and Personality: The Social Matrix of Human Action.* New York: Holt, Rinehart and Winston.

Kuhn, Thomas. 1970. *The Structure of Scientific Revolutions.* Chicago: University of Chicago Press.

Ladd, Florence. 1970. "Black Youths View Their Environment: Neighborhood Maps." *Environment and Behavior* 2 (Jun.): 64-79.

Lake, Dale, Matthew Miles, and Ralph Earle. 1973. *Measuring Human Behavior.* New York: Teachers College Press.

Lawrence, Paul and Jay Lorsch. 1969. *Developing Organizations: Diagnosis and Action.* Reading, MA: Addison-Wesley.

Lemke, Sonny, Rudolf Moos, Barbara Mehren, and Mary Gauvain. 1979. *Multiphasic Environmental Assessment Procedure (MEAP): Handbook for Users.* Palo Alto, CA: Social Ecology Laboratory and Stanford University School of Medicine.

Lewin, Kurt. 1951. *Field Theory in Social Science: Selected Theoretical Papers.* Edited by Darwin Cartwright. New York: Harper.

———. 1947. "Frontiers in Group Dynamics." *Human Relations* 1, 5-41.

———. 1946. "Action Research and Minority Problems." *Journal of Social Issues* 2, 34-46.

———. 1944. "The Dynamics of Group Actions." *Educational Leadership* 1, 195-200.

———. 1936. *Principles of Topological Psychology.* New York: McGraw-Hill.

Lippitt, Gordon, and Ronald Lippitt. 1978. *The Consulting Process in Action.* La Jolla, CA: University Associates.

Lippitt, Ronald, Jeanne Watson, and Bruce Westley. 1958. *The Dynamics of Planned Change: A Comparative Study of Principles and Techniques.* New York: Harcourt, Brace and World.

Lucas, R. 1963. "Wilderness Perception and Use: The Example of the Boundary Waters Canoe Area." *Natural Resources Journal* 3, 394-411.

Lewin, Kurt, Ronald Lippitt, and R. K. White. 1939. "Patterns of Aggressive Behavior in Experimentally Created 'Social Climates'." *Journal of Social Psychology*, 10, pp. 271-299.

Marrow, Alfred. 1969. *The Practical Theorist: The Life and Work of Kurt Lewin.* New York: Basic Books.

Maslow, Abraham. 1954. *Motivation and Personality.* New York: Harper and Row.

_____.1969. "Toward a Humanistic Biology." *American Psychologist* 24, 724-35.

May, Rollo. 1953. *Man's Search for Himself.* New York: Norton.

McKeachie, Wilbert. 1976. "Psychology in America's Bicentennial Year." *American Psychologist* 31 (Dec.): 819-33.

Menne, John W. 1967. "Technique for Evaluating the College Environment." *Journal of Educational Measurements* 4, 219-25.

Midwest Subcommittee on Prevention. 1975. *Report of the Midwest Subcommittee on Prevention.* Washington, D.C.: Division of Counseling Psychology of the American Psychological Association.

Milgram, Stanley. 1970. "The Experience of Living in Cities." *Science* 167 (Mar.): 1461-68.

Mischel, Walter. 1979. "On the Interface of Cognition and Personality—Beyond the Person-Situation Debate." *American Psychologist* 34 (Sept.): 740-54.

_____.1973. "Toward a Cognitive Social Learning Reconceptualization of Personality." *Psychological Review* 80 (Jul.): 252-83.

_____.1968. *Personality and Assessment.* New York: Wiley.

Moore, Ruth. 1975. *Man in the Environment.* New York: Knopf.

Moos, Rudolf. 1979a. *Evaluating Educational Environments.* San Francisco: Jossey-Bass.

_____.1979b. "Improving Social Settings by Social Climate Measurement and Feedback." In *Social and Psychological Research in Community Settings,* edited by Ricardo Muñoz, Lonnie Snowden, James Kelly, and Associates, pp. 145-82. San Francisco: Jossey-Bass.

_____.1973. "Conceptualizations of Human Environments." *American Psychologist* 28 (Aug.): 652-65.

Moos, Rudolf, and Barry Humphrey. 1974. *Group Environment Scale.* Palo Alto, CA.: Consulting Psychologists Press.

Moos, Rudolf, and Marvin Gerst. 1974. *University Residence Environment Scale.* Palo Alto, CA: Consulting Psychologists Press.

Morrill, Weston, Eugene Oetting, and James Hurst. 1974. "Dimensions of Counselor Functioning." *Personnel and Guidance Journal* 52 (Feb.): 354-59.

Murray, Henry. 1938. *Explorations in Personality.* New York: Oxford University Press.

Murrell, Stanley A. 1973. *Community Psychology and Social Systems: A Conceptual Framework and Intervention Guide.* New York: Behavioral Publications.

Olmosk, Kurt. 1972. "Seven Pure Strategies of Change." In *The 1972 Annual*

Handbook for Group Facilitators, edited by J. William Pfeiffer and John Jones, pp. 163-72. La Jolla, CA: University Associates.

Orleans, Peter. 1973. "Differential Cognition of Urban Residents: Effects of Social Scale on Mapping." In *Image and Environment: Cognitive Mapping and Spatial Behavior,* edited by Roger Downs and David Stea, pp. 115-30. Chicago: Aldine.

Orth, Maureen. 1975. "It's Me, Babe." *Newsweek,* November 17, p. 94.

Pace, C. Robert. 1979. *College Student Experiences.* Los Angeles: Higher Education Research Institute.

_____. 1969. *College and University Environment Scales Technical Manual.* 2d ed. Princeton, N.J.: Educational Testing Service.

Pace, C. Robert and George Stern. 1958. "An Approach to the Measurement of Psychological Characteristics of College Environments." *Journal of Educational Psychology* 49: 269-77.

Paddock, William and Paul Paddock. 1967. *Famine 1975!* Boston: Little, Brown.

Panati, Charles. 1976. "Mental Maps." *Newsweek,* March 15, p. 71.

Patton, Michael Quinn. 1978. *Utilization-Focused Evaluation.* Beverly Hills: Sage.

Pavlov, Ivan. 1927. *Conditioned Reflexes.* London: Oxford University Press.

_____. 1906. "The Scientific Investigation of the Psychical Faculties or Processes in the Higher Animals." *Science* 24: 613-19.

Perls, Frederick S., Ralph E. Hefferline, and Paul Goodman. 1951. *Gestalt Therapy.* New York: Julian Press.

Peterson, Richard. 1972. *Institutional Goals Inventory.* Princeton, N.J.: Educational Testing Service.

_____. 1965. *College Student Questionnaire.* Princeton, N.J.: Educational Testing Service.

Peterson, Richard, John Centra, Rodney Hartnett, and Robert Linn. 1970. *Institutional Functioning Inventory: Preliminary Technical Manual.* Princeton, N.J.: Educational Testing Service.

Pfeiffer, J. William and John Jones. 1977. "Ethical Considerations in Consulting." In *The 1977 Annual Handbook for Group Facilitators,* edited by J. William Pfeiffer and John Jones, pp. 217-24. La Jolla, CA: University Associates.

Polster, Erving and Miriam Polster. 1973. *Gestalt Therapy Integrated.* New York: Vintage Books.

Population Task Force of the Institute of Society, Ethics, and the Life Sciences. 1971. "Ethics, Population, and the American Tradition. A Study Prepared for the Commission on Population Growth and the American Future." Hastings-on-Hudson, N.Y.

Price, Richard. 1976. "Assessing Treatment Environments." Workshop presented at the Annual Meeting of the American Psychological Association, Washington, D.C., Sept.

_____. 1974. "Etiology, the Social Environment, and the Prevention of Psychological Dysfunction." In *Health and the Social Environment,* edited by Rudolf Moos, pp. 287-300. Lexington, MA: D.C. Heath.

Price, Richard and Cary Cherniss. 1977. "Training for a New Profession: Research as Social Action." *Professional Psychology* 8 (May): 222-31.

Proshansky, Harold M., William H. Ittelson, and Leanne G. Rivlin. 1970. *Environmental Psychology*. New York: Holt, Rinehart and Winston.
Rapoport, Robert N. 1960. *Community as Doctor: New Perspectives on a Therapeutic Community*. Springfield, IL: Charles C. Thomas.
Rappaport, Julian. 1977. *Community Psychology: Values, Research, and Action*. New York: Holt, Rinehart and Winston.
Reiff, Robert. 1975. "Of Carriages and Kings." *American Journal of Community Psychology* 3: 187-96.
_____. 1967. "Mental Health Manpower and Institutional Change." In *Emergent Approaches to Mental Health Problems*, edited by Emory L. Cowen, Elmer A. Gardner, and Melvin Zax, pp. 74-88. New York: Appleton-Century-Crofts.
Rich, Alexander and Harold Schoeder. 1976. "Research Issues in Assertiveness Training." *Psychological Bulletin* 83 (Nov.): 1081-96.
Robinson, John and Phillip Shaver. 1973. rev. ed. *Measures of Social Psychological Attitudes*. Ann Arbor, MI: Institute for Social Research.
Rogers, Carl. 1961. *On Becoming a Person: A Therapist's View of Psychotherapy*. Boston: Houghton-Mifflin.
_____. 1951. *Client Centered Therapy: Its Current Practice, Implications and Theory*. Boston: Houghton-Mifflin.
Rossi, Peter, J. Wright, and Sonia Wright. 1978. "The Theory and Practice of Applied Social Research." *Evaluation Quarterly* 2, pp. 171-92.
Ryan, William. 1971. *Blaming the Victim*. New York: Random House.
Sashkin, Marshall, William C. Morriss, and Leslie Horst. 1973. "A Comparison of Social and Organizational Change Models: Information Flow and Data Use Processes." *Psychological Review* 80 (Nov): 510-26.
Sauer, Louis. 1972. "The Architect and User Needs." In *Behavior, Design, and Policy Aspects of Human Habitants*. pp. 147-70. Green Bay, WI: University of Wisconsin-Green Bay.
Schaar, Karen. 1975. "Crowding: What's Bad for Rats May Be OK for Humans." *APA Monitor* 6: 7.
Schein, Edgar. 1969. *Process Consultation: Its Role in Organization Development*. Reading, MA: Addison-Wesley.
Schroeder, Charles. 1979. "Designing Ideal Staff Environments Through Milieu Management." *Journal of College Student Personnel* 20 (Mar): 129-35.
Schuh, John. 1979. "Assessment and Redesign in Residence Halls." In *Redesigning Campus Environments*, edited by Lois Huebner, pp. 23-36. San Francisco: Jossey-Bass.
Skinner, Burrhus F. 1948. *Walden Two*. New York: Macmillan.
Smith, Frank. 1976. "Index of Organizational Reactions." *JSAS Catalog of Selected Documents in Psychology* 6, No. 1265.
Smith, Nick. 1979. "Techniques for the Analysis of Geographic Data in Evaluation," *Evaluation and Program Planning* 2 (2): 119-26.
Sommer, Robert. 1974. *Tight Spaces: Hard Architecture and How to Humanize It*. Englewood Cliffs, N.J.: Prentice-Hall.
_____. 1969. *Personal Space: The Behavioral Bases of Design*. Englewood Cliffs, N.J.: Prentice-Hall.
Stea, David and James Blaut. 1973. "Some Preliminary Observations on Spatial

Learning in School Children." In *Image and Environment: Cognitive Mapping and Spatial Behavior,* edited by Roger Downs and David Stea, pp. 221-25. Chicago: Aldine.

Steele, Fred. 1973l *Physical Settings and Organization Development.* Reading, MA: Addison-Wesley.

———.1971. "Physical Settings and Organizational Development." In *Social Intervention: A Behavioral Science Approach,* edited by Harvey Hornstein, Barbara Bunker, W. Warner Burke, Marlon Gindes, and Roy Lewicki, pp. 244-54. New York: Macmillan.

Steinbeck, John. 1939. *The Grapes of Wrath.* New York: Viking.

Stenmark, David 1975. "Field Training, Apprenticeships, Modeling, Internships, and Other 'Community' Interludes." Paper presented at the Annual Meeting of the American Psychological Association, Chicago, Sep.

Stern, George. 1970. "People in Context." *Measuring Person-Environment Congruence in Education and Industry.* New York: Wiley.

Stogdill, Ralph. 1974. *Handbook of Leadership: A Survey of Theory and Research.* Riverside, N.J.: Free Press.

Struening, Ernest. 1975. "Social Area Analysis as a Method of Evaluation." In *Handbook of Evaluation Research,* vol. 1, edited by Ernest Struening and Marcia Guttentag, Beverly Hills: Sage.

Sullivan, Harry S. 1954. *The Psychiatric Interview.* New York: Norton.

———.1953. *The Interpersonal Theory of Psychiatry.* New York: Norton.

Taylor, James and David Bowers. 1972. *The Survey of Organizations.* Ann Arbor, MI: Institute for Social Research.

Thoresen, Carl and Michael Mahoney. 1974. *Behavioral Self-Control.* New York: Holt, Rinehart and Winston.

Thorndike, Edward. 1932. *The Fundamentals of Learning.* New York: Teacher's College Press.

———.1911. *Animal Intelligence.* New York: Macmillan.

Trist, Eric, G. Higgins, H. Murray, and A. Pollack. 1963. *Organizational Choice.* London: Tavistock.

Vaill, Peter. 1973. "An Informal Glossary of Terms and Phrases in Organization Development." In *The 1973 Annual Handbook for Group Facilitators,* edited by John Jones and J. William Pfeiffer, pp. 235-46. La Jolla, CA: University Associates.

von Bertalanffy, Ludwig. 1956. "General Systems Theory." *General Systems* (Yearbook of the Society for the Advancement of General Systems Theory) 1, pp. 1-10.

Walsh, H. Bruce. 1978. "Person/Environment Interaction." In *Campus Ecology: A Perspective for Student Affairs,* edited by James Banning, pp. 6-16. Cincinnati: National Association for Student Personnel Administrators.

———.1973. *Theories of Person-Environment Interaction: Implications for the College Student.* Iowa City: The American College Testing Program.

Walz, Gary, and Juliet Miller. 1969. "School Climates and Student Behavior: Implications for Counselor Role." *Personnel and Guidance Journal* 47 (May): 859-67.

Warren, Jonathan and Pamela Roelfs. 1973. *Student Reactions to College.* Princeton, N.J.: Educational Testing Service.

Warwick, Donald, and Herbert Kelman. 1973. "Ethical Issues in Social Intervention." In *Processes and Phenomena of Social Change*, edited by Gerald Zoltman. New York: Wiley.
Watson, John B. 1925. *Behaviorism.* New York: Norton.
———. 1916. "The Place of the Conditioned Reflex in Psychology." *Psychological Review* 23, 89-116.
Weisbord, Marvin. 1978. *Organizational Diagnosis: A Workbook of Theory and Practice.* Reading, MA: Addison-Wesley.
———. 1976. "Organizational Diagnosis: Six Places to Look for Trouble With or Without a Theory." *Organization and Group Studies* 1, 430-47.
WICHE. 1973. *The Ecosystem Model: Designing Campus Environments.* Boulder, Col.: Western Interstate Commission for Higher Education.
Wicker, Allen. 1979a. *An Introduction to Ecological Psychology.* Monterey, CA: Brooks/Cole.
———. 1979b. "Ecological Psychology: Some Recent and Prospective Developments." *American Psychologist* 34 (Sept.): 755-65.
Wigtil, James V. and Richard C. Kelsey. 1978. "Team Building as a Consulting Intervention for Influencing Learning Environments." *Personnel and Guidance Journal* 56 (Mar.): 412-16.
Willson, Meredith. 1950. *The Music Man.* New York: Frank Music Corporation.
Wolfensberger, Wolf and Linda Glenn. 1975. *PASS 3, Program Analysis of Service Systems: A Method for the Quantitative Evaluation of Human Services.* Toronto: National Institute on Mental Retardation.
Yalom, Irvin. 1975. *The Theory and Practice of Group Psychotherapy.* 2d ed. New York: Basic Books.
Yolles, Stanley F. 1966. "The Role of the Psychologist in Comprehensive Community Mental Health Centers." *American Psychologist* 21 (1): 37-41.

INDEX

action research, 10, 95, 102, 106, 117; comparison to planned change 96
Adler, Alfred, 4, 5
Agel, Jerome, 13
Allen, Andrea, 37
Alley, Sam, 111
Altman, Irwin, 30
American Psychological Association, 15, 161
applied behavioral science, 19-20, 22, 86-96, 102; Lewin and, 10
applied research, 78-82, 112; evaluation, 78-82, 112-13; modeling, 79; monitoring, 79; parameter estimation, 79
architectural design, 16-18, 28-29, 107-109
assessment, environmental, 1-2, 10, 45-77, 131-35; choice of method, 131-32; data categorization, 135-36; data review, 135; data summary, 133; definition of, 45-46; demographic data, 33-34; item writing, 59; perceptual data, 2; procedures, 130-46; response formats, 58-59; scope, 57-58
Astin, Alexander, 30-31, 48
Aubrey, Roger, 45
Aulepp, Lou Ann, 48, 56-57, 61, 102, 103

Bandura, Albert, 8, 32
Banning, James, 39, 40, 56, 79, 102
Barker, Roger, 22, 29-30, 32, 48
Bartz, Wayne, 19
Beckhard, Richard, 104, 118, 127
Beer, Michael, 118, 126-28
behavioral settings, 29-30
behaviorists and environment, 6-8

Bell, Cecil, 42, 67, 104, 106
Bell, Roger, 45
Bem, Daryl, 37
Benne, Kenneth, 86, 87, 159
Bergin, Allen, 8
Blake, Robert, 40
Blanton, Judith, 111
Boss, Medard, 11
Bowers, David, 48-49
Bradford, Leland, 159
Brandon, Richard, 76
Brickell, Henry, 90
Brunswik, Egon, 29, 41
Buber, Martin, 11

Caplan, Gerald, 16
Caplan, Nathan, 16, 98
Carson, Rachel, 18
Cashdan, Lisa, 158
Centra, John, 34
change agent, environmental, 118, 121; role of, 82-83
change, environmental, 82-83; approaches and strategies, 83-99; definition, 82-83; models, 99-112
change ideas, 137; sources of, 138
change implementation, 137-38; illustrative example, 141-42
change planning, 136-37; change ideas, 137; change recommendations, 137
change plan, the, 140-42
change recommendations, 61, 137, 138-40
change team, environmental, 121; formation of, 125-26; skills training, 128-30; team building, 126-28
Cherniss, Gary, 114
Chesler, Mark, 86, 87, 98

Chin, Robert, 86-87
Chrisman, Robert, 19
Clack, R. James, 15, 19, 79, 128, 132, 145, 146, 148
Clark, David, 83, 90
classical conditioning, 7
classification, environmental, 21-44; behavioral, 29-30, 31, 34; categories in, 27-33; matrix, 27, 35-36; models, 35-44
Classroom Environment Scale (CES), 52
client system, 121
Cobb, Sidney, 46, 63
Coch, Lester, 118
Collier, Abram, 123
Colman, Arthur, 113
community mental health, 15-16
Community-Oriented Programs Environment Scale (COPES), 52
community psychology, 15-16
community, sense of, 14-15
conditioning, classical and operant, 7-8
contracting, 125
Conyne, Robert, 15, 19, 57, 79, 101, 102, 112, 114, 128, 146, 148, 160
Cooper, Clare, 17
Corazini, John, 79, 100-101, 102
Correctional Institutions Environment Scale (CIES), 52
counseling service paradigm, 151,
Cowan, Michael, 61, 66, 104, 151
Craik, Kenneth, 29
Crowfoot, James, 86, 87

Daher, Douglas, 100-101, 102
Davis, Howard, 111, 113
DeBell, Garrett, 18
Delworth, Ursala, 48, 56-57, 61, 102, 103
design, environmental, 78-116, 121, 150-51; competencies, 153-54; cycle, 80-82; implications of, 151-59; training, 154-57
Dewey, John, 159
DeYoung, Alan, 100
Downs, Roger, 35, 43

Drum, David, 48
Duhl, Leonard, 30
Dunham, Randall, 49
D'Zurilla, Thomas, 159

ecology, 2, 18-19
Earle, Ralph, 49
ecological climate, 22, 24
ecosystem, 39-40, 56-61, 102-103
Egan, Gerald, 61, 66, 104, 151
Ehrlich, Paul, 18, 30
environment, components, 22-27; definitions of, 1-3, 21-22; effects of, 1-2; geophysical, 21-22; institutional, 1-3; institutional-physical, 23; physical, 1-3, 22; physical-social, 23; social, 1-3, 23; social-ecological, 37; social-environmental, 37; social-institutional, 23; technophysical, 22
Environmental Assessment Inventory, 146
Environmental Change Technology, 117-50; action phase, 130-42; assessment, 131-42; change planning, 136-42; change team formation, 125-26; contracting, 125; follow-up, 142-44; illustrative case, 145-48; implemented change, 137-38; initiation step, 122-25; preparation phase, 122-30; skills training, 128-30; team building, 126-28; withdrawal, 144
Environmental Design Research Association, 29
environment of reference (E_r), 22-27, 118; environmental referent form, 59-61; examples of 24-27, 56-57
Esser, Aristide, 17
ethics, 160-64; American Personnel and Guidance Association, 161; American Psychological Association, 161; guidelines for consultants, 161
existentialism, 11-12
Eysenck, Hans, 15

Fahle, Bernd, 158
Family Environment Scale (FES), 52
Farson, Richard, 33
Fawcett, Greg, 40, 102
feedback, 100, 133-35
field theory, 9-10
Figler, Howard, 48
follow-up, 142-44; monitoring 142-43; stabilization of change 143-44
force-field analysis, 88
Ford, Julian, 153, 155-57, 159
Francis, Mark, 158
Frankl, Victor, 11
Freedman, Jonathan, 30
French, John, 46, 63, 118
French, Wendell, 42, 67, 104, 106
Freud, Sigmund, 3-5
Frohman, Mark, 91, 106
Fromm, Erich, 5, 6

Gapp, Paul, 18
Garfield, Sol, 8
Gauvain, Mary, 49, 55
Gazda, George, 13
Geist, Allison, 98
Gibb, Jack, 14
Glenn, Linda, 56
Goldfried, Marvin, 159
Goodman, Ellen, 98
Goodman, Paul, 11
Goodstein, Leonard, 40
Goulet, Denis, 161
Greiner, Lawrence, 83, 86
Gregg, Gary, 98
Group Environment Scale (GES), 52-55
group modes of intervention, 13-14
Guba, Egon, 83, 90
Gump, Paul, 17, 29, 30
Guskin, Alan, 98
Guthrie, Edwin, 7

Hall, Calvin, 9
Hall, Edward, 17, 28, 30
Hamer, John, 15
Harding, Elizabeth, 146
Hartnett, Rodney, 34

Hausser, Doris, 49
Havelock, Mary, 83, 90-91, 95
Havelock, Ronald, 83, 90-91, 95
Haworth, Lawrence, 16
Hays, Donald, 45
Hefferline, Ralph, 11
Heidegger, Martin, 11
Heller, Kenneth, 98
Herzberg, Frederick, 65, 85
Heubner, Lois, 39, 40, 79, 102-103
Hiemstra, Norman, 22
Higgins, G., 65
Holahan, Charles, 28, 43, 100, 114
Holland, John, 31, 48; environmental classifications, 31
Horney, Karen, 5-6
Horst, Leslie, 83
Howard, Jane, 14
Hull, Clarke, 7
Humphrey, Barry, 34, 52
Hurst, James, 13-14, 102
Huse, Edgar, 83, 91, 94, 95, 124; action research model, 117-18
Hutchison, William, 114, 156
Hyne, Sue, 35, 44

initiation of environmental change, 121-25
Insel, Paul, 37, 100, 101, 156
Ittelson, William, 22, 28, 56
Ivey, Allen, 128

Jones, John, 161
Jones, Maxwell, 14, 131

Kahn, Robert, 30, 40, 61, 65, 103
Kaiser, Leland, 39, 56
Kast, Fremont, 40, 61, 65, 103
Katsarelas, Nick, 46
Katz, Daniel, 30, 40, 61, 65, 103-104
Kavanaugh, Michael, 106
Kay, F. Dewitt, 76
Keating, Lou Ann, 48, 79
Kelman, Herbert, 160
Kelsey, Richard, 127
Kiresuk, Thomas, 111
Klein, Donald, 15
Klevansky, Simon, 30

Koffka, Kurt, 8, 33-34
Kohler, Wolfgang, 8
Kolb, David, 91
Kotler, Milton, 15
Krasner, Leonard, 3, 8, 101, 113-14, 155, 158, 159
Kuhn, Thomas, 151

Lake, Dale, 49
Lawrence, Paul, 40, 41, 63
leadership, organizational, 65
Lemke, Sonny, 49, 55
Lewin, Kurt, 9-10, 12, 19, 47, 65, 83, 95; change model, 88-89, 117; compared with planned change, 93, 150
Lindzey, Gardner, 9
Linn, Joan, 45
Linn, Robert, 34
Lippitt, Gordon, 124, 154, 161
Lippitt, Ronald, 65, 78, 83, 91-94, 117, 124, 144, 154, 159, 161
Lorsch, Jay, 40, 41, 63
Lund, Sander, 111

Mahoney, Michael, 159
Malthus, Thomas, 18
mapping, 71-77, 111-13; cognitive, 71-74; ecological analysis, 76-77; geocode analysis, 75-76, 111-12; geographic, 74-75; social area analysis, 76-77
Marrow, Alfred, 95, 96
Maslow, Abraham, 11, 19, 65
Mausner, Bernard, 65
May, Rollo, 11
McKeachie, Wilbert, 100
McKinnon, Richard, 100-101, 102
McFarling, Leslie, 22
Mehren, Barbara, 49, 55
Menne, John, 33
Miles, Matthew, 49
Milgram, Stanley, 30
Military Company Environment Scale (MCES), 52
Mischel, Walter, 32, 37
"Model A," 61, 66-67
"Model B," 104-106

Monahan, John, 98-99
monitoring, 143
monitoring change, 79
Moos, Rudolph, 21, 27-28, 31-32, 34, 35-41, 44, 47-48, 49-56, 62, 99-101, 139, 156
Morrill, Weston, 13
Morriss, William, 83
Mouton, Jane, 40
Multiphasic Environmental Assessment Procedure (MEAP), 49, 55-56
Murray, Henry, 31, 65
Murrell, Stanley, 16, 46

Nelson, Stephen, 98

Oetting, Eugene, 13
Olmosk, Kurt, 84-88
open-system, 61; Kast and Rosenzweig approach, 61, 65-66; "model A," 61, 66-67; six-box approach, 61-65
Orth, Maureen, 15

Pace, Robert, 31, 33-34
Paddock, Paul, 18
Paddock, William, 18
Panati, Charles, 43
Patton, Michael, 113
parameter estimation, 79
Pavlov, Ivan, 6
Pecorell, Patricia, 49
people radicalism, 13
Perls, Frederick S. (Fritz), 11
personality theory, 3-12
Peterson, Richard, 34
Pfeiffer, J. William, 161
phenomenologists and environment, 8-12; gestalt psychology, 9
physical settings, functions of, 67-71
planned change, 91-94; compared with Lewin model, 93-94
Pollack, A., 65
Population Task Force of Institute of Society, Ethics and the Life Sciences, 156-61.
Preston, Thomas, 98
Price, Richard, 46, 101, 114

Program Analysis of Service Systems (PASS), 56
Proshansky, Harold, 22, 28, 56
psychoanalysts and environment, 4-6
psychosocial climate, 31-33

Ragle, John, 102
Rapaport, Robert, 14
Rapaport, Julian, 98
Reiff, Robert, 15
research-development-diffusion, 90-91
Rich, Alexander, 159
Rivlin, Leanne, 22, 28, 56
Robinson, John, 49
Rogers, Richard, 114
Rogers, Carl, 11
Rogers, Willard, 46, 63
Rosenzweig, James, 40, 61, 65, 104
Rossi, Peter, 79
Ryan, William, 98

Salasin, Susan, 111, 113
Sartre, Jean Paul, 11
Sashken, Marshall, 83, 91, 106
Sauer, Louis, 17
Schaar, Karen, 28
Schein, Edgar, 40, 65, 154
Schroeder, Charles, 101, 102
Schroeder, Harold, 159
Schuh, John, 102
Schwab, John, 45
Schwartz, Steven, 158
self theory, 11
sense of community, 14-15
sensing interviews, 132
Shaver, Phillip, 49
Sheltered Care Environment Scale, 52-56
Skinner, B. F., 7
skills training, 128; in charge, 130; in communication, 128; in group discussion, 128-29; technical, 129-30
Smith, Frank, 49
Smith, Nick, 35, 43, 76-77
Snowden, Lonnie, 37
Snyderman, Barbara, 65
social climate, 52, 62
social ecology, 37-39, 99-101

Soleri, Paoli, 28
Sommer, Robert, 17, 28, 30, 109
stabilization of change, 143-44
Stea, David, 35, 43
Steele, Fred, 21-22, 28, 41-42, 56, 67-71, 101, 106, 109, 110, 114, 144, 156
Stein, Peter, 158
Steinbeck, John, 18
Stenmark, David, 16
Stern, George, 31, 48
Struening, Ernest, 43
Sullivan, Harry Stack, 5-6, 158
system blame, 98-99

Taylor, James, 48-49
team building, 126; goal-setting model, 127; interpersonal, 127; role models, 127-28
Thoreson, Carl, 159
Thorndike, Edward L., 6-7
Tolman, Edward, 7
Trist, Eric, 65

Ullman, Leonard, 3, 158
University Residence Environment Scale (URES), 52
user behavior, 17-18
user participation, 100

Vaill, Peter, 64
values, 160-61
victim blame, 98-99
von Bertalanffy, Ludwig, 41

Walsh, H. Bruce, 48
Warheit, George, 45
Warwick, Donald, 160
Watson, Jeanne, 78, 83, 91-94, 117, 144, 154
Watson, John B., 6-7
Weisbord, Marvin, 61, 64-65, 104
Wertheimer, Max, 8-9
Western Interstate Commission on Higher Education (WICHE), 39, 40, 56
Westley, Bruce, 78, 83, 91-94, 117, 144, 154
White, R. K., 65

Wicker, Allen, 29
Wigtil, James, 127
Wilcox, Brian, 100, 114
Willson, Meredith, 21
Winkel, Gary, 22, 28
Wissler, Anne, 49
withdrawal of change agent, 144
Wolfensberger, Wolf, 56
Work Environment Assessment Scale, 146

Work Environment Scale (WES), 52
Wrenn, Robert, 79
Wright, Sonia, 79
Wright, J., 79

Yalom, Irvin, 13
Yolles, Stanley, 16

Zawacki, Robert, 42, 67, 104-106

ABOUT THE AUTHORS

Robert K. Conyne is Associate Vice Provost for Student Life and while writing this book, he was on sabbatical leave from Illinois State University as a visiting scholar at the Community Psychology Program and the Counseling Services of the University of Michigan.

Dr. Conyne is Editor of the *Journal for Specialists in Group Work*. He has published extensively in the areas of environmental assessment and group processes, with articles and reviews appearing in the *Personnel and Guidance Journal, Professional Psychology, Contemporary Psychology, Psychotherapy: Theory, Research, and Practice, Journal of College Student Personnel,* and other journals.

Dr. Conyne holds an A.B. degree from Syracuse University, M.S. and Ph.D. degrees from Purdue University, and he was a postdoctoral intern at the Counseling Center of the University of California at Berkeley.

R. James Clack is Associate Director of the Counseling-Psychological Services Center of The University of Texas at Austin. His responsibilities include the provision and administration of clinical, preventive, and developmental counseling, and career and learning services on the Austin campus.

Dr. Clack has published widely in the areas of consultation, developmental programming, career development, and the utilization of paraprofessionals in the delivery of mental health services. He has extensive experience in management training, organizational consultation, and planned change in business, industry, health services, governmental and educational institutions.

Dr. Clack holds a B.S. degree in Education, and M.S. and Ph.D. degrees in Counseling and Personnel Services from Purdue University.

BF
353
C768
1981

69125

WITHDRAWN
From Library Collection

DATE DUE

DEC 2 1 1991			
APR 2 7 1992		JY 14 2007	
FEB 0 9 1995			
FEB 2 5 2002			
FEB 2 1 2003			

Ireton Library
Marymount College
Arlington, VA 22207

WITHDRAWN
From Library Collection